The Right to Privacy Revisited

This book focuses on the right to privacy in the digital age with a view to see how it is implemented across the globe in different jurisdictions.

The right to privacy is one of the rights enshrined in international human rights law. It has been a topic of interest for both academic and non-academic audiences around the world. However, with the increasing digitalisation of modern life, protecting one's privacy has become more complicated. Both state and non-state organisations make frequent interventions in citizens' private lives. This edited volume aims to provide an overview of recent development pertaining to the protection of the right to privacy in the different judicial systems such as the European, South Asian, African and Inter-American legal systems.

The chapters in this book were originally published as a special issue of *The International Journal of Human Rights.*

Özgür Heval Çınar is Lawyer and Associate Professor at the University of Greenwich, School of Law and Criminology, UK. He completed his PhD at the School of Law, University of Essex. Previously, he was a post-doc fellow at the University of Oxford between 2012–2016. He has authored several books such as *Freedom of Religion and Belief in Turkey: Religion, Society and Politics* (2021), *Introduction to EU Law* (2021), *Introduction to the English Legal System* (2021), *The Right to Conscientious Objection to Military Service and Turkey's Obligations Under International Human Rights Law* (2014).

Dr Aysem Diker Vanberg is Lecturer in Law at the Department of Law at Goldsmiths, University of London. She is a recognised authority on data protection law, competition law digital markets and online platforms. Her work has been cited by academic and legal practitioners in the UK and globally. Prior to joining Goldsmiths, Aysem worked at the University of Greenwich and Anglia Ruskin University as a Senior Lecturer and as an Associate Lecturer and Research Associate, at the University of Essex. She holds a PhD from the University of Essex, an LLM from the University of Bremen and an LLB (Hons) from the University of Ankara (Turkey). She is also a qualified Turkish lawyer. Before moving to the UK, she worked as a lead In-house counsel for multinational companies including MAN Nutzfahrzeuge AG and Cimpor Cimentos de Portugal.

The Right to Privacy Revisited

Different International Perspectives

Edited by
Özgür Heval Çınar and Aysem Diker Vanberg

Routledge
Taylor & Francis Group
LONDON AND NEW YORK

First published 2022
by Routledge
2 Park Square, Milton Park, Abingdon, Oxon, OX14 4RN

and by Routledge
605 Third Avenue, New York, NY 10158

Routledge is an imprint of the Taylor & Francis Group, an informa business

British Library Cataloguing-in-Publication Data
A catalogue record for this book is available from the British Library

ISBN13: 978-1-032-17189-0 (hbk)
ISBN13: 978-1-032-17190-6 (pbk)
ISBN13: 978-1-003-25219-1 (ebk)

DOI: 10.4324/9781003252191

Typeset in Minion Pro
by codeMantra

Publisher's Note
The publisher accepts responsibility for any inconsistencies that may have arisen during the conversion of this book from journal articles to book chapters, namely the inclusion of journal terminology.

Contents

Citation Information

The following chapters were originally published in *The International Journal of Human Rights*, volume 25, issue 1 (2021). When citing this material, please use the original page numbering for each article, as follows:

Chapter 1
International law, surveillance and the protection of privacy
Kristian P. Humble
The International Journal of Human Rights, volume 25, issue 1 (2021) pp. 1–25

Chapter 2
The current case law of the European Court of Human Rights on privacy: challenges in the digital age
Özgür Heval Çınar
The International Journal of Human Rights, volume 25, issue 1 (2021) pp. 26–51

Chapter 3
Informational privacy post GDPR – end of the road or the start of a long journey?
Aysem Diker Vanberg
The International Journal of Human Rights, volume 25, issue 1 (2021) pp. 52–78

Chapter 4
Playing catch up – privacy regimes in South Asia
Smitha Krishna Prasad and Sharngan Aravindakshan
The International Journal of Human Rights, volume 25, issue 1 (2021) pp. 79–116

Chapter 5
The long arm of GDPR in Africa: reflection on data privacy law reform and practice in Mauritius
Alex B. Makulilo
The International Journal of Human Rights, volume 25, issue 1 (2021) pp. 117–146

Chapter 6
From privacy to data protection: the road ahead for the Inter-American System of human rights
Carlos Affonso Souza, Caio César de Oliveira, Christian Perrone and Giovana Carneiro
The International Journal of Human Rights, volume 25, issue 1 (2021) pp. 147–177

Notes on Contributors

Carlos Affonso Souza is Professor of Law at UERJ and at the Pontifical Catholic University of Rio de Janeiro (PUC-Rio), Brazil. Carlos has PhD and a master's degree in Civil Law from Rio de Janeiro State University (UERJ). Visiting professor at the University of Ottawa and an affiliated fellow at the Information Society Project, Yale Law School. Co-founder and Director of the Institute for Technology & Society of Rio de Janeiro (ITS Rio).

Sharngan Aravindakshan is a programme officer at the Centre for Communication Governance at National Law University, Delhi. He works on issues at the intersection of technology and national security, which besides surveillance and privacy also include international and domestic laws on cybersecurity and national security. Sharngan holds B.A.LL.B. from Gujarat National Law University, Gandhinagar.

Giovana Carneiro is an undergraduate student at the Rio de Janeiro State University (UERJ), Faculty of Law, Brazil. Diploma on Private International Law (The Hague Academy of International Law, The Hague, The Netherlands, 2019). Junior Researcher at Institute for Technology & Society of Rio de Janeiro (ITS Rio).

Özgür Heval Çınar is Lawyer and Associate Professor at the University of Greenwich, School of Law and Criminology, UK. He completed his PhD at the School of Law, University of Essex. Previously, he was a post-doc fellow at the University of Oxford between 2012–2016. He has authored several books such as *Freedom of Religion and Belief in Turkey: Religion, Society and Politics (2021), Introduction to EU Law (2021), Introduction to the English Legal System (2021), The Right to Conscientious Objection to Military Service and Turkey's Obligations Under International Human Rights Law* (2014).

Dr Aysem Diker Vanberg is Lecturer in Law at the Department of Law, at Goldsmiths, University of London. She is a recognised authority on data protection law, competition law digital markets and online platforms. Her work has been cited by academic and legal practitioners in the UK and globally. Prior to joining Goldsmiths, Aysem worked at the University of Greenwich and Anglia Ruskin University as a Senior Lecturer and as an Associate Lecturer and Research Associate, at the University of Essex. She holds a PhD from the University of Essex, an LLM from the University of Bremen and an LLB (Hons) from the University of Ankara (Turkey). She is also a qualified Turkish lawyer. Before moving to the UK, she worked as a lead In-house counsel for multinational companies including MAN Nutzfahrzeuge AG and Cimpor Cimentos de Portugal.

Kristian P. Humble is Principal Lecturer in International Law at the School of Law and Criminology, University of Greenwich, London, UK, where he is the Programme Leader for the LLB Programme. Kristian has taught undergraduate and postgraduate modules in human rights, international law, and international criminal law. His research focuses on best practice in legal education, social justice, human rights, and international law.

Alex B. Makulilo is Professor of Law and Technology at the Open University of Tanzania, Tanzania. He is the Co-Director and Chairperson of the African Law and Technology Institute. His most recent publication African Data Privacy Laws (2016), is a pioneering work in the field of data privacy in Africa. Professor Makulilo has also published widely journal articles on many aspects of computer law and information technology.

Caio César de Oliveira is Fellow at the Institute of Technology and Society of Rio de Janeiro (ITS-Rio), Brazil. Master's degree from the University of São Paulo (USP). Director of the New Lawyers Commission at the São Paulo Lawyers Institute (CNA/IASP). Lawyer.

Christian Perrone, Ph.D. Candidate and Fulbright Scholar at Georgetown University on International Law and the Internet. LL.M. Cambridge University (UK); Diploma EUI on International Human Rights. Former Secretary of the Inter-American Juridical Committee (OAS) and Human Rights Specialist at the Inter-American Commission on Human Rights and the Inter-American Court of Human Rights. Lawyer and Senior Researcher at Institute for Technology & Society of Rio de Janeiro (ITS Rio).

Smitha Krishna Prasad is Director at the Centre for Communication Governance at National University, Delhi, India. At the Centre she leads the work for the Technology & Society team, which focuses on work related to law, policy and awareness/capacity building activities in the context of privacy and surveillance, freedom of speech and expression, and the access to internet. Her research interests relate to international and domestic laws on privacy, data protection and surveillance with a focus on sectors where the intersection of law, policy and technology have an increased impact on the right to privacy, among other things. Smitha holds on LL.M. degree in International Legal Studies from the New York University School of Law; as well as a B.A.LL.B. from Symbiosis Law School, Pune.

Introduction

Özgür Heval Çınar and Aysem Diker Vanberg

The right to privacy is one of the fundamental rights enshrined in international human rights law. It is essential to the autonomy and protection of human dignity, and as such it serves as a foundation upon which many other human rights (e.g. freedom of thought, conscience and religion and freedom of expression) is build. It is recognised by numerous international human rights instruments such as Article 12 of the Universal Declaration of Human Rights, Article 17 of the International Covenant on Civil and Political Rights, Article 8 of the European Convention on Human Rights (ECHR), Article 7 of the Charter of Fundamental Rights of the European Union and Article 11 of the American Convention on Human Rights.

The right to privacy should be respected by everyone including state and non-state actors. However, with the advent of digitalisation protecting one's privacy has become a more complex task. Both state and non-state actors make frequent interventions in citizens' private lives. Data-intensive technologies, such as artificial intelligence applications, enable these actors to track, analyse, predict and manipulate human behaviour to an unprecedented degree. For instance, our movements are monitored through our smartphones, computers or devices data can also be gathered on individuals via their search history, social media accounts, credit cards as well as AI-operated devices (e.g. Alexa). This monitoring is carried out by states on security grounds and by non-state actors under the premise of offering a better and personalised experience for their users. Nevertheless, if these data-intensive technologies are used without any effective legal safeguards, they carry significantly risks to the right to privacy and other human rights.

In the light of above, it will be very timely to explore to what degree the right to privacy, one of the most important freedoms for the existence of human dignity, has been restricted in the digital world, and examine the challenges facing this right from different international perspectives. In particular, this book aims to provide an overview of recent development pertaining to the protection of the right to privacy in the different judicial systems such as the European, South Asian, African and Inter-American legal systems. Thus, it is very unique as there have not been any publications with similar content covering the issue as extensively as we did and it is a first in this regard.

The right to privacy has been a topic of interest for both academic and non-academic audiences around the world. Many articles, first and foremost newspaper articles, academic and non-academic articles are being published. In this respect, a comprehensive study of the latest situation regarding the right to privacy violations will be useful to many people who take an interest in this edited book, and it is evident that this book will make a significant contribution to the literature by providing a broader perspective on the issue that transcends national boundaries. As stated above, in this book we focus on the right to privacy in the digital age with a view to see how it is implemented across the globe in different jurisdictions. As a result, the right to privacy is examined in a total of six chapters.

The first chapter explores the United Nations (UN) mechanism as the right to privacy has historically not been at the forefront of discussions within the international community and the UN. This position changed after the Edward Snowden and Cambridge Analytica revelations. This chapter is written by Mr. Kristian P. Humble and is entitled "International law, surveillance and the protection of privacy". In this chapter, Mr. Humble focuses on how the UN, the international community and international law aim to bring surveillance practices in line with human rights law and what privacy means in the modern digital age. Especially, the first part of this chapter looks at the inherent right to privacy; the second part covers the recent developments from the UN and international law perspective. Finally, the chapter looks at the challenges ahead in the modern age of surveillance and digital communication. This chapter concludes that there are some positive steps being made in the international community for the protection of privacy, however, the law, in particular the international law framework must be clearer and more robust to protect the individuals from the state and private actors.

The second chapter analyses the current case law of the European Court of Human Rights' (ECtHR) as it has played a pivotal role in shaping and developing the right to privacy for all Council of Europe member states. The second chapter is written by Dr. Özgür Heval Çınar and is entitled "The Right to Privacy in the 21st Century and the European Court of Human Rights' Case Law". In this chapter, Dr. Çınar examines Article 8 of the ECHR, its historical origins, definition, and scope. The chapter also examines the current case law of the ECtHR in light of the current developments in the digital world. Moreover, this chapter specifically endeavours to find answers to the following questions: How in private life can the balance be struck between the gathering of personal data and the maintenance of security? What does the term personal data mean? In what situations may it be valid to limit this freedom? What are the threats to this freedom in our lives which digital devices dominate? By whom are these threats being created? What is the attitude of the ECtHR towards these threats? Dr. Çınar concludes that the right to privacy is undoubtedly one of the most fundamental of human rights and is crucial in safeguarding human dignity and autonomy. The ECtHR has not only reached judgments on the application of the right to privacy but also clarified that the right to privacy has a wide scope that incorporates rights relating to family, home and communication in addition to private life. Hence, it is incumbent on states to enact legal provisions to introduce necessary and effective measures as soon as possible.

The third chapter focuses on the right to privacy in the context of European Union (EU) Law with a particular focus on the General Data Protection Regulation (GDPR), as sound data protection laws are crucial for the protection of fundamental human rights including the right to privacy. The third chapter is written by Dr. Aysem Diker Vanberg and is entitled "Informational privacy post GDPR – end of the road or the start of a long journey?". The GDPR is a far-reaching legal instrument that regulates the collection and use of personal data by private actors, individuals and by governments. Hence this chapter analyses and discusses the impact of the GDPR on the right to privacy particularly in the context of data protection. It also aims to explore whether the GDPR in itself is adequate to ensure the right to privacy in the EU and whether the protection provided by the GDPR can be supplemented by other means. The chapter finds that while the GDPR is a significant step in the right direction to protect informational privacy, it is certainly not the end of the journey. It argues that on its own, the GDPR cannot fully address the imbalance of power between data subjects and data controllers. Hence, it needs to be complemented by other regulatory tools such as the ePrivacy Regulation, EU competition law and Consumer Protection rules. Furthermore, some provisions in the GDPR must be revisited in the near future to ensure they do not become obsolete due to technological advancements.

The fourth chapter examines the right to privacy taking into consideration the South Asian context. This chapter is written by Ms. Smitha Krishna Prasad and Mr. Sharngan Aravindakshan and it is entitled "Playing catch up – privacy regimes in South Asia". As noted by authors the landscape of privacy laws in the South Asian Association of Regional Cooperation (SAARC) countries, which consists of India, Pakistan, Sri Lanka, Nepal, Bhutan, Bangladesh, Maldives and Afghanistan, is fragmented. In most of these countries, privacy is only an elitist concern, which meant that privacy as a legal and policy issue was not high on the priority list for most governments in the region, resulting in little focus on the development of a comprehensive legislative framework or architecture for privacy. For instance, India is still engaged in massive digitization drives to ensure digital penetration and access to all sections of its population. This chapter attempts to examine the growing consolidation and harmonization of privacy and surveillance laws in major South Asian countries and take stock of South Asia's emerging privacy jurisprudence. Driven by reactions to increasingly frequent data collection and profiling attempts by the government, as well as the side effects of growing digital markets, the privacy discourse in South Asia is evolving with a heightened awareness of privacy as a core fundamental right. At the same time, some governments in the region are also keen to explore the benefits of the digital economy and are increasingly developing economic policies that focus on the use of data as a 'resource' for the State and the industry. Apart from outlining these developments, the chapter delves into and identifies the source of privacy rights in these countries, whether derived from the constitutions of the respective countries or otherwise provided for through specific legislation. The chapter also traces and examines the legal architectures of privacy and surveillance in the region, including national profiling databases. It then zooms out to pinpoint possible trends and influences. The authors conclude that while the South Asian privacy landscape is marred by loosely regulated surveillance and weak safeguards against personal data exploitation, there is an increase in the consolidation of laws governing privacy in the past decade. However, these legislation attempts do not seem to be suggestive of coherent policy or law making at the regional level.

The fifth chapter concentrates on the African legal system with a particular focus on Mauritius. This chapter is written by Professor Alex B. Makulilo and it is entitled "The long arm of GDPR in Africa: reflection on data privacy law reform and practice in Mauritius". The focus of this chapter is Mauritius as it has a leading role in the privacy policy reforms and the internationalization of its data protection systems in Africa. Furthermore, the impact of the GDPR in Africa is examined in this chapter because the GDPR is an effective legal instrument in Africa to safeguard the right to privacy. In this respect, this chapter contributes to the literature to understand how the GDPR is implemented outside Europe. It should be noted that the recently adopted GDPR in the EU has certainly set the highest standards of all data privacy policies across the world. In theory, such standards have provided more control to individuals over their personal data. Due to the strengthened third-party obligations in the GDPR for data export to non-EU countries and fear of loss of foreign investment, if such countries fail to provide adequate protection of personal data, the GDPR exerts a profound influence on data privacy law reform and practice outside Europe. In this chapter, Professor Makulilo analyses the impact of the GDPR in Africa by using Mauritius as an intrinsic case study. Accordingly, the development of the data protection system in Mauritius from the repealed Data Protection Act 2004 to the current Data Protection Act 2017 is analysed in detail, drawing on the largest body of reported complaints, appeals and judicial decisions so far decided by courts. This chapter concludes that the GDPR had a profound impact on law Mauritius data protection system and there has been little or no influence from the other human rights instruments applicable to Mauritius.

Finally, the sixth chapter examines the Inter-American System of Human Rights (IAHRS) as this System is in stark contrast to the European system that recognizes the right to data protection as an autonomous right – differentiating it from the right to privacy. This final chapter is written by Prof. Carlos Affonso Souza, Mr. Caio César de Oliveira, Mr. Christian Perrone & Ms. Giovana Carneiro and is entitled "From privacy to data protection: the road ahead for the Inter-American System of human rights". The IAHRS is a regional human rights system responsible for monitoring, promoting and protecting human rights in the 35 independent countries of the Americas that are members of the Organization of American States. The chapter highlights that out of all thirty-five States of the Organisation of American States (OAS), only eighteen have a specific data protection regulation; seven are discussing the Bill and eleven do not have a specific data protection regulation. These numbers clearly indicate that data protection is violated dangerously in most of the OAS countries. This chapter presents the stage of development of the IAHRS in relation to the protection of the right to privacy and data protection and also demonstrates the challenges that such a system will have to face as it moves towards the effective guarantee of such rights in the OAS countries. The chapter concludes that as privacy and data protection grow in importance around the world, the IAHRS will face the challenge of protecting them under the umbrella of many different, cultural, economic and legal landscapes. Despite these inherent difficulties, the System has proven reliable in the past to adapt and carve out, in a creative way, standards for the protection of human rights that are in tune with technological developments.

In conclusion, the above chapters once again demonstrate that it is imperative for all the countries in the world to make the necessary legislative changes and to ensure that they establish an effective legal framework for the protection of privacy. If the existing restrictions and the unlawful interferences to this right (by state or non-state actors) are maintained or even extended, individuals will no longer enjoy this right. This will have wider repercussions and may adversely affect other fundamental rights such as freedom of thought, conscience and religion and freedom of expression. In this respect, we hope that this book will prove useful to those who endeavour to understand the value of this right in different judicial systems. Furthermore, the book is aspiring to start an international dialogue in terms of finding effective legal safeguards against violations of this right.

We gratefully acknowledge the help of all contributors to this edited book. Without you, this title would not be here. We would also like to thank Routledge Taylor & Francis Group for bringing this project to fruition. Finally, we would like to thank others including our peer reviewers and our families who have offered invaluable assistance, support and encouragement for this book.

International law, surveillance and the protection of privacy

Kristian P. Humble

ABSTRACT
The right to privacy is a fundamental human right under international law. The right to privacy for an individual is the right to hide or obscure elements of their life from the wider public. In the modern age, the need for privacy is becoming increasingly difficult in light of modern communication companies which seek to make once which was considered private, public. The right to privacy has historically not been at the forefront of discussions within the international community and the United Nations. This position changed after the Edward Snowden and Cambridge Analytica revelations. The focus from the international community is on addressing not only the practices of state sponsored surveillance but also surveillance undertaken by modern communications companies. This article will focus on how the United Nations, the international community and international law aim to bring surveillance practices in line with human rights law and what privacy means in the modern digital age. The first part of the article will look at the inherent right to privacy, the second part will cover the recent developments from the United Nations and international law and the third part will look at the challenges ahead in the modern age of surveillance and digital communication.

1. Introduction

The right to privacy is seen as a fundamental human right contained in the Universal Declaration of Human Rights (UDHR)[1] and the International Covenant on Civil and Political Rights (ICCPR).[2] The right to privacy, however, has historically not been at the forefront of discussions within the international community and the United Nations. This position changed in 2013 after the Edward Snowden revelations. The international community was focused on addressing not only on the practices of state sponsored surveillance but also surveillance undertaken by modern communications companies.[3]

The basis of the international community and the United Nations, in particular, was the application and interpretation of Article 17 of the ICCPR and more recently the United Nations Resolution of Privacy in the Digital Age[4] and how to bring surveillance practices in line with human rights law and what is privacy means in the modern digital age.

The modern international law jurisprudence holds states accountable for their actions (not in all cases) based on the effective control test.[5] There has also been a suggestion of a different approach which is based on virtual control within the legal boundaries of holding states accountable over there surveillance activities while upholding the individual's right to privacy over their own communications.[6]

Recent events such as 2013 Edward Snowden and 2018 Cambridge Analytica revelations has shown that there needs to be an international legal solution to communication surveillance by states sometimes referred to as the Five Eyes[7] states and by communication-based companies such as Facebook. Activities which use surveillance without an individual's permission is in clear breach of Article 17 of the ICCPR. Despite the exposure of such practices (Snowden and Cambridge Analytica in particular) there has been a slow process of an agreement of how to bring these practices in line with international human rights law.

This article will deal with some of these challenges. The first part of the article will look at inherent right to privacy, the second part will cover the recent developments from the United Nations and international law, the third part will look at the challenges ahead in the modern age of surveillance and digital communication.

2. The meaning of privacy

The international community has been slow in responding to changes in technologies which are based on communication and data collection, leaving international law trying to catch up and regulate a growing concern for the protection of privacy of states and the individual.

Article 17 of the ICCPR 1966 states privacy as the following:

(1) No one shall be subjected to arbitrary or unlawful interference with his privacy, family, home or correspondence, nor to unlawful attacks on his honour and reputation.
(2) Everyone has the right to the protection of the law against such interference or attacks.

In 1988 this was further expanded in General Comment No 16 on Article 17 ICCPR.[8] This Comment explained:

(1) Article 17 provides for the right of every person to be protected against arbitrary or unlawful interference with his privacy, family, home or correspondence as well as against unlawful attacks on his honour and reputation. In the view of the Committee this right is required to be guaranteed against all such interferences and attacks whether they emanate from State authorities or from natural or legal persons. The obligations imposed by this article require the State to adopt legislative and other measures to give effect to the prohibition against such interferences and attacks as well as to the protection of this right.
(2) In this connection, the Committee wishes to point out that in the reports of States parties to the Covenant the necessary attention is not being given to information concerning the manner in which respect for this right is guaranteed by legislative, administrative or judicial authorities, and in general by the competent organs established in

> the State. In particular, insufficient attention is paid to the fact that article 17 of the Covenant deals with protection against both unlawful and arbitrary interference. That means that it is precisely in State legislation above all that provision must be made for the protection of the right set forth in that article. At present, the reports either say nothing about such legislation or provide insufficient information on the subject.

The ICCPR was in 1966 was not equipped to look at the threat to individual privacy from data collection and digital technologies because these technologies simply did not exist. Therefore, the definition of privacy is regarded as narrow in today's technological advances in communication and data collection. The 1988 General Comment only goes further to distinguish the incoming threat of data collection by states and the protection of states from individual's private data being interfered with. Again, however, a full appreciation of technologies concerning communication and information were not fully understood as the use of these technologies and the internet were in their infancy.

The way individuals communicate and the collection of data by states and technology companies seems to be commonly understood as being part of the digital age. But there needs to be discussion to look again at the General Comment from 1988 and an update for this new decade and beyond. The discussion was enhanced[9] by the United Nations Special Rapporteur Frank La Rue[10] and by the General Assembly.[11] The reason for an update is clear, there needs to be a fundamental understanding of what the right to privacy means and what it must protect in light of the obligations of not only states but the more difficult notion of companies under international law.

The current 'General Comment to Article 17'[12] states that 'the gathering and holding of personal information on computers, databanks and other devices by public authorities or private bodies must be regulated by law'.[13] Also, it can be seen that this has been agreed upon by the Human Rights Committee (HRC).[14]

This guiding statement of Article 17 has been followed in a number of European Court of Human Rights (ECtHR) decisions. Indeed, the United Nations and the international community can take note of the ECtHR's decision in *Botta v Italy*,[15] *MK v France*,[16] *S and Marper v the UK*[17] and *Bensaid v the UK*[18] that the notion of 'private life is not an exhaustive decision'.[19] The court, therefore, does not feel that a definition on what is a private life can ever be fully comprehensive and include all aspects that an individual might feel are private. The ECtHR also stated that the very 'protection of personal data is of fundamental importance to a person's enjoyment of respect for his or her personal data and family life'.[20]

The United Nations and the international community, therefore, should also take into account the Court of Justice of the European Union (CJEU)'s decisions on this matter. A landmark decision came in *Schrems v Data Protection Commissioner*.[21] This is seen as one of the most important international privacy cases in recent history. The case was based on a complaint against Facebook brought to the Irish Data Protection Commissioner (IDPC). In the complaint, Schrems challenged the transfer of his data to the United States by Facebook in light of Facebook USA alleged involvement with the PRISM mass surveillance program.[22] The Court of Justice of the European Union (CJEU) made the Safe Harbor arrangement of collection and data transfer between EU and US invalid. Schrems complaint was based on EU data protection law, which does not allow data transfers to non-EU countries, unless the company transferring and storing the data can guarantee adequate protection. The Court found that there was not the adequate protection needed in line with the EU data protection law and deemed that the Safe Harbor agreement 'must be declared invalid'.[23] The Court also expressed that:

> legislation permitting the public authorities to have access on a generalized basis to the content of electronic communications must be regarded as compromising the essence of the fundamental rights guaranteed by Article 7 of the Charter of Fundamental Rights of the European Union.[24]

2.1. Is there a right to obscurity in the digital age?

Privacy is an essential human need and an essential fundamental human right. The difficulty comes that the term privacy itself can be an abstract concept which at times is difficulty to define but all humans need the knowledge to know that elements of their private lives will be private and kept from others.

With the rise of new technologies, it is difficult to know where this fundamental right to privacy extends or even exists. With the internet and social media, it has become almost impossible to protect these fundamental rights and almost impossible for an individual to become invisible and keep themselves completely private.

Under the modern framework of international law, the protection of privacy for individuals depends entirely on constitutional limitations and states willingness to be adhere to international legal treaties and by bound by them. International law has however benefited from international custom as a source of law which means that the practice of certain types of actions will be enough to be recognised as binding on state parties. Article 38 of the International Court of Justice (ICJ)[25] Statute lists the sources of law in this regard and specifically sets out the importance of customary international law.[26] Customary international law has the status of law because the ICJ considers custom as 'evidence of a general practice accepted by law' and therefore 'part of the corpus of general international law'.[27] International customary law has at its core decision making value through state practice which can then evolve into a legal norm through consistent usage and then a final stage that this custom is accepted by the international community.[28] This is seen as a unique passage of law making within international law itself that the recognition of a custom or right can be enforced internationally without the express written agreement and consent of the sovereign power.

Therefore, to paraphrase the UDHR, a human right is based on an idea that there exists within the international sphere that a universal standard of rights which should be held in higher regard to local and cultural customs which are essential for dignity of human life.[29]

The need for privacy is seen in all cultures and civilisations, a need as humans that certain types or actions are of a private nature and should be away from general observation. Clarity to what the actions are and what constitutes privacy has and is a difficult subject to define.

Post suggested that:

> Privacy is a value so complex so entangled in competing and contradictory dimensions, so engorged with various and distinct meanings that I sometimes despair whether it can be usefully addressed at all.[30]

This inherent need for privacy is also coupled with some sort of expectation that the state that one resides in will protect their privacy. The protection of this privacy will be from unwanted observation from other members of the public and from the state itself.

From Solove concept of privacy, in order to determine the action or behaviour that might cause an infringement of privacy and what level of protection might be needed it would be paramount to what the understood term of privacy meant. There would also need to be a distinction between the right to privacy and the concept of privacy.[31]

Rengel explained that:

> The concept of privacy involves a definition of what it entails as well and how it is valued, while the right to privacy refers to the recognition that privacy should be legally protected.[32]

Therefore, it is impossible to formulate an argument for the obscurity in cyberspace without having a definition firstly of what constitutes privacy and secondly what then should be legally protected as a privacy issue for individuals.

As this article has suggested privacy has consistently been defined in the context of personal autonomy or having the innate control over the personal intimacies of personal identify or having control over the personal data which is available about yourself.[33] Many definitions of privacy vary from one element of privacy to another but what is clear is that privacy at its core is about the protection of oneself from the outside world.

Privacy can also be described as 'claim of individuals, groups or institutions to determine for themselves when how and to what extent information about them is communicated to others'[34] or 'privacy is the condition of human life in which acquaintance with a person or with affairs of his life which are personal to him is limited'.[35]

Solove has put privacy into six different concepts or general types based on his research:

(1) The right to be left alone.
(2) Limited access to the self, the ability to shield oneself from unwanted access by others.
(3) Secrecy, the concealment of certain matters from others
(4) Control over personal information, the ability to exercise control over information about oneself.
(5) Personhood, the protection of ones' personality, individuality and dignity and;
(6) Intimacy, control over or limited access to ones' intimate relationships or aspects of life.[36]

These categories are on the face of it common sense approaches to privacy matters that most individuals would agree that on some level all human beings need a level of the right to be left alone, secrecy, control or personhood. However, the problem exists in that some individuals will value some privacy matters over others. Some, for example, may not value intimacy as an important protection. This can be seen in the use of Instagram to catalogue personal and private sometimes intimate images of oneself. So, the intrinsic problem lies in the notion that an overall definition of privacy may at times be out of reach or have to be contended on a more personal level.

Solove's own definition of privacy is that:

> The value of privacy must be determined on the basis of its importance to society, not in terms of individual rights. Moreover, privacy does not have universal value that is the

same across all contexts. The value of privacy in a particular context depends upon the social importance activities that it facilitates.[37]

Therefore, Solove is also here looking at contextualising privacy, privacy which needs to change with time and maybe what privacy means to individuals and not the wider world interpretation of it. What an individual might hold dear in the scope of privacy might be very different to how another individual wants their privacy protected.

Privacy as most would ascertain is a general right to be left alone, for an amount of secrecy, to keep from the outside world aspects of oneself that an individual want or needs to keep private. As Newell explains privacy can be then described in as a number of different protective rights from control over personal information, freedom from surveillance, protection from invasions into someone's home, personal autonomy and control over one's body.[38]

Another viewpoint here is that the right to privacy is wrapped up in the notion of self-worth and these notions by the very fact of their existence means that society itself can function more efficiently and in turn can proceed with purpose when these rights are protected. Regan suggests that 'I argue that society is better off … when privacy exists. I maintain that privacy serves not just individual interests but common, public and collective purposes'.[39] Reiman suggests that 'privacy functions as a means of protecting freedom, moral personality and a rich and critical inner life'.[40]

The right to privacy of course has long been recognised in the international community. There are several international conventions and human rights treaties which mention privacy as a central issue. In conjunction with Article 28 of the ICCPR the HRC was formed which investigates or 'monitors' states implementations of rights including those pursuant to privacy.[41] The HRC issued a General Comment on Article 17 of the ICCPR which embodies the right to privacy, discussing and clarifying concepts such as 'arbitrary interference' 'family' 'home' and 'correspondence'. Although it must be stated again that the ICCPR is unclear as to what it intended by these 'general comments'.[42]

The General Comment does, however, look at the legal aspect to how the ICCPR should be able to have an interpretation to the right to privacy within the scope of international law. According to the HRC the term 'unlawful' as it appears in Article 17 sets out that, no one's privacy must be interfered with unless reasoned by law.[43]

The right to privacy is not only recognised in some of the most important international and regional human rights documents but they have also been recognised in almost every constitution in the world. States without written constitutions like the UK, for example, have extended privacy protection through jurisprudence, procedural rules and other protections. Furthermore, privacy has become a common element in most states.[44] Although the right to privacy is not an absolute right and at times is infringed when other matters are at stake (like in light of public protection or criminal sanction) there must be a fine act of balancing the international community's inherent recognition of the right to privacy and the private act it may or may not protect.

The right to privacy includes the very idea that human interaction will often take place in the public sphere. This means, that an individual will only give up their personal space when they feel safe to so. But in cyberspace this is a difficult concept to ascertain. It has been stated that a right to obscurity in the digital age is not much more than a desirable goal and has little chance of being achieved in the reality.[45] Obscurity can be described as a 'state of unknowing or being unidentifiable online'.[46] Out in the public space, it is impossible for an observer to identify someone identity or personal data because they do not have the correct pieces of this puzzle to fit together, as they do not have access to any personal information. For instance, an observer who observes a conversation will be unlikely to ascertain any personal information about the individuals taking part in the conversation simply by observing them.

Online obscurity is more complex but a person can remain obscure if a piece of vital personal information is missing like identity or social connections. But with some of these vital personal pieces fitting together, like for example social connections, the online observer can, if they have right tools, infiltrate private information much easier than if they were simply observing a conversation taken place in public.

Obscurity would only be fully realised through regulation that protects an individual's information in which they wish to keep private. Therefore, if a right to privacy has been recognised within international treaties and national domestic legislation then surely obscurity is another function of privacy.

Hartzog and Strutzman have suggested other frameworks that could lead to a protection of obscurity and protection of privacy on the internet.[47] They have suggested that the protection of obscurity may be easier to implement than that of privacy recognition, due in the main to the problematic nature of a widely accepted definition of a right to privacy. Obscurity they suggest could form a compromise remedy of protection. This would mean in essence instead of mandating that websites to remove sensitive information, the courts could propose some element of obscurity. So, companies storing personal information would have to keep the information online as it had been received, therefore, if the individual did not want it to be exposed then it would not be exposed.

Hartzog and Strutzman suggested framework, however, does bring with it a number of other problems in which the individual in the protection information may not be initially satisfied with. This again still puts the individual information received and what to do with it in the hands of the receiving company, the trusting of the company not to expose personal or sensitive personal information. In light of Cambridge Analytica, this seems problematic. What is needed is a stronger legal mandate to obscurity on the internet.

Hartzog and Strutzman suggested four factors which could be used by the courts to determine whether some aspects should be deemed private or public. They suggested that if certain elements were missing from the public then they are closer to being obscure and should come with some element of a protection of privacy attached to them. These factors suggested are:

(1) Search visibility (ease of discovery in search systems)
(2) Unprotected access (degree of access restriction)
(3) Identification (degree to which individual is identified by direct or indirect disclosure)
(4) Clarity (ability for observer to comprehend or discover information)[48]

Hartzog and Strutzman suggested the following as guidance:

> The presence of these factors diminishes obscurity, and their absence enhances it. Thus, in determining whether information is obscure online, courts should consider whether any of these factors were present in their determination. Information that is entirely unobscured

> is completely obvious, and vice versa. Like in fair use disputes, courts should engage in a case-by-case analysis of the factors, examining each one individually, then as a whole to determine the degree of online obscurity.[49]

To expand the understanding of these four factors, Hartzog and Strutzman used the following scenarios:

> Scenario 1 is a blog that is visible only to invited users and is not searchable by general search engines like Google. It is close to being completely obscure because it is missing two of the most important factors for finding it. Scenario 2 is a Twitter account that uses only a first name and a blurry photo to identify the poster. While this information is more obvious than the information in Scenario 1 because it is freely searchable and accessible, it is still slightly obscure because only certain Internet users would be able to identify the poster of the content or completely comprehend any idiosyncratic posts.[50]

Therefore, these determining factors as suggested by Hartzog and Strutzman are based on which elements are present for the courts to deem them to be obscure. If a user posts their name, a picture of themselves online in which they are easily identifiable then this cannot be a case of privacy and the individual cannot be assumed to have been trying to be obscure. If however elements within these four factors are missing as in the scenarios above then the court could determine that there was an element of obscurity intended to be observed.

There have been several US cases which the court has shown a balancing of the action taken by the user in determining whether the action is deemed private and obscure. In *United States v Gines-Perez*[51] the Court held that a right to claim privacy is unavailable to a person if they place information on a public forum without taken any steps to protect the information from discovery from the general public. In contrast in *Pietrylo v Hillstone Restaurant Group*[52] and an employee set up a private closed network page on Myspace with invitation only to join. The group was used mainly to convey frustration with their employer. When one of the managers obtained the password to the account, the creator of the group brought a case against the manager for an invasion of privacy. The Court held in favour of the infringement of privacy on the grounds that the group had been intended to be private and obscured from public view as it was by invitation only and each member had its own username and password.

Both the right to obscurity and the right to privacy are interlinked but are not helped by the current international guidelines not being clear enough on the protection of these rights. But clear guidelines on obscurity in the definition of what is private and what is public could help in making the protection and what should be protected clearer.

3. Privacy protection under international law

It is understood that in certain circumstances states and their governments carry out surveillance and data collection within the borders of their own territories. However, this does raise the question as to whether they can carry out such acts in foreign states.

The scope of the ICCPR is clearly set out in Article 2(1) and sets out the following 'states must respect and to ensure' the rights recognised in the treaty 'to all individuals within its territory and subject to its jurisdiction'.[53] The question of subject of under their jurisdiction raises questions of whom is under a state's jurisdiction. Does this include individuals that are not within the territory of state?

However, global surveillance within different states and different legal frameworks makes a clear distinction between external and internal communications. Most states (namely the Five Eyes[54]) have legislation which governs these actions. In the UK it is the Regulation of Investigatory Powers Act 2000 (RIPA),[55] in the United States of America (USA or US) it is the US Foreign Intelligence Surveillance Act 1978,[56] Australian Intelligence Services Act[57] and Canadian National Defence Act 1985.[58] These legislative frameworks show the obligations of protection of nationals and those within the state's territory and non-nationals who are living outside states territory.

For the UK under ss.8(1) and (2) of the RIPA communications which are internal may only be used in surveillance when a warrant is issued and only on evidence of suspicion of unlawful activity.[59] External communications are defined as communication sent or received outside the territory of the British Islands.[60]

This problematic element which contrasts with ICCPR and Comment No 16 is that the conditions of evidence and warrant set out ss.8 (1) and (2) do not apply to external communications. This controversial element here is that the UK governments would seem to suggest that all activities of UK residents through digital communications platforms such as Google, Twitter and Facebook as their headquarters can be under surveillance as their data is held outside a British territory in the United States.[61]

This, therefore, gives the UK government through its intelligence gathering agencies permission to use all these communications which are coming in and out of the UK by UK residents using companies such as Google, Twitter and Facebook. Another caveat to this is that under a general warrant under s 8(4) RIPA 2000 both residents of the UK and foreign nationals can have their communications monitored.

The controversial nature of this was commented on by the HRC in a 2015 report[62]:

> Regulation of Investigatory Powers Act 2000 (RIPA) that makes a distinction between internal and external communications, provides for untargeted warrants for the interception of external private communications and communication data, which are sent or received outside the United Kingdom without affording the same safeguards as in the case of interception of internal communications ... the UK must review the regime regulating the interception of personal communications and retention of communication data with the view to ensuring that such activities both within and outside the State party, conform to its obligations under the International Covenant of Civil and Political Rights including Article 17.[63]

However, despite this request from the United Nations, the UK made no concession on this above point. In the updated Investigatory Powers Act 2016 s 136(3) still allows for surveillance by their security forces to issue mass warrants to intercept 'overseas related communications'.[64] So again, just reconfirming the infringement of an individual's right to privacy protection as the RIPA 2000 does and on the face of it contrary to the ICCPR Article 17.

Therefore, it is unclear on the extent to which information is being used by state agencies on the permission from governments. Many states seem to fragrantly absolve themselves from the obligations placed on them by ICCPR. The US government has refuted the obligations placed on it by ICCPR stating it is not bound by them. The US ratified the ICCPR in accordance with actions occurring outside its territory in 1992. Therefore, the US asserts that it is not legally bound to comply with ICCPR in respect to any surveillance operations over non-US communications systems or activities which are not housed in the US. This position asserts that the US states that the ICCPR obligations are restricted to very specific circumstances. These circumstances are when an individual is both within a state's territory and subject to its jurisdiction. Therefore, if these two conditions are not satisfied then the foreign individual concerned does not benefit from privacy protection under the ICCPR.[65]

In the UK state surveillance, the Investigatory Powers Tribunal (IPT) has looked at the issue of the UK's international law obligations and human rights protections of individuals privacy in *Human Rights Watch v Secretary of State*.[66] The Court here was concerned with the interception, storage and use of information and communications by the Government Communications Headquarters (GCHQ). The case concerned a group of UK residents and a group of individuals that were not residing in the UK. Regarding the question of the rights to privacy for the individuals not residing in the UK the court expressed that 'under Article 8 of the [European Convention on Human Rights (ECHR)] the UK owes no obligation to persons who are situated outside its territory in respect of electronic communications between them which passes through the state'.[67] The IPT when investigating, therefore, considered two issues in relation to infringement of privacy. The first issue of standing (whether such an individual could make a claim from being directly affected) the tribunal decided that all the applicants had standing if they could provide the information necessary for the investigation. The controversial element was the second issue of extraterritorial application of the ECHR. The Tribunal concluded that the ECHR was not applicable to individuals living abroad even if they have been the subject to surveillance by the state.

Extraterritorial application concerns the issue of whether the ECHR applies to individuals abroad and whether states owe human rights protection to those individuals living outside their territory.[68] The discussion is concerned with the interpretation of the term 'jurisdiction' within the ECHR. The IPT, therefore, was submitting the question that is an individual under the jurisdiction of the UK if they have been under surveillance by the state but the individual is not domiciled within the UK.

The controversial issue of extraterritorial application decision by the IPT strikes is at the very centre of the right to privacy. Communications via the digital medium do not have respect for national borders and neither do digital communication companies or state government. Logic would suggest that the right to privacy should not be depended on an individual's location and whether they are protected by article 8 of the ECHR.

The findings in *Human Rights Watch v Secretary of State* have been controversial and have been criticised.[69] As the IPT decisions cannot be subject to a direct appeal in the UK, therefore, the IPT decisions could be challenged by the ECtHR.

3.1. ICCPR: effective control v virtual control

If states are primarily basing the jurisdiction of privacy on territory this would seem to not fit easily with the circumstances which are set out within international law. However, all human rights courts and bodies, such as the International Court of Justice (ICJ), the HRC and the Inter-American Commission on Human Rights (IACHR) that privacy issues may exist beyond merely a state's territory and exist outside a state's territory i.e. extraterritorially.

This simply means a state is therefore bound by international law in relation to individuals who may not be domiciled within the state borders but who are under the control of its jurisdiction. The HRC has adopted the following approach (similar to effective control) to determine not only the jurisdiction but also the protection of an individual's privacy where they are not domiciled within the state in questions borders:

> A state party must respect and ensure the rights laid down in the International Covenant on Civil and Political Rights to anyone within the power or effective control of that State Party even if not situated within the territory of the State Party.[70]

The IACHR established similar principles:

> The inquiry turns not on the presumed victim's nationality or presence within a particular geographical area but on whether under specific circumstances the State observed the rights of a person subject to its authority and control.[71]

How international law obligations may apply outside a state's geographical territory is spilt into two different categories: spatial and personal models. The spatial model sees jurisdiction as effective overall control over a specific geographical area, but the personal model sees it as a physical control over the individual in question.

The spatial model was established in the ECtHR case *Loizidou v Turkey*. In this case, the Court established 'a state's responsibility was engaged when as a consequence of lawful or unlawful military action, it exercised effective control of an area outside its national territory'.[72] In the International Court of Justice case *DRC v Uganda*, it was held that the ICCPR applies 'extraterritorially when a state is occupying territory of another state'.[73]

However, both these examples seem to apply to military exposition and control but do not go far enough in everyday protection of individuals right to privacy. Milanovic stated that in some circumstances during conflict states could control areas without being in another state's territory. For example, the use by a state of drones during conflict would have effective control over an area without physically being in another states territory.[74]

The case of *Lopez Burgos v Uruguay*[75] is important to note here, even though not directly about privacy, it is important in the context of effective control of individuals and whether they should have the same protection of their rights regardless of where they are domiciled. In this case, the applicant was alleged to have been kidnapped and tortured in Argentina by Uruguayan security and intelligence forces due to his trade union activities, despite having a visa to enter Austria and having political refugee statues granted by the UNHCR. The HRC emphasised in this case that an individual right and the protection of them do not diminish once they are domiciled in a foreign state. The HRC expressed these obligations in the following way:

> It would be unconscionable to so interpret the responsibility under Article 2 of the ICCPR as to permit a State party to perpetrate violations of the Covenant on the territory of another State which violations it could not perpetrate on its own territory ... a State party must respect and ensure the rights laid down in the Covenant to anyone within the power or effective control of that State Party even if not situated within the territory of the State Party ... regardless of the circumstances in which such power or effective control was obtained.[76]

Therefore, a state must have under international law a human rights obligation by the means of the effective control over an individual. In times of conflict this rule would need to be extended to encompass the obligation of a state where there is the privacy of communications by an individual who is residing in a foreign state.

The effective control test works well in times of conflict due to the physical nature of the definition and the finding of international courts but is harder to make it fit with modern privacy concerns over surveillance and interception of individual's private communications.

Margulies[77] has suggested that the existing effective control test is 'inadequate for the cyber and communications realm as it places the emphasis on the exercise of physical over persons or territory which is difficult to relate to cyberspace'.[78] Therefore, Margulies suggested that the US which has unprecedented virtual power and the narrowly defined standard of privacy requiring physical control means that it is easy to exploit this gap by ignoring their human rights obligations. The US, for example, has relationships with communications companies allowing direct access to surveillance transmitting devices, undersea cables and other carriers of internet and telephonic communications.[79]

Then international law must protect privacy by looking at the obligations in the controlling of communications not the effective control over physical areas or physical individuals. Nyst[80] argues that instead of looking at control as in physical control of territory, it must be looked at in terms of when data or communications are intercepted within that states territory, the state in question should owe obligations to those individuals regardless of their location on the basis Nyst suggests of 'interface-based jurisdiction' that a state is not allowed to 'interfere with communications that passes through its territorial borders'.[81]

Nyst has the same thinking of Milanovic[82] who distinguishes between the positive obligation of states to protect human rights and to preventing human rights violations by third parties and negative obligation of states to respect human rights that only require states to refrain from interfering with the rights of individuals without sufficient justification.[83] Milanovic, therefore, is suggesting that within this construct it sees jurisdiction as a negative duty to not interfere and therefore all violations as negative when interfering with privacy.[84]

Both Nyst and Milanovic approaches here look at the weakness of the privacy debate couched in the confines of the personal and spatial models and put at the centre of their thinking that there must be an emphasis on the negative duty that states cannot interfere with rights that are protected.

There is also a larger picture here which is not just about the protected right of interference of communication and storing of data. There is also the subject of collusion and the sharing of personal data between states which makes the obligation and protection of privacy so difficult to police against. The agreements between the US and other states allow governments to simply engage in the notion of 'collusion for circumvention'.[85] GCHQ is allowed to essentially spy on anyone except British nationals[86] and the NSA through the PRISM surveillance program is allowed to spy on anyone that is not American.[87]

The PRISM program allows the NSA to collect communication from US internet communications companies. The collection of this data is governed by Section 702 FISA Amendments Act 2008 which allows communication data, encrypted data and search entries from companies such as Google, Yahoo and Microsoft to be transferred to the NSA.[88]

The documents leaked by Edward Snowden suggested that PRISM is 'the number one source of raw intelligence area for the NSA analytic reports and makes up approximately 91% of NSA internet acquired data'.[89] The US government has defended the use of PRISM stating that is can only be used on US nationals with a warrant and it has prevented act of Terrorism.[90]

Then the data information collected by GCHQ and the NSA is shared between the two agencies and therefore enables each agency to circumvent any national restrictions that are in place protecting its own citizens right to privacy, as they are able to access this information that has been gathered on their own citizens by foreign governmental agencies.[91]

There has also been a suggestion of the 'virtual control test'. This was proposed by Margulies[92] who suggested that a virtual control test would make the ICCPR and other international human rights treaties applicable when a state can assert 'virtual control' over an individual's communications even if the state does not have control over the territory the individual is located.[93] Margulies suggests that virtual control would be when a state intercepts, stores and analyses an individual's communications.

Of course, this test is a suggestion and has not be accepted or adopted by the international community as the expansion or different approach to privacy and the protection of it. Paust has criticised the approach as it has little or no shared legal expectation about personal jurisdiction and privacy.[94]

However, such an approach does not fit with the jurisprudence of the ECtHR in the case of *Jaloud v Netherlands*.[95] For example, in this case, the court took a more expansive approach and extraterritorial jurisdiction in privacy matters was suggested, because the state can 'exercise authority and control over individuals right to life which made the physical nature of effective control unimportant'.[96]

A virtual control test would ensure equal treatment of all individuals not dependent on their location because the establishing a virtual control test would not depend on where the communications took place but rather on whether a state can have control of it even if its lacks control over the territory or physical person.

The HRC has addressed this matter head on suggesting extraterritorial surveillance does not affect the right to privacy and the ICCPR. The HRC suggested:

> The Committee is concerned about the surveillance of communications in the interest of protecting national security conducted by the National Security Agency (NSA) conducted both within and outside the United States.[97]

United Nations Office of the High Commissioner also addressed the issue:

> Digital surveillance may engage a State's human rights obligations if that surveillance involves the State's exercise of power or effective control in relation to digital communications infrastructure, wherever found for example through direct tapping or penetration of that infrastructure. Equally where a State exercises regulatory jurisdiction over a third party that physically controls the data that State also would have obligations under the Covenant.[98]

The Special Rapporteur observed:

> State's jurisdiction is not only engaged where State agents place data interceptors on fibre-optic cables travelling through their jurisdictions but also where a State exercises regulatory authority over the telecommunications or Internet service providers that physically control the data.[99]

The UN General Assembly when adopting Resolution 68/167 expressed:

> At the negative impact that surveillance including extraterritorial surveillance in particular when carried out on a mass scale may have on the exercise and enjoyment of human rights.[100]

Therefore, it can be seen that a virtual control test is needed as the elements which make up the effective control test over privacy do not fit the digital age. It is impossible to know where and how physical control is made in the traditional sense and where in the traditional sense territorial control is ascertained. This is because with digital communications, all such communications are sent through various different territories and jurisdictions before the reach their destination of the user. So, what becomes important, is whether the virtual control can be implemented regardless of where the individual is located or their nationality.

3.2. United Nations and the future of surveillance

The international community has taken steps to look at enhancing the protection of privacy since the adoption of the ICCPR in 1966 and the subsequent HRC's adoption of General Comment No 16 on the right to privacy in 1988.[101] These steps do include a focus on human rights and surveillance practices of the UN High Commissioner for Human Rights and the UN Special Rapporteurs on Freedom of Expression and Counter-Terrorism. The adoption of both UN General Assembly Resolutions and the UN Human Rights Council Resolutions on the right to privacy showed a focus on the issues by the international community. The 2015 creation of a UN Special Rapporteur on the Right to Privacy shows the focus on international importance of privacy. The HRC has also addressed surveillance legislation in its Concluding Observations to States. Also, the ECtHR, the CJEU and the Inter-American Commission and Court on Human Rights have developed a jurisprudence on right to privacy.

There are of course the arguments that these steps are not progressive enough. Most of these advancements are merely regional agreements or soft law principles without much real binding force on states and their behaviour towards the right to privacy.

However, some of these advancements have started to influence the behaviour of states towards the intrusion of states into individual's privacy. Canada's decision to stop the sharing of intelligence data with its Five Eyes partners was in direct response to the evidence of the unlawful surveillance of Canadians.[102] In 2014 the German Parliamentary Committee investigating the spy scandal involving the National Security Agency (NSA) has led to a lessening of the cooperation between the Federal Intelligence Agency (BND) and the NSA.[103] Also, there has been an increase in privacy cases being decided by German Courts.[104]

The UN has reaffirmed its commitment to the question of the protection of data in the digital age in Human Rights Council Resolution adopted in 2017 which reaffirmed its commitment to the issue by reaffirming many privacy issues that had previously been decided.

In 2015 via Resolution 28/16 the UN Human Rights Council decided to appoint (after international community interest in the OHCHR Report into privacy) a Special Rapporteur on the right to privacy for a period of three years.[105] The resolution directed the

Special Rapporteur to report on alleged violations of the right to privacy including in particular concerns arising from new technologies. With this mandate in mind all member states were urged to cooperate fully with the office of the Special Rapporteur.

The main findings from the Special Rapporteur can be seen in the right to privacy report; Report of the Special Rapporteur on the right to privacy from 27 February 2019.[106] In the report, the Special Rapporteur states that the 'right to privacy can facilitate the enjoyment of other human rights. Equally its infringements constrain the enjoyment of other human rights'.[107] He is also critical of the states not taking seriously the regulations on privacy that they have signed up to stating: 'there are several historical examples of Member States ratifying international instruments on human rights while lacking the genuine will to take the necessary measures for their implementation'.[108] The example used is former German Democratic Republic who signed the ICCPR in 1973 but was still openly using a surveillance regime against its citizens. The report went on to state that today there were similar contradictions. Many states commit themselves to protecting the right to privacy but are also acting in ways which puts this privacy at risk.[109]

The report used a Sieghart quote to explain that the right to privacy is integral to personal autonomy, the links between privacy, information flows, autonomy and power exist.[110] Sieghart suggests the following:

> In a society where modern information technology is developing fast, many others may be able to find out how we act. And that, in turn, may reduce our freedom to act as we please – because once others discover how we act, they may think that it is in their interest, or in the interest of society, or even in our own interest to dissuade us, discourage us, or even stopping us from doing what we want to do, and seek to manipulate us to do what they want to do.[111]

The above position the Special Rapporteur linked to privacy in the following way[112]:

> Shorn of the cloak of privacy that protects him, an individual becomes transparent and therefore manipulable. A manipulable individual is at the mercy of those who control the information held about him, and his freedom, which is often relative at best, shrinks in direct proportion to the extent of the nature of the options and alternatives which are left open to him by those who control the information.[113]

The report therefore clearly sets out the importance of the protection of privacy and it states 'infringing upon privacy is often part of a system which threatens other liberties'.[114] The report also reaffirmed the position of the HRC`s resolution of March 2017[115] that 'States should ensure that any interference with the right to privacy is consistent with the principles of legality, necessity and proportionality'.[116]

The main privacy recommendations of the report included the following[117]:

> 47. The incorporation by UN Member States into their domestic legal system of the standards and safeguards set out in Convention 108+ Article 11,[118] for the protection of the fundamental right to privacy, especially:
>
> (a) the creation of legal certainty by ensuring that any and all privacy-intrusive measures.
>
> (b) the establishment of the test of 'a necessary and proportionate measure in a democratic society'.
>
> (c) the establishment of one or more independent oversight authorities empowered by law and adequately resourced by the State.

> 48. (a) All UN Member States should amend their laws to empower their independent authorities entrusted with oversight of intelligence activities, to specifically and explicitly, oversight of all personal information exchanged between the intelligence agencies of the countries for which they are responsible.

In conclusion[119] the Special Rapporteur again expressed the importance of the right to privacy for individuals within the international community:

> 102. The confidence of individuals to share ideas and to assemble is also fundamental to the health of societies and democracy. The loss of privacy can lead to a loss of this confidence including confidence in Government and institutions established to represent the public interests, withdrawal from participation, which can adversely impact and undermine representative democracies.
>
> 103. While privacy rights are not costless, or free of risks to governments, the challenges are outweighed by our collective interest in democracy. The right to privacy for women, as well as children and individuals of diverse sexual orientations, gender identities, gender expressions and sex characteristics, is critically important for all of the reasons outlined above and reported in submissions.
>
> 108. Transparency is needed in how private companies use personal data of users, and respond to reports of online harassment. Greater gender diversity among those shaping online experiences is important for making products and platforms safer, more socially-responsible and accountable.

Therefore, throughout the findings of the Special Rapporteur and specifically the recommendations and conclusions from the report that the right to privacy is an area which needs protection and the cooperation of states within the UN to insure that individual`s privacy or the obscurity of certain information is a protected right.

4. Cambridge Analytica and the right to privacy

This part of this article will focus on the way forward for the right to privacy after the Cambridge Analytica scandal and how this may be a focus for reevaluation of the what is privacy and who should hold the key to private information of individuals. Whether this is the inherent right to privacy which is incumbent in international treaties or the right to obscurity in cyberspace one element is clear and that there is a need for tightening up of the law in this area to be clear for those companies that hold individual's information on what will constitute a breach and punishment for the misuse of personal data.

On 17 March 2018, the New York Times and the Guardian published stories exposing that the personal data of over 50 million Facebook users were in the possession of a company called Cambridge Analytica.[120] Cambridge Analytica was a company[121] which had links not only to the 2016 US election but also the 2016 UK Brexit Referendum.[122]

Cambridge Analytica was a British political data consulting firm which combined data mining, data brokerage and data analysis with strategic communication which used specifically during election campaigns.[123] The personal data of up to 87 million Facebook users were acquired via the 270,000 Facebook users who used an app called 'This is Your Digital Life'. By giving this third party app permission to acquire data (in 2015) this also gave the app access to information which was stored on the apps user's associate networks. Therefore, this resulted in data of about 87 million users, the vast majority of who had not given Cambridge Analytica the permission to access their personal data.[124]

Cambridge Analytica was based on a system engineered by Michal Kosinski. The system was based around a profiling system of general online data from likes on Facebook and data collected from smartphones. Kosinski suggested that with a limited number of 'likes' individuals can be analysed more efficiently and individual psychological targeting is a powerful tool to influence people.[125] Cambridge Analytica would then collect data on potential voters using this data via such actions as demographics, consumer behaviour and internet activity. According to The Guardian, the data used psychological data derived from millions of Facebook users without permission.[126] Other sources of information included the 'Cruz Crew' which was a mobile app that tracked physical movements and contacts.[127]

The use and collection of personal data without permission raises privacy issues and ethical concerns. But Cambridge Analytica company base was in the United States and privacy laws are not enacted with protecting privacy. The Cruz Crew app's database has been described as 'political-voter surveillance'.[128]

Cambridge Analytica scope was wide and influence widespread. In India, Cambridge Analytica was used by the Indian National Congress to carry out analysis of the electorate and influence voters in the 2010 elections. It was found that 355 Indian Facebook users had installed a Cambridge Analytica app which then, in turn, exposed the data of 562,455 other users. The Indian National Congress was also given data information by Cambridge Analytica for the 2019 general elections.[129] Cambridge Analytica ran secret campaigns in Kenya for the 2013 and 2017 elections.[130] There are also accusations that Cambridge Analytica had influence on elections in Australia, Malta and Mexico.[131]

However, by far the most controversial influence Cambridge Analytica had was alleged to have had was on the US 2016 Presidential elections and the 2016 EU Referendum in the UK.

Cambridge Analytica became involved in the 2016 UK European Union Membership Referendum (commonly known as Brexit) using data to convince 'persuadable' voters to vote to leave the European Union.[132] Articles that appeared in February and May in 2017 in the Observer and the Guardian suggested respectively that Cambridge Analytica had influenced the Vote Leave campaign and Donald Trump's 2016 presidential campaign.[133] It was claimed that Cambridge Analytica had produced a document claiming that it could affect the outcome of the referendum with the data it had collected. The document was entitled 'Big Data Solutions for the EU Referendum' and claimed it could single out vote leave voters, donors, politicians and journalists.[134]

In March 2018 Christopher Wylie a former Cambridge Analytica employee told the UK Electoral Commission that a firm linked to Cambridge Analytica helped the official Vote Leave campaign by circumventing the financing laws in place during the EU referendum.[135]

Cambridge Analytica involvement in the 2016 presidential primaries for the Republican Party became known in July 2015.[136] As of December that same year, Cambridge Analytica claimed to have collected up to 5,000 data points on over 220 million US citizens.[137] After Ted Cruz dropped out of the Republican presidential nomination race, Cambridge Analytica started to work closely with Republican candidate Donald Trump.

On 18 May 2017, the US Congress started to investigate Cambridge Analytica in connection with possible Russian interference in the 2016 US election campaign.[138] It was suggested the Cambridge Analytica breached data privacy by spreading Russian propaganda using micro targeting.[139] In 2018 it was found that Cambridge Analytica had used 50 million Facebook users personal data without permission while assisting Donald Trump's presidential campaign. This information it was suggested was used to influence the US election in Donald Trump's favour.[140]

In the UK the Information Commissioners Office (ICO) conducted an investigation into data analytics for political purposes and in response to the Cambridge Analytica scandal obtained new and stronger powers as the UK Data Protection Act 2018. In November 2018 the ICO published its report to Parliament on the use of data in political campaigns and highlighted:

> A disturbing disregard for voters' personal privacy by players across the political campaigning system from data companies and data brokers to social media platforms, campaign groups and political parties.[141]

Mark Zuckerberg (CEO Facebook) announced in March 2019 that Facebook would build a 'privacy focused messaging and social networking platform'.[142] He was criticised for failing to address whether the company would stop purchasing information from data analysts, harvesting data from individuals not using Facebook.[143]

The importance of the discussion on Cambridge Analytica is its impact on the wider discussion on the protection of privacy. After the scandal broke it seems that the international community has been forced into action on the right to privacy and access to data issues. This has seen investigations in Italy Germany and Canada. These investigations have all led to the call on Facebook to regulate its use of personal data.

Within the discussions of this article, Cambridge Analytica and the focus it put on privacy does not seem to have influenced any enhancements in fundamental international legal protection of privacy. It seems that it has had a greater influence on regional discussion and region reform. If international law had a more robust approach to how privacy should be protected and more measures which are not on a voluntary basis, then international human rights law would and should be the basis of protection from the privacy breach seen by Cambridge Analytica and any future incarnation.

Therefore, without the necessary framework in place it would seem privacy protection from international law and the United Nations in the case of Cambridge Analytica would be difficult.

5. Future development of privacy protection under international law

There is data protection, as this article has set out in UDHR, ICCPR and an interpretation of data protection guaranteed by the UNHRC. The protection of privacy within international law is uncertain due to several competing factors.

International human rights treaties (like the ICCPR) do not mention the need for data protection specifically and the guidance and guarantees are very broad which leaves little room for direct guidance for the courts.

International legal framework is fragmented between international human rights law, regional legal agreement and national legal agreements. For example, there is a fundamental rights approach in EU law[144] in the protection of individual privacy contrasting with the US approach[145] based on a more consumer protection approach. As Kittichaisaree and Kuner state few states agree with position of the US that international law does not preclude unauthorised intelligence gathering as long as the activity does not involve commercial or industrial espionage or the destruction of data.[146]

A future development of protection under international law could take three main areas of privacy rights protection.

Firstly, there is a need for a more precise normative framework based on what is privacy and obscurity for the courts or a new legal framework to address. This could be based on Hartzog and Strutman four factors for recognition of what is private and what is public privacy as discussed early in this article.[147]

Secondly, to draft a new international agreement dealing with data protection. This would have the profound advantage of setting out a clear, precise framework based around privacy protection. However, there are obstacles to such an agreement. An agreement between all states on what is privacy and the need to balance the need of data protection for the individual against the wider needs of society. For example, states would still uphold the right of infringement of privacy in light of terrorism concerns. There might also be the practical barrier that a treaty-based solution might not provide the most adequate remedy in an area which is as fast moving as data protection and future technologies.

Thirdly, international law could accept that data protection is too fragmented to have one centralised hierarchical system of protection. Kittichaisaree and Kuner suggest that this would allow data protection to develop on a regional and national level through international cooperation, therefore allowing privacy protection that could develop over time that states could adopt voluntarily at a national level providing a common internationalised approach to the protection of privacy.[148]

It is clear, what is needed is a holistic approach from the international community, which brings together implementation of data protection laws at a national level which could then influence a more progressive development of the protection of individual privacy at an international level.

6. Conclusion

Individuals place a great deal of importance on the notion of privacy. There is an inherent right of the individual to protect one's personal and private thoughts and actions. The right to protect privacy is important in establishing and forming human relationships. There is also a very real link between the need for privacy and the connection to dignity as human beings.

As this article has shown at the international level there is evidence through treaty level implementation to the continuing discussion at the UN level that privacy and the existence of privacy is a fundamental right which exists as a universal principle of human existence. The need to protect this right is something which is becoming increasingly important and increasingly difficult within the digital age. The difficulty comes in the fact that much of our protected privacy is now within the digital sphere making the protection from surveillance and intrusion from the state much harder to regulate.

The right to privacy can be recognised as the following:

> Privacy is a fundamental human right that has been defined as the presumption that individuals should have an area of autonomous development, interaction and liberty, a 'private sphere' with or without interaction with others and free from state intervention and free from excessive unsolicited intervention by other uninvited individuals.[149]

The evidence that the right to privacy is now considered to be within the higher scope of international law can be seen by its protected status within several international law doctrines and within international customary law. Of course, there is a cavate to this which is prevalent within the international law sphere that this right to privacy is not an absolute right and in most cases this right is balanced against the interest of states.

The legal definition of a right to privacy needs to be a continuous process. The development and advances of new technology means that this area needs to be constantly adaptable to change. These developments will constantly make the application and protection of the need of an individual's privacy much more complex. As technology advances the temptation of states to use individual data becomes greater.

The current legal framework in international law is at times unclear. The UN through the Special Rapporteur is clear in reinforcing the rights protected under the ICCPR, UDHR, HRC`s General Comment no 17 and others but states are, especially through the Five-Eye states infringing individual rights, collecting data on individuals and using such data without permission.

Privacy and its protection are a complex notion and there are not any failsafe routes to individual privacy protection. There is a fundamental right to be left alone and elements of this article have discussed whether an individual has a right to obscurity in the digital age. This article shows there are positive steps being made in the international community for the protection of individual privacy. However, it is clear that the law and international law in particular, must be clearer and more robust to protect the individual from interference from the state and private companies.

Notes

1. Universal Declaration of Human Rights, 10 December 1948, GA/Res/217A.
2. International Covenant on Civil and Political Rights, 23 March 1976, 999 UNTS 171, Art. 17.
3. United Nations Human Rights Council, *Report by the Special Rapporteur on the Promotion and Protection of the Right to Freedom and Protection of the Right to Freedom of Opinion and Expression*, 2013, UN Doc., A/HRC/23/40.
4. Human Rights Council, *UN Resolution on the Right to Privacy in the Digital Age*, 2017, UN Doc., A/HRC/RES/34/7.
5. There are under international law two distinct control tests, one over territory and one over persons. The effective control test is based on acts of private individuals or groups controlled by the state. From *Nicaragua v United States*, ICJ Rep.14, (1986), 115.
6. United Nations General Assembly, *Report of the Office of the United Nations High Commissioner for Human Rights; the Right to Privacy in the Digital Age*, 2014, UN Doc. A/HRC/27/37, para 20.
7. The often referred to Five Eyes comprises the US National Security Agency, the UK General Communication Headquarters, Canada's Communications Security Establishment, New Zealand's Government Communications Security Bureau and the Australian Signals Intelligence Directorate.
8. United Nations Human Rights Commission, *General Comment No 16 Article 17 (Right to Privacy), The Right to Respect of Privacy, Family Home and Correspondence and Protection of Honour and Reputation*, 8 April 1988, UN Doc., HRI/GEN/Rev9.
9. Notably from the Human Rights Committee (HRC).
10. United Nations Human Rights Council, *Report by the Special Rapporteur on the Promotion and Protection of the Right to Freedom and Protection of the Right to Freedom of Opinion and Expression*, 2013, UN Doc. A/HRC/23/40.

11. United Nations General Assembly, 18 December 2013, Res 68/167 UN Doc., A/RES/68/167, United Nations General Assembly, 18 December 2014, Res 69/166 18, UN Doc. A/RES/69/166.
12. United Nations Human Rights Commission, *General Comment No 16 Article 17 (Right to Privacy), The Right to Respect of Privacy, Family Home and Correspondence and Protection of Honour and Reputation*, 8 April 1988, UN Doc. HRI/GEN/Rev9.
13. Ibid., para 10.
14. United Nations Human Rights Committee, *Consideration of Reports Submitted by States Parties Under Article 40 of the Covenant, Concluding Observations in Spain*, 2009, UN Doc. CCPR/C/ESP/CO/5, para 11.
15. *Botta v Italy, ECHR*, Appl. No 21439/93, (1994).
16. *MK v France*, ECHR, Appl. No 19522/09, (2013).
17. *S and Marper v UK*, ECHR, Appl. No 30542/04, (2008).
18. *Bensaid v UK*, ECHR, Appl. No 44599/98, (2001).
19. *S and Marper v UK*, ECHR, Appl. No 30542/04, (2008), para 47.
20. *Botta v Italy, ECHR*, Appl. No 21439/93, (1994).
21. *Maximilan Schrems v Data Protection Commissioner*, CJEU, C-362/14, (2015).
22. PRISM is a code name for a mass surveillance program which the US National Security Agency (NSA) collects internet communications from various US based companies.
23. *Maximilan Schrems v Data Protection Commissioner*, CJEU, C-362/14, (2015) para 92.
24. Ibid., para 94.
25. Statute of the International Court of Justice, 26 June 1945, 33 UNTS, 993.
26. See above, Article 38, (1)(b).
27. *North Sea Continental Shelf Cases, ICJ*, Reports 3, 28, (1969).
28. Philip Alston, *Human Rights Law* (New York: New York University Press, 1996), 3–8.
29. Unite Nations General Assembly, Universal Declaration of Human Rights, 10 December 1948, 217A, (III).
30. Robert C. Post, 'Three Concepts of Privacy', *Georgetown Law Journal* 89 (2001): 2087.
31. Daniel J. Solove, 'Conceptualizing Privacy', *California Law Review* 90, no. 4 (2002): 1087.
32. Alexandra Rengel, 'Privacy as an International Human Right and the Right to Obscurity in Cyberspace', *Groningen Journal of International Law* 2, no. 2 (2014): 38.
33. T. Gerety, 'Redefining Privacy', *Harvard Civil Rights-Civil Liberties Law Review* 12 (1977): 236 and William Parent, 'Privacy Morality and the Law', *Philosophy and Public Affairs* 12, no. 4 (1983): 323.
34. Alan Westin, *Privacy and Freedom* (New York: Atheneum, 1970), 330.
35. Hyman Gross, 'The Concept of Privacy', *New York University Law Review* 42, no. 1 (1967): 34–5.
36. Daniel J. Solove, *Understanding Privacy* (Cambridge: Harvard University Press, 2009), 13.
37. Ibid., 39. Political scientist Priscilla Regan states that privacy interests are not individual interests but the interests of society. She explains that individual perceptions fail to appreciate the importance of privacy for individuals fails to recognise its importance as common, public and collective values. See Priscilla Regan, *Legislating Privacy: Technology, Social Values and Public Policy* (Chapter Hill: University of North Carolina Press, 1995).
38. P.B. Newell, 'Perspectives on Privacy', *Journal of Environmental Psychology* 15, no. 2 (1995): 88–105.
39. Priscilla Regan, *Legislating Privacy: Technology, Social Values and Public Policy* (Chapter Hill: University of North Carolina Press, 1995).
40. Jeffrey H. Reiman, 'Driving to the Panopticon: A Philosophical Exploration of the Risks to Privacy Posed by the Highway Technology of the Future', *Santa Clara High Tech Law Journal* 11, no. 1 (1995): 27.
41. Article 28 International Covenant on Civil and Political Rights 1966.
42. General Assembly Report of the Human Rights Committee 43rd Session, 1988, A/43/40.
43. Ibid, para 3.
44. Alexandra Rengel, *Privacy in the 21st Century* (Leiden: Martinus Nijhof Publishers, 2013).

45. Woodrow Hartzog and Fred Strutzman, 'The Case for Online Obscurity', *California Law Review* 101 (2013): 1.
46. Ibid., 112.
47. Ibid., 113.
48. Ibid.
49. Ibid., 36
50. Ibid.
51. *United States v Gines-Perez*, D.P.R., F Suppl. 214 (2002) 205.
52. *Pietrylo v Hillstone Restaurant Group,* D.N.J, WL 6085437 (2008).
53. International Covenant on Civil and Political Rights, March 23 1976, 999 UNTS 171, Art. 17, Art. 2(1).
54. Five Eyes comprises the US National Security Agency, the UK General Communication Headquarters, Canada's Communications Security Establishment, New Zealand's Government Communications Security Bureau and the Australian Signals Intelligence Directorate.
55. United Kingdom, Regulation of Investigatory Powers Act, 2000, Sec., 8(4) and Investigatory Powers Act, 2016.
56. United States, Foreign Intelligence Surveillance Act, 1978. Sec., 1881a(a).
57. Australia, Australian Intelligence Services Act, 2001, Sec., 9.
58. Canada, Canadian National Defence Act, 1985, Sec., 273.64(1).
59. United Kingdom, Regulation of Investigatory Powers Act, 2000, Sec., 8(2).
60. Ibid., Sec., 20.
61. *Privacy International v GCHQ*, IPT/13/92/CH (16 May 2014).
62. United Nations Human Rights Council, *Concluding Observations on the Seventh Periodic Repost of the UK and Northern Ireland*, 17 August 2015, UN Doc., CCPR/C/GBR/Co/7.
63. Ibid., 31
64. United Kingdom, Investigatory Powers Act, 2016, Sec. 136(3).
65. United Nations Human Rights Commission, *Summary Record*, 1405th Meeting, 24 April 1995, UN Doc., CCPR/C/SR 1405, para 20. United States Department, *Second and Third Periodic Report of the USA to the UN Committee on Human Rights Concerning the International Covenant on Civil and Political Rights*, 21 October 2005.
66. *Human Rights Watch Inc and Others v The Secretary of State for the Foreign and Commonwealth Office and Others,* ALL ER, (2016) 105.
67. Ibid., 106.
68. Marko Milanovic, *Extraterritorial Application of Human Rights Treaties: Law, Principles, and Policy* (Oxford: Oxford University Press, 2011), 8.
69. Scarlet Kim, 'ECHR Jurisdiction and Mass Surveillance: Scrutinising the UK Investigatory Power Tribunal's Recent Ruling', *EJIL:Talk!* (June 9, 2016).
70. United Nations Human Rights Commission, *General Comment No 31 The Nature of the General Obligations Imposed on State Parties to the Covenant*, 2004, UN Doc. CCPR/C/21/Rev.1/Add1326, para 10.
71. *Alexandre v Cuba*, IACHR, Case 11.589, Report No 109/99, (1999), para 37.
72. *Loizidou v Turkey*, EHRR, 20, (1995), 98.
73. *Case Concerning Armed Activities on the Territory of the Congo in Democratic Republic of Congo v Uganda,* ICJ, (2000), 111.
74. Marko Milanovic, 'Human Rights Treaties and Foreign Surveillance: Privacy in the Digital Age', *Harvard International Law Journal*, 81 (2015):113.
75. *Lopez Burgos v Uruguay*, Communications No 52, UN Doc., CCPR/C13/D/52/1979, (1979).
76. Ibid., para 10.
77. Peter Margulies, 'The NSA in the Global Perspective: Surveillance, Human Rights and International Counterterrorism', *Fordham Law Review* 82 (2014): 2137.
78. Ibid., 2150.
79. Ibid.
80. Carly Nyst, 'Interface Based Jurisdiction Over Violations of the Right to Privacy', *EJIL:Talk!* (November 16, 2013).

81. Ibid., 48.
82. Ibid., 126.
83. Ibid., 50.
84. Ibid., 129.
85. Parliamentary Assembly of the Council of Europe 'Mass Surveillance', Doc. 13734, 2015, para. 30–33.
86. Allowed to spy on British nationals only with reasonable suspicion.
87. Parliamentary Assembly of the Council of Europe 'Mass Surveillance', para. 53.
88. The Washington Post, 'NSA Slides Explain the PRSIM Data Collection Program', *The Washington Post*, June 6, 2013.
89. Glen Greenwald, 'NSA Taps into Internet Giants' Systems to Mine Data', *The Guardian*, June 6, 2013.
90. Stepeh Ovide, 'US Officials Releases Details of PRISM Program', *Wall Street Journal*, June 8, 2013.
91. Ibid., 53.
92. Peter Margulies, 'The NSA in the Global Perspective: Surveillance, Human Rights and International Counterterrorism', *Fordham Law Review* 82 (2014): 2139.
93. Ibid., 2157.
94. Jordan J. Paust, 'Can You Hear Me Now? Private Communications, National Security and the Human Rights Disconnect', *Chicago Journal of International Law* 15, no. 2 (2015): 612.
95. *Jaloud v Netherlands*, ECHR, Appl. No 47708/08, (2014).
96. Ibid.
97. United Nations Human Rights Council, *Concluding Observations on the Fourth Periodic Report of the USA*, April 23, 2014, CCRP/C/USA/CO/4, para. 22.
98. Ibid., para 34.
99. United Nations, *Report of the Special Rapporteur on the Promotion and Protection of Human Rights and Fundamental Freedoms While Countering Terrorism*, 2014, UN Doc. A/69/397, para. 41.
100. United Nations General Assembly, Res 68/167, 18 December 2013.
101. Human Rights Committee, General Comment 16, 22nd session, 21 UN Doc. HRI/GEN/1/Rev.1, (1988) 21.
102. Associated Foreign Press, 'Canada Spy Agency Stops Sharing Intelligence with International Partners', *The Guardian*, January 28, 2016.
103. The Guardian, 'German court backs murder's right to be forgotten online', *The Guardian*, November 27, 2019.
104. Ibid.
105. The Special Rapporteur is mandated by Human Rights Council Resolution 28/16 to submit an annual report to the Human Rights Council and the General Assembly on information, trends, obstacles and violations related to the right to privacy.
106. United Nations, *Report of the Special Rapporteur on the Right to Privacy*, 2019, Unedited Version, A/HRC/40/63.
107. Ibid., para. 4.
108. Ibid., para. 5.
109. Ibid., para. 6.
110. Ibid., para. 8.
111. Peter Sieghart, *Privacy and Computers* (London: Latimer, 1976), 24.
112. United Nations, *Report of the Special Rapporteur on the Right to Privacy*, 2019, Unedited Version, A/HRC/40/63, para. 9.
113. Joseph Cannataci, *Privacy & Data Protection Law* (Oslo: Norwegian University Press, 1987), 60.
114. United Nations, *Report of the Special Rapporteur on the Right to Privacy*, 2019, Unedited Version, A/HRC/40/63, para. 10.
115. Ibid., para. 2.
116. Ibid., para. 17.

117. Ibid., para. 46, 47 and 48.
118. Convention 108+ Article 11 is a Council of Europe Convention for the Protection of Individuals with regard to Automatic Processing of Personal Data CETS No 108.
119. United Nations, *Report of the Special Rapporteur on the Right to Privacy*, 2019, Unedited Version, A/HRC/40/63, para. 102, 103 and 108.
120. There were a number of individuals who helped expose Cambridge Analytica; Carole Cadwalladr (journalist), Christopher Wylie (a former employee of Cambridge Analytica), Shahmir Sanni (a volunteer with the Vote Leave Campaign in the UK Brexit Referendum), and Professor David Carrol, a Professor, who has engaged in a lengthy battle to obtain his data from Cambridge Analytica.
121. The company was partly owned Robert Mercer, an American hedge-fund manager who supports manly conservative political causes. The CEO was Alexander Nix. Nix has suggested has that Cambridge Analytica was involved in forty four US political races in 2014. In 2016, Cambridge Analytica worked for Donald Trump's presidential campaign as well as for Leave.EU. CA's role in those campaigns has been controversial and is the subject of ongoing criminal investigations in both UK and US. See David Hakim, 'Data Firm Says Secret Sauce Aided Trump; Many Scoff', *The New York Times*, October 28, 2018. Also see Carol Cadwalladr, 'Watchdog to launch inquiry into misuse of data in politics, *The Guardian*, October 29, 2019.
122. Privacy International, 'Guide to International Law and Surveillance', *Privacy International*, https://privacyinternational.org/long-read/993/guide-international-law-and-surveillance-20 (accessed November 8, 2019).
123. Editorial, 'Who is Cambridge Analytica and What Did It Do?', *Reuters*, https://www.reuters.com/article/us-facebook-cambridge-analytica-factbox/factbox-who-is-cambridge-analytica-and-what-did-it-do-idUSKBN1GW07F (accessed November 10, 2019).
124. Alex Hern, 'How to Check Whether Facebook Shared Your Data with Cambridge Analytica', *The Guardian*, April 10, 2018.
125. Michal Kosinski, David Stillwell and Thore Graepel, 'Private Traits and Attributes are Predictable from Digital Records of Human Behavior', *Proceedings of the National Academy of Sciences*, 110 (2013): 5805.
126. Harry Davies, 'Ted Cruz Using Firm that Harvested Data on Millions of Unwitting Facebook Users', *The Guardian*, https://www.theguardian.com/us-news/2015/dec/11/senator-ted-cruz-president-campaign-facebook-user-data (accessed October 30, 2019).
127. Michael Biesecker and Julie Bykowicz, 'Cruz App Data Collection Helps Campaign Read Minds of Voters', *AP News*, https://apnews.com/2db0fc93cf664a63909e26e708e91c67/cruz-app-data-collection-helps-campaign-read-minds-voters (accessed October 30, 2019).
128. Ibid.
129. Ibid.
130. Jina Moore, 'Cambridge Analytica Had Role in Kenyan Election Too', *New York Times*, https://www.nytimes.com/2018/03/20/world/africa/kenya-cambridge-analytica-election.html (accessed November 3, 2019).
131. Channel 4 News, 'Data, Democracy and Dirty Tricks', *Channel 4 News*, https://www.channel4.com/news/data-democracy-and-dirty-tricks-cambridge-analytica-uncovered-investigation-expose (accessed November 10, 2019).
132. The Guardian, 'Cambridge Analytica Files', *The Guardian*, https://www.theguardian.com/news/series/cambridge-analytica-files (accessed November 10, 2019).
133. Carole Cadwalladr, 'The Great British Brexit Robbery How Our Democracy was Hijacked', *The Guardian*, https://www.theguardian.com/technology/2017/may/07/the-great-british-brexit-robbery-hijacked-democracy (accessed November 15, 2019).
134. Joe Murphy, 'Cambridge Analytica Bragged: We Have Vast Data for Brexit Vote', *London Evening Standard*, https://www.standard.co.uk/news/uk/cambridge-analytica-bragged-we-have-vast-data-for-brexit-vote-a3797441.html (accessed November 13, 2019).

135. Carole Cadwalladr, 'I Made Steve Bannon's Psychological Warfare Tool: Meet the Data War Whistleblower', *The Guardian*, https://www.theguardian.com/news/2018/mar/17/data-war-whistleblower-christopher-wylie-faceook-nix-bannon-trump (accessed January 18, 2020).
136. Kenneth Vogel, 'Cruz Partners with Donor's "Psychographic" Firm', *Politico*, https://www.politico.com/story/2015/07/ted-cruz-donor-for-data-119813 (accessed November 5, 2019).
137. Carole Cadwalladr, 'I Made Steve Bannon's Psychological Warfare Tool: Meet the Data War Whistleblower', *The Guardian*, https://www.theguardian.com/news/2018/mar/17/data-war-whistleblower-christopher-wylie-faceook-nix-bannon-trump (accessed December 18, 2019).
138. Massimo Calabresi, 'Inside Russia's Social Media War on America', Time, https://time.com/4783932/inside-russia-social-media-war-america/ (accessed November 18, 2019).
139. Ibid.
140. The Great Hack. Directed by Jehane Noujaim and Karim Amer. United States: Netflix.
141. Privacy International, 'Cambridge Analytica, GDPR 1 Year on a Lot of Words and Some Action', *Privacy International*, https://privacyinternational.org/news-analysis/2857/cambridge-analytica-gdpr-1-year-lot-words-and-some-action (accessed 3 November 2019).
142. Zeynep Tufekci, 'Zukerberg's So Called Shift Towards Privacy', *New York Times*, https://www.nytimes.com/2019/03/07/opinion/zuckerberg-privacy-facebook.html (accessed November 3, 2019).
143. Roger McNamee, 'Mark Zuckerberg Says He Wants to Fix the Internet. Don't Take Him Seriously', *The Guardian*, https://www.theguardian.com/commentisfree/2019/apr/02/mark-zuckerberg-fix-the-internet (accessed January 26, 2020).
144. EU Directive 95/46.
145. Kriangsak Kittichaisaree and Christopher Kuner, 'The Growing Importance of Data Protection in Public International Law', *EJIL: Talk*, https://www.ejiltalk.org/the-growing-importance-of-data-protection-in-public-international-law/ (accessed March 6, 2020).
146. Ibid.
147. Woodrow Hartzog and Fred Strutzman, 'The Case for Online Obscurity', *California Law Review* 101 (2013): 1.
148. Kriangsak Kittichaisaree and Christopher Kuner, 'The Growing Importance of Data Protection in Public International Law', *EJIL: Talk*, https://www.ejiltalk.org/the-growing-importance-of-data-protection-in-public-international-law/ (accessed March 6, 2020).
149. Martin Scheinin, 'Report of the Special Rapporteur on the Promotion and Protection of Human Rights and Fundamental Freedoms While Countering Terrorism', *UN Human Rights Council* (28 October 2009): A-HRC-13-37.

Disclosure statement

No potential conflict of interest was reported by the author(s).

The Right to Privacy in the 21st Century and the European Court of Human Rights' Case Law

Özgür Heval Çınar

ABSTRACT

The right to privacy is one of the rights enshrined in international human rights law. However, with the increasing digitalisation of modern life, protecting one's privacy has become more complicated. Both state and non-state organisations make frequent interventions in citizens' private lives. Legislations exist to ensure such interventions are carried out proportionately and with the permission of the relevant authorities. In this article a close look will be taken at Article 8 of the European Convention on Human Rights, its historical origins, definition and scope. The article will also examine current case law of the European Court of Human Rights in the light of the current developments in the digital world.

1. Introduction

Members of the human race have, since time immemorial, shared common spaces with other human beings, while also possessing a personal and private life. The term private life is used to denote a private space which a person claims possession of and permits others to enter. Hence, private life provides us with protection against arbitrary and baseless interventions by state and other organisations. It is the individual who has control of the space, into which s/he does not want others to pry.[1] The origin of this right lies in human dignity and is the basis of all human rights. The important thing is to enhance the rights of individuals and their standard of living in order that they may achieve their aspirations. This right has a broad-spectrum including elements such as physical space, home, family life and correspondence. It has consequently been protected by international human rights law and by the domestic legislation of many countries.

Private life is a fundamental right that deserves universal respect by every state. It achieved recognition in international human rights law after the Second World War. However, since this right is a complex one it is covered in various areas of law. These include property rights, health, insurance and financial law.

Rapid technological developments in the twenty-first century have led to increased surveillance of individuals' private lives. Monitoring can take place by means of smartphones and computers and data on consumers is easily obtained from search engines, social media and credit card use. This monitoring is in general carried out by states on security grounds.

This article has been republished with minor changes. These changes do not impact the academic content of the article.

In this article, apart from taking a brief look at the antecedents of private life, the definition and range of this right will be put under the microscope. An examination of the definition of this right in Article 8 of the European Convention on Human Rights ('ECHR' and/or 'the Convention') will also be undertaken. Hence, this article will explore in the light of the current case law of the European Court of Human Rights ('ECtHR' and/or 'the Court') to what degree the right to privacy, one of the most important freedoms for the existence of human dignity, has been restricted in the digital world, and examine the challenges facing these freedoms. Indeed, the reason it is different to many previous studies is that it makes a detailed examination of ECtHR judgments relating to developments in the digital world, something that is absent from the literature. Thus, this article will look closely at it will make a major contribution to the literature. Moreover, the article will endeavour to find answers to the following questions: How in private life can the balance be struck between the gathering of personal data and the maintainance of security? What does the term personal data mean? In what situations may it be valid to limit this freedom? What are the threats to this freedom in our lives which digital devices dominate? By whom are these threats being created? What is the attitude of the ECtHR towards these threats?

2. Definition and history of the right to privacy

The term private life is derived from the Latin word *privatus* meaning 'separate from public life, belonging to the individual'.[2] The term private life is sometimes used as a synonym for the concept of intimate relations. However, this is not correct, as private life is the 'private space' that a person shares with those they trust, that they keep separate from all other persons and do not want others to learn about. This space is not one included in an individual's private space, but one which s/he also shares with close family members and friends. In short, it embodies not only a person's private space, but also a part of non-private space.[3]

The origins of this right can be observed in primitive communities. In communities where no dividing walls or screens existed 'imaginary walls' were used to create abstract private areas. The Yagua people in the northeast of Peru who live in houses without inner walls or screens turn and face the wall of the house when they wish to have a private space. When they do this, the message they convey is that they are not present in that space. In Europe, with the collapse of the Western Roman Empire and the emergence of powerful tribes, people looked to have more protected houses, and privacy gained in significance.[4] The increasing importance of privacy was accompanied by protection being introduced for the inviolability of domicile and the right to privacy. For instance, the 'Justices of the Peace Act' of 1361 envisaged the arrest of those who eavesdropped or followed other people.[5] With urbanisation in the 16th century, the beginning of industrialisation and invention of the printing press, steps were taken to protect privacy. In 1710 it was made illegal to open letters in England without official permission. In the nineteenth century in the United States of America debates took place regarding respect for private life. Following the Second World War there was increasing international interest in this subject. Technological advances in the twenty-first century have made it abundantly clear that there is an urgent need for this right to be given serious protection.[6]

While in certain international documents, for instance, Article 8 of the Convention, the term 'private life' is used, in Article 12 of the Universal Declaration of Human Rights (UDHR) and Article 17 of the International Covenant on Civil and Political Rights (ICCPR) the term 'privacy' is used. In short, the term private life means the right to privacy. Furthermore, in international documents there is not a clear, concise definition of private life. Article 8 of the ECHR contains no definition at all, and in the ECtHR judgment *Niemietz v. Germany* was the following:

> The Court does not consider it possible or necessary to attempt an exhaustive definition of the notion of 'private life'. However, it would be too restrictive to limit the notion to an 'inner circle' . . . .[7]

There are also problems regarding the meaning of private life and uncertainty over establishing its scope in the literature. Arthur Miller felt it was a difficult concept to define on account of a troubling ambiguity and inclination to vanish.[8] And Julie C. Innes said: 'Exploring the concept of privacy resembles exploring an unknown swamp… We turn to the legal and philosophical literature on privacy in the hope of gaining a foothold. Instead, we find chaos; the literature lacks an accepted account of privacy`s definition and value'.[9]

Nevertheless, difficulties encountered in defining the right does not mean it is of no importance or does not exist. This right is crucial as regards human dignity, freedom and democracy and a prerequisite for a democratic society. It has been described as the most fundamental of all freedoms, offering an individual the opportunity to be creative and ensuring they can engage in social relations with others, while also protecting autonomous life and physical tranquillity.[10] The Special Rapporteur to the Human Rights Council said the following in a report in 2016:

> Recognizing that the right to privacy can enable the enjoyment of other rights and the free development of an individual's personality and identity, and an individual's ability to participate in political, economic, social and cultural life, and noting with concern that violations or abuses of the right to privacy might affect the enjoyment of other human rights, including the right to freedom of expression and to hold opinions without interference, and the right to freedom of peaceful assembly and association . . . [11]

It is evident how this right has been infringed, both by state and non-state bodies, especially given recent technological advances. The United Nations (UN) Special Rapporteur noted in 2016 that ten per cent of citizens worldwide had been the victim of human rights violations regarding their personal data. Moreover, this right has yet to be provided with legal protection by more than 70 UN member states.[12]

3. Scope of the right to privacy (Article 8)

The right to privacy is protected in international human rights law. The main international documents have all safeguarded this right. For instance, article 12 of the UDHR, article 17 of the ICCPR, article 8 of the ECHR, articles 7 and 8 of the European Union (EU) Charter of Fundamental Rights, article 5 of the American Declaration of the Rights and Duties of Man (ADRDM) and article 11 of the American Convention on Human Rights (ACHR) are the relevant provisions. While the above articles answer the question as to why the right to privacy needs protection, no answers are provided as regards when, how and by whom this freedom should be safeguarded.[13]

The Council of Europe is one of the most important institutions in Europe. It was established after the Second World War, guaranteeing rights and freedoms in the Convention, which came into force on 3 September 1953. In order for these rights and freedoms to be guaranteed the ECtHR was created.

Article 8 of the ECHR states:

(1) Everyone has the right to respect for his private and family life, his home and his correspondence.
(2) There shall be no interference by a public authority with the exercise of this right except such as is in accordance with the law and is necessary in a democratic society in the interests of national security, public safety or the economic well-being of the country, for the prevention of disorder or crime, for the protection of health or morals, or for the protection of the rights and freedoms of others.

A general framework regarding this freedom is outlined in the first paragraph of this article. The freedom in question provides protection for an individual's private life and also to family life, the home and confidentiality of correspondence. In the second paragraph, it is stated that these rights are not absolute and that in certain circumstances the public authorities may intervene. In the chapters below an examination will be made as to in which circumstances such interventions may take place.

Private life is a concept too broad to be defined with all its aspects.[14] This concept cannot be expressed through the narrow concept of privacy and is interpreted by the ECtHR in a dynamic way, taking into consideration social and technological developments. This right incorporates a sphere that provides everyone with the opportunity to develop a free personality. In *Niemitz v. Germany* the Court stated:

> [private life] would be too restrictive to limit the notion to an "inner circle" in which the individual may live his own personal life as he chooses and to exclude therefrom entirely the outside world not encompassed within that circle. Respect for private life must also comprise to a certain degree the right to establish and develop relationships with other human beings.[15]

When ECtHR judgments are examined, it will be seen that those concerning private life are in three categories. The first category is one that may be called that of 'physical, psychological or moral integrity'. This includes issues such as victims of violence, reproductive rights, forced medical treatment and compulsory medical procedures, mental illness, health care and treatment, end of life issues, disability issues, issues concerning burial, environmental issues, sexual orientation and sexual life and professional or business activities. The second category is that of 'identity and autonomy'. This category incorporates the right to personal development and autonomy, right to discover one's origins, religious and philosophical convictions, desired appearance, right to a name/identity documents, gender identity, right to ethnic identity, statelessness, citizenship and residence and marital/parental status. The last category is under the heading 'privacy'. This category includes the right to one's image and photographs, the publishing of photos, images and articles, protection of individual reputation and defamation, data protection, right to access personal information, information about one's health, file or data gathering by security services or other organs of the State, police surveillance and stop and search police powers and privacy during detention.[16] In these categories 'privacy' constitutes the main element of this article, and below a more detailed examination of this topic within the framework of ECtHR judgments will be made. However, before the term privacy is explored, it would be fruitful to examine briefly the terms of 'family life', 'home' and 'correspondence' in the light of the ECtHR's case law.

Family life, too, has undergone many social and legal changes since the Convention came into force in 1953, and the Court has interpreted this concept according to contemporary circumstances. It has adopted a flexible approach, taking into consideration the diversity of modern family arrangements, the consequences of divorce and developments in medicine.[17] The first issue the Court examines is to establish whether the persons involved in the case have close personal links. For instance, in the event of it being proved to be legal and natural, a family based on marriage and the relationship of this family to the children of this family are within the scope of this right. However, it has been made clear that if the relationships of unmarried persons living together are stable, they will be accepted within the concept of family.[18] But in order to talk about a concept of family it is not necessary for the persons to be living together. Hence, people who are not living together on account of divorce, separation or wish are also within the scope of this right.[19] While the Court in general seeks a blood tie between persons, it has on one occasion handed down a judgment finding that those without a blood tie may have a family life. For example, in the case of *X, Y and Z v. the United Kingdom (UK)* the Court found that a female-to-male transsexual who had a child using AID (artificial insemination) had set up a family life.[20] It noted that a co-habiting same-sex couple in a stable relationship could have the same kind of family life as a heterosexual couple.[21]

Another right safeguarded within the scope of this article pertains to home.[22] The term 'home' is an 'autonomous' concept.[23] The meaning of autonomous is as follows: the way states that are signatories to the Convention define the concept of home in their domestic legislation and what are classified as dwellings are not binding for the ECtHR. According to its case law, home is the physically defined area where private life and family life develops.[24] As regards whether a place will be accepted by the ECtHR as a home, it uses a factual criterion as to whether there are 'sufficient and continuous links with that place'. For instance, it is not necessary that the persons own the place in question.[25] The Court has found a property owned by a person to be a home if they continually intend to return there and if they have connections to the property in question.[26] Furthermore, workplaces have also been put into the scope of home, with 'caravan', 'bungalow', 'summer house' and 'second homes' also being accepted as 'home'.[27] Even a hotel room may be accepted as a home as long as 'sufficient and continuing links' have been established.[28]

Lastly, the right to correspondence is safeguarded by Article 8. A person's right to respect for their correspondence is a right to correspond with others without interruption or censor.[29] This includes an individual's communication with others by means such as letter, electronic mail, telephone, internet, telex or fax.[30] Apart from individuals, legal entities are also able to benefit from this right.[31] In *Bernh Larsen Holding AS and others v. Norway* three Norwegian companies received a demand from the tax authorities to provide a copy of all their data from a joint server. The companies made an application to the Court claiming a violation of paragraph 1 of Article 8 of the

Convention had taken place. The ECtHR examined the application within the framework of the right to respect for the home and correspondence right, finding there had been an intervention in both rights, but reaching the conclusion that these rights had not been violated.[32] Moreover, conversations that are the subject of correspondence do not in any case have to be about private life, as professional topics are also within the scope of this protection. For instance, a lawyer's conversation with a client may come within the scope of article 8.[33]

4. Positive and negative obligations under Article 8

Since the rights in this article are in the category of 'qualified right', the state authorities are legally permitted to interfere in certain situations. In order for restrictions to be placed on this freedom there are three stage tests that must be applied:

(1) Any state intervention must be legal (in accordance with law). This includes statutes, decree laws, codes, regulations and court judgments.[34] The legislation in question should be sufficiently precise and incorporate a provision to protect against arbitrary measures by the authorities.[35] In other words, the law in question should contain foreseeability and accessibility safeguards against arbitrariness in implementation.[36]

(2) One of the legitimate aims cited in Article 8(2), that is, national security, public safety or the economic well-being of the country, the prevention of disorder or crime, the protection of health or morals, or the protection of the rights and freedoms of others, should be used as justification.

This is a question asked by the Court at the second stage. Since it is up to the respondent State to make clear the purpose or purposes of the interference, and the fact that reasons that may be cited for any interference are so all-encompassing – for instance, in the interests of national security – a State is usually able to construct a reasonable justification to support interference. Applicants very often claim that the justification asserted by the State is not the 'real' grounds for the interference at issue, but the Court has not been open to accepting such claims. On the contrary, the Court has generally not examined in detail the justifications cited by the State as the reason for its actions, often combining the aims cited – such as the protection of health and morals and the protection of the rights and freedoms of others – into one reason.[37] Hence, the Court has very rarely taken the step of rejecting the reasons given by States, and accepted that they were acting in pursuit of the stated aims. This has been the case even when the applicant may disagree.[38]

(3) It 'must be necessary in a democratic society'. This means that any intervention must 'be a pressing social need',[39] and that this intervention 'be proportionate to the legitimate aim pursued'.[40] As for a 'democratic society', it is a society based on the principles of pluralism, tolerance and open-mindedness.[41] For a State to have 'some' justification for taking the measures in question is obviously not sufficient as any interference must be 'necessary'. As regards the meaning of 'necessary', in *Handyside v. the UK* the Court said that while

> ... it is not synonymous with "indispensable" ... neither has it the flexibility of such expressions as "admissible", "ordinary", "useful", "reasonable" or "desirable".[42]

National authorities are granted a margin of appreciation when it comes to the matter of pressing social need.[43] The reason for states having a margin of appreciation is on account of the fact that as some cases are very complex and sensitive, national authorities may be able to better evaluate each case in their own circumstances and ascertain the appropriate steps to take.[44] Of course this margin of appreciation changes according to the existing circumstances, the issue in question and its antecedents.[45]

In addition to State parties having a margin of appreciation, they also have obligations within the framework of this right. In brief, while the margin of appreciation is being used States have to constantly fulfil the positive and negative obligations arising from the Convention. As a matter of fact, these obligations arise from Article 1 of the Convention. In this article, it is stipulated that High Contracting Parties shall secure to everyone in their jurisdiction the rights and freedoms defined in the Convention. Hence, it is the negative obligation of States to ensure there is no arbitrary interference in the exercise of this freedom. Thus, the fundamental purpose of Article 8 is to protect individuals against the arbitrary interference of public authorities.

There are also positive obligations incumbent on States to make sure that legal entities act respectfully towards each other.[46] However, the meaning of the concept 'respect' here has not been defined by the Court. Hence, respect differs in each situation. While it has been defined according to circumstances what respect necessitates, States have a very broad margin of appreciation. The State should look to see whether a fair balance has been struck between the general interests of the individual and those of society.[47] In brief, within the scope of positive obligations are the 'obligation to take measures' and 'obligation to be effective'. Examples of the obligation to take measures may be listed as follows: to enact legal provisions with regard to the issue in question, to carry out supervision and carry out a fair and unbiased investigation. Within the framework of these measures States should achieve effective outcomes.[48]

5. European Court of Human Rights' current case law on the right to privacy

As mentioned above all four main rights contained in Article 8 will not be covered in this article. Since the topic of this special edition is privacy, the ECtHR's case law regarding this right, what it encapsulates, in what circumstances it may be restricted and its relationship to other rights and freedoms will be examined.

As constantly expounded by the Court, 'private life' is a concept that is not easy to define. It includes matters of a personal nature, such as an individual's name and photo and a person's physical and psychological integrity. The main purpose of Article 8 of the Convention is to safeguard the development of an individual's personality and their relations with others without external interference. Hence, a person's area of interaction with others, even if it takes place in public, may possibly come within the scope of private life.[49]

5.1. Privacy and personal data

Another significant right connected to privacy is 'an individual's right to protect his privacy'. While one aspect of the right to privacy is 'the right to be left alone', another is 'the right of an individual to control information about themselves', that is, 'the right to control personal data'.[50]

The Court considers the collection of data relating to an individual's private life and the holding and use of this data under Article 8. For instance, the case of *S. and Marper v. the UK* involved two applicants. The first of these, Mr S., was arrested in January 2001 and charged with attempted robbery. He was eleven years old at the time. His fingerprints and DNA samples were taken but he was later found not guilty. Mr Marper, the second applicant, also had his fingerprints and DNA samples taken after being arrested in March 2001 and charged with harassment of his partner. Before a pre-trial review took place, Mr Marper and his partner repaired their relationship and in June 2001 the charges were dropped. Both Mr S and Mr Marper asked for their fingerprints and DNA samples to be destroyed, but the police refused. The Court found that the gathering and holding of personal data, even when it was not used, constituted a violation of Article 8.[51] This judgment highlights the limits of police powers as regards the gathering and holding of personal data for crime prevention, and the human rights implications of such retention by national authorities of DNA and fingerprint data for use on criminal identification databases.[52]

After this judgment, in April 2010, the Crime and Security Act was introduced in the UK. However, after the change of government in May 2010, it was not enacted. In its place the Coalition Government brought in a new Protection of Freedoms Bill to bring the law in England and Wales into line with Scotland which was eventually adopted in May 2012 as the Protection of Freedoms Act and came into force at the end of 2013. In May 2011, the Supreme Court declared that existing Association of Chief Police Officer (ACPO) guidelines relating to the retention of DNA, fingerprints and Police National Computer (PNC) records were unlawful on account of being incompatible with the ECHR.[53] These developments are in fact a good example of the positive obligations pertaining to the measures High Contracting Parties should take in domestic law in line with judgments of the Court.

Additionally, the Court considers the type of data collected and held, how it is used and potential effects. Thus, in *Klass and others v. Germany* the Court found that states could not justify the blanket monitoring of individuals on the grounds of espionage and counter terrorism.[54] The Court stressed that interference with the rights of individuals must be subject to 'an effective control' and that the principle of proportionality was important.[55]

In its judgments the Court often refers to the Convention for the Protection of Individuals in connection with Automatic Processing of Personal Data (the Convention on Personal Data).[56] In Article 1 of the above Convention, it is stated that its aim is the safeguarding of individuals' right to privacy with regard to automatic processing of personal data. This Convention incorporates provisions concerning the automatic processing of personal data. Article 2 of this Convention outlines the concept of personal data in the following way: 'any information relating to an identified or identifiable individual ... ' Although the Convention includes individuals, High Contracting Parties may, if they wish, also extend protection to legal entities. However, as this is dependent on the will of States, the fact that the Convention does not provide complete protection to legal entities is worthy of criticism. Moreover, according to paragraph c of this article this includes storing data, applying logical or mathematical processes to the data, making changes, deleting data, retrieval and distribution. Additionally, Article 3 makes clear that personal data processed by both the public and the private sector are within the scope of the Convention. Article 4 states:

'Each State shall introduce the necessary provisions in its domestic law to protect the fundamental principles concerning data protection that are listed here'.

According to Article 5 data to be automatically processed must meet the following criteria:

> (a) obtained and processed fairly and lawfully; (b) stored for specified and legitimate purposes and not used in a way incompatible with those purposes; (c) adequate, relevant and not excessive in relation to the purposes for which they are stored; (d) accurate and, where necessary, kept up to date; (e) preserved in a form which permits identification of the data subjects for no longer than is required for the purpose for which those data are stored.

Article 6 deals with sensitive data. Personal data concerning racial or ethnic origin, political opinions, religious or other beliefs, health and sexual life and criminal convictions are examples of special personal data.

The ECtHR takes its definition of personal data from Article 2(a) of the above Convention.[57] According to the Court the protection of personal data is vital as regards a person exercising their right to respect for their private life.[58] With regard to personal data the Court only takes into account individuals, in parallel with Article 2 of the Convention. For instance, the Court examined the claims of three Norwegian companies, in *Bernh Larsen Holding AS and others v. Norway* within the scope of 'right to respect for home' and 'right to respect for correspondence', not 'right to respect for private life' in Article 8(1) of the ECHR. In this way the Court did not allow legal entities to take advantage of the right to protection for personal data.[59] This approach of the Court is open to criticism, as to accept legal entities as the subject of the right to respect for the home and correspondence, but to exclude them with regard to personal data does not seem consistent.

Furthermore, in Court judgments the divulging of personal data, the sharing of this data with other organisations, not allowing access to information, the failure to correct erroneous personal data or the rejection of demands for personal data to be deleted, surveillance of telephones, revealing of names and addresses without the permission of the individual, the gathering of a person's data, their storage, use and the failure to allow the opportunity to disprove the veracity of data held have all been found to be in violation of Article 8.[60]

When Court judgments are examined it is seen that the following are generally within the category of personal data: name, postal address, email address, IP address, bank accounts, medical data, GPS data, camera records, photographs, voice and blood records, fingerprints and DNA records.[61] In other words, the Court separates data into two categories: specific and other data. Specific data relates to data referred to in Article 6 of the Convention on Personal Data such as 'racial origin', 'political opinions or religious or other beliefs', 'health or sexual life' or 'criminal convictions'. However, the issue here concerns other data not referred to in the article, but which may give a clue to a person's identity. The case law of the ECtHR needs to be examined in connection with this issue. In the Court's judgments the concept of personal data includes a person's profile, photographs, fingerprints, DNA profile, cell samples, personal medical data, voice, security number, home address and personal spending.[62] Moreover, the Court identifies data according to it being either of a personal or public nature. That is, it considers a person's picture to be of a personal nature, while their political activities are classed as being of a public nature.

5.2. A person's photographs

The Court makes the observation that a person's photographs identify them due to their unique character. Hence, they are important for a person's personal development. In the event of a well-known person's photographs being shared, this is particularly true and can have serious consequences. The reason for this is that it is important to find the middle ground between a person's reputation, as protected by Article 8, and Article 10, that safeguards freedom of expression. Regarding this point the Court poses these questions:

> contribution to a debate of general interest; how well known is the person concerned and what is the subject of the report?; prior conduct of the person concerned; content, form and consequences of the publication; circumstances in which the photos were taken; and severity of the sanction imposed.[63]

Hence, every person, including people in the public eye, may reasonably expect that there will be safeguards in place to protect their private life. In *Von Hannover v. Germany (no. 2)*, two German newspapers published photographs of members of a royal family on holiday. The Monaco royal family applied for an injunction to prevent further publication of the photographs in question, claiming that their right to private life had been violated. The German courts complied with the first *Von Hannover* ECtHR judgment, finding that two of the photographs contravened the right to privacy as they were not relevant to any public concern in the accompanying text. However, since the third photograph showed a Prince who was not well, and the health of members of the royal family was considered a matter of public concern, the ECtHR concluded there had been no violation of the Article 8 right to privacy in the ECHR. In coming to this conclusion, the Court adhered to the 5-point analysis it had outlined in the original *Von Hannover* case. The ECtHR concluded that, despite the photos featuring a public official, the accompanying articles were not relevant to the photographs. Hence, while the articles contained topics of public interest, two of the three photographs in the article did not, and that therefore, the domestic courts had not been wrong to prevent further publication of the two photographs in question. Secondly, the ECtHR found that the individuals in question were definitely public figures, on account of their political positions. So, once more the domestic courts had been right in their judgment. Thirdly, the ECtHR also concluded that, while the Applicants might have previously cooperated with the media, this did not mean they had given permission for the photographs in question to be published. Fourthly, the Court concluded that the photographs were not in essence offensive in nature. Lastly, the ECtHR judged that the domestic courts had not been wrong in their implementation of German law as regards harassment or other circumstances covering the taking of a photograph. Therefore, the domestic courts were not at fault as regards this part of their judgment. In conclusion, the ECtHR did not find that the German courts' implementation of the judgment in the previous *Von Hannover* case had been wrong. As a result, the ECtHR unanimously found there had been no violation of the Article 8 right to privacy in the ECHR.[64]

For Princess Caroline to be deemed a 'public figure' contrasts with the Court's earlier *Von Hannover* judgment of 2004 (*Von Hannover (No.1)*), when she was considered to be a 'private' individual, 'in whom the interest of the general public and the press was based solely on the membership of the reigning family, whereas she herself did not exercise any official functions'.[65] In *Von Hannover (No.2)*, the Court did not accept that the applicants could be deemed to be 'ordinary private individuals'. Therefore, 'they must be regarded as public figures'. However, the Court in the original case had not said Princess Caroline was an 'ordinary' private individual, instead saying she was a 'private' individual who was well known. Nevertheless, it appears that the scope of what constitutes a Convention-compliant publication has widened, even if it has become less clear. It does seem apparent that 'public figures' who wish to prevent the publication of photographs will find it more difficult, especially if they appear in articles that are considered to meet the general interest threshold. The ECtHR's conclusion that the decision of the German Court was within the margin of appreciation points to be an understanding that the middle ground between Article 8 and Article 10 will not on every occasion be as the court saw it in the first *von Hannover* judgment. Taking into consideration how a similar situation would have been addressed under English law, it is a matter of conjecture whether the judgment will have an effect in this country. Nevertheless, publishers may see the judgment as welcome recognition that the concept of privacy varies across Europe.[66]

Apart from this, in the circumstances of the police taking a person's photograph, what will happen? At this juncture the Court would examine whether the taking of photographs was a private or public matter and whether the photographs would be used deliberately or whether there was the possibility of making a public statement.[67] In *Friedl v. Austria* a photograph of the applicant was taken by the police on a demonstration and a file relating to the applicant was concealed. The Court did not find a violation in this case, listing three reasons why: (1) since the police had not entered the applicant's home to take the photo, the 'inner circle' of his private life had not been intruded upon; (2) the photographs in question were of a public gathering, which the applicant participated in; (3) the reason for taking the photos was to record the nature of the demonstration and how those involved behaved to assist any subsequent investigation.[68]

The Court stated that the file in question might contain the person's criminal record and documents concerning the investigation in addition to the photographs taken by the police.[69] In *McVeigh v. the UK* the applicants, who were questioned, searched, fingerprinted and photographed under anti-terrorism legislation, claimed that the retention of relevant records was an interference in their private life. Initially, the Commission looked at the question of the taking and retention of fingerprints as part of investigative procedures. It reached the conclusion that some of the measures taken interfered with the applicants' private life, while keeping an open mind regarding whether solely the retention of fingerprints could be considered interference. The Court accepted the argument that the information was necessary for intelligence purposes, and conceded that there was a pressing social need to combat terrorism, a factor it considered to be more important than insignificant violations of the applicants' rights.[70] The McVeigh judgment was an indication that the Court was prepared to be flexible regarding Convention norms in order to assist states in exceptional circumstances.[71] In *Murray v. the UK*, after being arrested the applicant's personal details and photograph were recorded. This was deemed to be acceptable within the framework of the process of combatting terrorism. The Court found that all of the personal details recorded were relevant to legal procedures. This case gives the impression that the Court will examine the information recorded by the police and security forces as regards its nature and extent, allowing for the wide margin of appreciation which is usually applied.[72]

However, public authorities should take care not to abuse their powers on the grounds of protecting national security. The Court therefore wants to be satisfied that there are sufficient and effective assurances against all manner of abuse. For instance, in *Leander v. Sweden* the applicant was prevented from taking up a permanent post and his part-time employment was ended by the authorities on account of their seeing him as a security risk due to some secret information.[73] The person in question made an application claiming a violation of his right to respect for his private life under paragraph 1 of Article 8, claiming that in addition to the information being concealed from him and used, he was not given the opportunity to refute the allegations against him. Although the Court accepted that the personnel control system had interfered in the applicant's private life, it pointed out, taking into consideration the existing measures to prevent abuse of the applicant's rights, that this system was necessary in a democratic society. In the twelve-point list that the Court believed the Swedish government utilised to ensure sufficient protection against abuse, the Court attached importance to certain measures that aim to reduce the effects of personnel control procedures to the required minimum level. They are as follows:

(i) the existence of personnel control as such is made public through the Personnel Control Ordinance;
(ii) there is a division of sensitive posts into different security classes;
(iii) only relevant information may be collected and released;
(iv) a request for information may be made only with regard to the person whom it is intended to appoint;
(v) parliamentarians are members of the National Police Board;
(vi) information may be communicated to the person in question; the Government did, however, concede that no such communication had ever been made, at least under the provisions in force before 1 October 1983;
(vii) the decision whether or not to appoint the person in question rests with the requesting authority and not with the National Police Board;
(viii) an appeal against this decision can be lodged with the Government;
(ix) the supervision effected by the Minister of Justice;
(x) the supervision effected by the Chancellor of Justice;
(xi) the supervision effected by the Parliamentary Ombudsman;
(xii) the supervision effected by the Parliamentary Committee on Justice.[74]

This case indicates significant points pertaining to how control of the proper implementation of the system should be, and is for this reason important. Hence, the Court stated that it attached great importance to the fact that supervision of the system was given to independent bodies such as Parliament, the Justice Ministry, Parliamentary Ombudsman and Parliamentary Committee on Justice.[75]

5.3. Accessing personal data held by the state

Another issue is whether a person whose data has been gathered by the public authorities has the right to access it. That said, the question also arises as to whether this can be extended to include the gathering of data by individuals and legal entities in addition to the data-collection by public authorities. In the case of *Gaskin v. the UK* the applicant was in public foster-care until reaching adulthood. After becoming an adult, the applicant wished to access the file relating to his care, but his wish was rejected. The applicant argued his rights arising from Article 8 had been violated. The Court found that as the records in question related to a person's private and family life the case came within the framework of Article 8. The Court endeavoured to strike a balance between public interest (holding of social service records in a confidential system) and the private and family life of the individual. Hence, the Court stated:

> persons in the situation of the applicant have a vital interest, protected by the Convention, in receiving the information necessary to know and to understand their childhood and early development. On the other hand, it must be borne in mind that confidentiality of public records is of importance for receiving objective and reliable information, and that such confidentiality can also be necessary for the protection of third persons.[76]

The Court holds that where such a system is in use the rights of the individual who wants to access records concerning his private and family life must be safeguarded in the event of the non-availability of a contributor to the records or their refusing permission. A system of this kind can only comply with the principle of proportionality if it ensures that an independent authority has the final say regarding the question as to whether access has to be allowed when a contributor fails to reply or refuses to give permission. In the case in question no such option existed for the applicant. The Court consequently found that the procedures followed did not respect Mr Gaskin's private and family life as enshrined in Article 8 of the Convention, and that a violation of that provision had occurred.[77]

The Gaskin case is seen as a notable victory for individuals who were put in public care at a young age. Such people are now granted limited access to their own records in order that they may learn about their childhood. However, the records of those who grew up in the care of the independent sector (the charities) are not covered by provisions contained in the Data Protection Act. Access to such files is only possible if these organisations grant permission. Nevertheless, the Gaskin case is considered a landmark case in the UK. The Data Protection Act has special provisions granting people previously in public care access to all manner of social services records, both electronically kept records and those in a paper-based filing system. Whereas prior to the judgment in the Gaskin case individuals could only access electronically stored data under Data Protection Act, computer systems and all other filing systems are now covered. The Information Commission was also established as an independent appeal body after this case.[78]

5.4. Disclosure of personal data to third parties

Is the revealing of personal data to third parties or the public a violation of Article 8? First of all, during the investigation and trial of a crime in the event of information relating to the suspect or accused what will happen? In *Doorson v. the Netherlands* the Commission stated that the showing by the police of a photograph of the applicant to a third party did not constitute a violation of Article 8. Firstly, this was because the photograph had been used for the purpose of investigation. Secondly, there was no public access to the photograph or other information concerning the applicant. And, finally, the photograph had been taken legally during an arrest procedure.[79] It also found that the police informing the public was legitimate and since the incidents were a summary based on the truth no violation of Article 8 had taken place.[80] This case is also a good example of the circumstances in which Article 8 is taken together with Article 6. The Court for the first time expressed its opinion on the relation between a fair trial and the rights of the witness.[81]

Moreover, the sharing of personal data with third parties results in conflict between public interest and a person's privacy and in addition to this their honour and reputation. In other words, in practice the protection of the right to respect and dignity clashes with freedom of expression. Hence, the freedom of expression is safeguarded by Article 10. One of the criteria of restriction is the 'protection of the reputation and rights of others'. The ECtHR uses the following criteria in striking a balance between the right to respect for private life and freedom of expression: (i) Whether the information in question contributes to an argument that is in the public interest; (ii) Whether the subject of the news item or the person commented on is a public figure; (iii) Previous behaviour of the person in question; (iv) The content of the publication, its form and consequences; (v) The circumstances of the photograph-taking; (vi) The severity of the sanction in question.[82]

It is important to state that the ECtHR only accepts penal sanctions/prison sentences in the case of hate speech or abetting a crime. Rather than penal sanction it considers measures taken during judicial procedures to be a sufficient legal remedy for attacks on a person's right to respect and reputation.[83]

It is not acceptable for the Convention to be interpreted in a way that requires individuals to put up with being the target of accusations of criminal activity without a factual basis levelled at them by State officials. The public reasonably expects the authorities to have concrete information regarding such accusations.[84] An example of such a case is *Egill Einarsson v. Iceland.* The applicant, a well-known figure in Iceland, was called a 'rapist' on Instagram with an accompanying photograph. The Court found that such a comment could constitute interference with the private life of the applicant, since it was sufficiently serious. It stated that Article 8 should be interpreted in a way that even when public figures create controversy through their actions and public comments, they should not be expected to endure public accusations of violent criminal acts without a factual basis.[85]

As regards the Internet, the Court has stressed the importance of gauging the degree of seriousness.[86] Millions of comments are posted online every day, and many of these comments can be considered offensive or even defamatory. However, most of these comments are trivial and with a limited publication and are therefore unlikely to seriously damage a person's reputation. In the case in question, the applicant argued that comments in a blog had damaged his reputation. In its deliberations the Court concurred with the national courts in their conclusion that while most of the comments in question were offensive, they were in reality only a form of 'vulgar abuse' frequently encountered on the Internet. Moreover, the Court considered that the more specific and potentially damaging allegations made would, in all probability, have been seen by those who read them as speculation which could not be taken literally.[87]

This judgment narrows the scope of freedom of expression by finding that a breach of the applicant's right to respect for his private life had been caused by the rejection of a defamation claim regarding his being called a 'rapist' online. The ECtHR made this judgment in spite of the importance attached by the domestic courts to the applicant's previous statements of a derogatory nature made against women, and the fact he was a well-known person who attracted public interest. One of the most worrying aspects of this judgment is that the Court did not take into consideration the character of online comment, and how they are understood by users. Such an observation was conspicuous by its absence in this judgment, but the Court has addressed this issue in other decisions.[88]

For instance, in *Tamiz v. the UK,* the Court dealt with the scope of the right to respect for private life as safeguarded by Article 8 relating to the freedom of expression of service providers such as Google Inc enshrined in Article 10.[89] This case encapsulates an interesting example of conflict between Article 8 and Article 10, in that our personal information is on the internet, while, on the other hand, the public has a right to access information. In the present time individuals' personal information is frequently used on search engines like Google. Hence, this situation is in fact a classic example of personal data being shared with the entire public. This is also a good example of the 'right to be forgotten'. This right involves a person securing the prevention of access to their personal data. This right first became a topical issue in the *Google v. Spain* judgment of the Court of Justice of the EU in 2014.[90]

In *Tamiz v. the UK*, the ECtHR acknowledged that online communication is very often on the 'lower register of style', noting that the allegations made regarding the applicant would, in all likelihood, be understood by those reading them 'as conjecture which should not be taken seriously'.[91] The Court in this judgment, too, neglected to properly acknowledge that domestic courts are best able to evaluate the meaning of comments in their social and cultural context. Nevertheless, this judgment broadens the scope of expression in stating that the UK's 'real and substantial tort' test is acceptable as regards striking a reasonable balance between the rights to freedom of expression and to personal reputation in the event of libellous statements being made in comments in online blogs. The test in question seriously restricts the degree of liability of blog hosting service providers. As a result, this also serves to reduce the possibility of businesses and other actors being put off by the fear of liability from creating websites that encourage the free debating of ideas.[92]

The case of *M.L. and W.W. v. Germany* addressed the question of internet archives featuring previously reported news for the first time at the ECtHR. The two applicants had been found guilty of murdering a popular German actor in 1991. In 2000, the media reported that they had made an application to have the case reopened. In 2007, the applicants went to court to attempt to have their names removed from those media reports, to protect their anonymity. After German Courts ruled against the applicants on the grounds that the right of the public to be informed of matters of public interest would then be violated, they went to the ECtHR. The Court remarked that the case incorporated conflict between two fundamental Convention rights: the applicants' right to respect for their private life under article 8 and the media's right to freedom of expression enshrined in article 10. The Court noted that the right to freedom of expression did not refer only to the right enjoyed by the specific media outlets in this case, but that it included the general freedom of the press to inform the public. The Court placed this case in the context of digital channels of communication having increased the risk for privacy. It examined the conflict between the two rights, weighing the relative importance of the contribution made by the articles to a general interest debate; the infamy of the applicants and the object of the report; M.L. and W.W's. previous behaviour towards the media; and the content, form and effect of the publication. The Court found that public interest in coverage of the crime and conviction existed, and also in the efforts to reopen the case, and that in general the public is interested in being informed about past events. The Court noted that to require the media to either remove personal information from their archives or no longer store their work would profoundly affect the freedom of expression. The Court also observed that on account of their murder conviction M.L. and W.W. were well known, and that this meant the public were likely to take an interest in developments. Furthermore, M.L. and W.W. had actively endeavoured to ensure press participation in their attempts to reopen the case. The Court mentioned relevant media reports, noting that the judicial decision had been accurately and objectively reported. It also noted that there was limited access to the reports, as they only appeared on news pages of websites which were only available to subscribers. Hence, the Court found that, having struck a balance between the two rights in question, there had been no violation of article 8.[93]

To sum up, the ECtHR endorsed the protection of media archives under article 10 of the Convention, and drew attention to the potentially serious effect of the request to remove personal details from articles in the archives of media organisations.[94] In this judgment the right to be forgotten was touched upon, in that in the digital world the freedom of expression and data protection imperatives are interrelated. Therefore, both domestic courts and international courts have to be prepared to hand down judgments in an efficient and just manner.[95]

In *Khadija Ismayilova v. Azerbaijan* the Court found there had been a violation of Article 8. The case involved the revealing of the applicant's personal data and financial and personal relationships in a press statement made by prosecution authorities, which the authorities claimed was part of a report regarding a criminal investigation.[96] In *J.S. v. the UK*, the Court found a complaint by the applicant about personal data in a press statement made by the prosecution service was manifestly ill-founded.[97] In this case the information in question did not include the applicant's name, age, school attended, or any other personal data, not going beyond what is normally issued to the media regarding court proceedings.[98]

In the case of *Satakunnan Markkinapörssi Oy and Satamedia Oy v. Finland* the Grand Chamber of the ECtHR found no contravention of the right to freedom of expression and information.[99] Satakunnan Markkinapörssi Oy (Satakunnan) had, since 1994, been engaged in gathering tax data from the Finnish tax authorities and publishing data relating to individuals' taxable income and assets in the *Veropörssi* newspaper. There were other companies involved in such publishing in Finland, but not as much as Satakunnan. The Grand Chamber reached the conclusion there had been no violation of Article 10. It based its judgment on a narrow, public interest, interpretation of journalism and granted a wide margin of appreciation to the verdict of the domestic authorities.[100] In fact, the Grand Chamber agreed with the domestic courts as regards the wide margin of appreciation it allowed in balancing the right to freedom of expression against the right to respect for a private life. The Grand Chamber was unable to conclude that *en masse* publication of tax data made a contribution to a public interest debate. It also considered that despite certain tax data being publicly accessible in Finland, it was necessary to distinguish between this situation and the way in which data was published by the companies, since this made the data accessible to an unintended extent. The Grand Chamber thus found that the restrictions imposed were legal and had the legitimate aim of protecting taxpayers' right to privacy.[101]

The above case narrows the concept of expression in that no breach of the right to freedom of expression was found in the event of domestic authorities and courts placing restrictions on the publication of taxation data in catalogues, even if the data was already accessible to the public. The judgment is puzzling in that it agrees with the domestic courts that the publication of data *en masse* in a journalistic file cannot be considered publication for journalistic purposes, or in the public interest. Moreover, the Court did not mention the fact that Finland has never made clear by means of administrative and judicial decisions, what the acceptable limits are as regards how and to what degree taxation data may be published in the country. The decisions merely stipulated that the applicants were not permitted to publish taxation data 'in the manner and to the extent that had been the case in 2002'. This leads to confusion as regards to which publication of this sort of data will come within the journalistic derogation from data protection law and, consequently, could have an alarming effect on data journalism.[102]

5.5. Monitoring by CCTV or different technological equipment

Control of personal information does not only occur through the internet, as surveillance of our movements can also be carried out in public spaces by CCTV or other technological equipment. The question that arises now is what will happen to the footage recorded by video surveillance of public spaces. The Court generally considers these circumstances under Article 8.

In *Peck v. the UK*, a Brentwood Borough Council CCTV camera filmed the applicant in a street only seconds after he had cut his wrists with a knife in an attempt to commit suicide. Several months later, the Council used two photographs from that CCTV footage in a published article concerning the role of CCTV in crime prevention. In the photographs the applicant's face was not obscured, whereas in the CCTV footage that was also shown on regional television the applicant's face was concealed at the request of the Council. The applicant went to court to seek a judicial review of the Council's decision to use the CCTV footage. After his application was rejected and the decision ratified by the Court of Appeal he applied to the ECtHR.[103] After the release of the CCTV footage, the actions of the applicant were made accessible to a much larger number of people, vastly more than being seen by a passer-by or a security observation, and to an extent the applicant could never have foreseen. Hence, the Council's actions were a grave interference with his right to respect for private life. The Council could not justify its disclosure without the permission of the applicant, or failing to take reasonable steps to ensure his identity was concealed. The applicant's later appearances on the media did not reduce the serious implications of the interference. Since the publishing of the footage by the Council was not sufficiently safeguarded it constituted a disproportionate interference with the applicant's rights under Article 8. In brief, this case is an example of the ECtHR considering that incidents which occur in public can still fall within the scope of a person's private life and, therefore, an individual can have a reasonable expectation of privacy.[104]

The Court also stated that the publication of photographs taken by the police or public authorities of persons in custody without their consent constitutes a violation of Article 8. However, in the case of the disclosure of photographs of a suspected terrorist, a breach of Article 8 was not found on account of the state being granted a broader margin of appreciation.[105]

State monitoring of communications is an issue that causes fierce debate in modern times. Although State public authorities are allowed a margin of appreciation on the question of evaluating policy in this field, they are entitled to carry out unlimited covert surveillance of persons within their jurisdiction. Nevertheless, the Court has emphasised that States cannot use any measures they deem legitimate on the grounds of fighting espionage and terrorism; rather, adequate and effective measures to prevent abuse must be applied regardless of the type of surveillance used.[106] The clandestine monitoring of citizens is only acceptable when it is absolutely necessary in order to protect democratic institutions.[107] There must be concrete reasons for all procedures utilised, and they must be proportionate to the legitimate aims pursued.[108]

In *Weber and Saravia v. Germany* the first applicant, Ms. Gabriele Weber, a German citizen resident in Montevideo, the capital of Uruguay, was a freelance journalist who investigated issues subject to surveillance by the Federal Intelligence Service (armaments, drug trafficking, etc.). As part of her job, she travelled all over Europe. The second applicant, Mr. Cesar Richard Saravia, was a Uruguayan national living in Montevideo, who was working for Montevideo City Council. When Ms. Weber was on assignments, Mr Saravia took phone messages for her, forwarding them to her. The applicants claimed that the Fight against Crime Act in Germany allowed surveillance of telecommunications without any concrete justification, using secret passwords. They argued that such monitoring was used to prevent journalists from doing effective research regarding sensitive issues covered by the above Act. The Court found that the interference in question was 'necessary in a democratic society' in order to meet the respondent State's aim, since the surveillance had sufficient safeguards against misuse. Strict conditions relating to the communication and use of personal data existed, restricting the utilisation of information obtained to what was necessary. Moreover, personal data was destroyed to prevent abuse, and individuals under surveillance were informed as soon as possible of any restriction imposed on the confidentiality of their communications.[109] Although the Court has yet to make a clear judgment regarding whether personal data obtained from foreign intelligence services leads to a breach of Article 8, as can be seen in this judgment, a state's national security interests are given priority over the rights of individuals. Although of course this does not mean that states can do anything in the name of national security, as the Court points out that domestic legislation must contain sufficient safeguards in law to protect individuals and to avoid abuse of power. In this context, this is a significant judgment.

The ECtHR issued a long-awaited judgment in *Big Brother Watch and others v. the UK*.[110] This judgment came in the first mass electronic monitoring case against the UK, which examined the issue of mass interception of communications. This judgment was the conclusion of a protracted challenge to the espionage powers possessed by Britain, which had been exposed by Edward Snowden in 2013. The Court found that these powers, which enable the UK to carry out mass surveillance, constituted a violation of the rights to privacy and freedom of expression. Firstly, the Court found that Britain's use of mass interception violated the right to privacy enshrined in Article 8 of the

ECHR on account of the 'absence of robust independent oversight of the selectors and search criteria used to filter intercepted communications',[111] and the freedom of expression under Article 10. It also found that these rules were illegal, since interception of communications data was a serious violation of privacy. Finally, the Court found that allowing mass interception of communications conflicted with the principle of proportionality as regards interference only being of a degree necessary in a democratic society. The Court added that any interception must be in accordance with the six minimum requirements cited in *Weber and Saravia v. Germany*, to reduce the risk of abuse of power. The Regulation of Investigatory Powers Act 2000 (RIPA) allows the security services to scrutinise 'related communications' data, with no limitations attached, which was not considered to be sufficient protection and therefore constituted a violation of Article 8 of the ECHR. Although this was certainly an important victory for human rights organisations, it is also true that the judgment was based the on the rather technologically outdated principles established more than a decade before in Weber and Saravia. The surveillance capabilities of security services in Europe are now many times greater. Digital monitoring is now carried on indiscriminately and *en masse*. Hence, individuals who have absolutely nothing to do with terrorism and organised crime are more likely to be affected by mass interception of data. There may well be widespread disgruntlement that the Court did not establish more updated principles to cope with the latest digital bulk monitoring systems.[112]

5.6. Disclosure of medical data and confidentiality

According to the Court, it is necessary for there to be respect for the privacy of medical data. This requirement is not solely to do with an individual's privacy, but also concerns confidence in the medical profession and health services in general.[113] Hence, since the disclosure of a person's medical data will sometimes lead to individuals applying for medical assistance, the Court has noted that in these circumstances disclosure will endanger the health of a person or community.[114] For instance, in *Z. v. Finland* the applicant claimed the disclosure of medical data including an HIV situation at a rape trial constituted a violation of Article 8. According to the Court, the rights of a patient and of the community in general regarding the protection of medical data may be of less importance than the public benefit of the investigation of a crime and the public nature of the resulting trial. Every case must be evaluated according to its unique character and the state's margin of appreciation be taken into consideration. In this case the Court held that the disclosure of the witness's medical records was 'necessary' in the meaning of paragraph 2 of Article 8. However, the Court ruled that no legitimate purpose had been served by the disclosure of the witness's name and HIV status in the appeal court judgment. The Court reached the conclusion that Article 8 of the Convention had been breached on account of court files containing details of the applicant's medical records (HIV status) being made public ten years later, given the possibility of the person still being alive.[115] While this case is important for the emphasis it placed on the confidentiality of personal data, the principle of respect for private life is not solely the responsibility of organisations or companies. States are responsible for data protection, too. Accountability should be allotted and distributed to all relevant entities at a national level.[116]

Additionally, the disclosure by medical institutions of medical data to journalists and a prosecutor's office, and the collection of a patient's medical records by a body tasked with supervising the quality of medical care were also found to have violated the right to respect for private life.[117] However, the provision of medical data to social security authorities is important as regards a person benefitting from insurance, therefore it is necessary for insurance companies to have access to the person's medical history. Furthermore, since in the event of the insurance companies disclosing the medical data in question legal action may result, the existing measures were considered to be proportional and, hence, no violation of Article 8 had taken place.[118]

According to the Court the gathering of DNA samples also comes within the scope of the right to privacy. Moreover, the collection and retention of cellular material, and storing of DNA profiles extracted from it, has been categorised as interference with the right to respect for privacy as enshrined in the Convention.[119] However, this prohibition is not a blanket one, as it does not automatically include the taking and storing of DNA profiles of those persons convicted of crimes, for the purpose of use in any criminal trials that may take place in the future. As mentioned above, unless interference of this nature is deemed to be 'in accordance with law', in that it can be justified as being a legitimate aim under paragraph 2 of Article 8 and as being 'necessary in a democratic society', then it will be considered a violation of Article 8. [120]

The ECtHR, while widening the boundaries of Article 8, is also indicating that this freedom is not unconditional. Hence, when considering the negative and positive obligations that states have relating to the restriction of this right, one must carefully apply the three-stage test. In other words, in order to avoid a violation of Article 8, there must be a legal provision, which must be implemented in pursuit of a legitimate aim and be proportionate and necessary in a democratic society. If this is not the case, then there will be a possibility that the principle of proportionality may be breached, constituting a violation of Article 8.

Furthermore, since the right to protection of personal data is not an absolute right, a balance needs to be struck between both other rights in the Convention and other legal interests in Article 8. Hence, this right is one that is linked to other articles in the Convention. For instance, Article 10. Several cases have been mentioned above in which this right is connected to the freedom of expression. Article 8 has also been interpreted in combination with Article 14, that prohibits discrimination, in numerous cases. This is particularly true in cases concerning same-sex couples or gender-based discrimination. Apart from this, connections have also been made with interference with home relating to states' positive obligations with regards to property rights (Article 1 of Protocol No. 1) and the right to life (Article 2). In *Kolyadenko and Others v. Russia,* the ECtHR found that the City of Vladivostock Administration and the Promorskiy Regional Administration of Russia had contravened Articles 2 and 8 of the Convention. This case involved the authorities failing in a duty to maintain the Pionerskaya River and not introducing the necessary legal and remedial measures to prevent flooding. These failures led to serious damage to property (right to property) and endangered the lives (right to life) of Vladivostock residents. Articles 2 and 8 enshrine the rights to life and to respect for the home. The Court concluded that Article 2 had been violated both substantively and procedurally, on account of the State failing to make an adequate judicial response to the claims of violation of the right to human life. The Court found the Russian State to be responsible for the damages suffered by residents as a result of the violations.[121]

Finally, as regards Article 8 of the ECHR, clear and detailed legal provisions are required that set forth the rules and guarantees governing the circumstances under which personal data may be gathered, the period of retention, how they may be used and in what circumstances they will be destroyed.[122] For instance, in the context of the retention of personal data, for there to be no difference in the period of retention of criminal records for those convicted of a crime, without differentiating the nature of the offence, and for there to be no legal provision relating to the deletion of these records constitutes a violation of Article 8 of the Convention.[123] The retention for indefinite periods of the fingerprints, cellular samples and DNA profiles of applicants who have been acquitted on criminal offences is a violation of Article 8. Hence, this situation constitutes a contravention of the principle of not holding personal data for longer than is necessary. Individuals have the right to access information in records relating to them held by public authorities. The lack of recognition for such a right or the failure to ensure access within a reasonable time may also be considered a violation of Article 8.[124] According to the ECHR, the widespread and reckless use of modern technological techniques in the criminal justice system jeopardises the right to respect for private life and significantly undermines the protection provided by Article 8.[125]

6. Conclusion

To set down a precise definition and explanation of the concept of private life is virtually impossible. Freedom of ideas, expression, religion and conscience in social life also come within the scope of this freedom. Even accepting the difficulty in defining the concept of private life and establishing its limits does not mean it does not exist. It is undoubtedly one of the most fundamental of human rights and is crucial in the safeguarding of human dignity and autonomy. The right to privacy is the right of an individual to have a private life without encroachment. This freedom therefore provides safeguards against interference of an arbitrary and unwarranted nature by either the state or non-state actors. States have negative and positive obligations, one of which is to ensure that effective mechanisms are implemented to protect this freedom of individuals. These obligations have been enshrined in international human rights law and in the domestic legislation of many countries.

The ECtHR in particular has not only reached judgments on hundreds of applications on this subject, it has also made many points with reference to private life. Hence, with technological developments, changes are taking place in our social relations. As a result, as mentioned above, the definition and scope of private life becomes even more difficult. Therefore, the case law of the ECtHR is illuminating. As pointed out in this article, Article 8 of the Convention also incorporates rights relating to family, home and communication, apart from private life. Both states and large companies occasionally interfere in the rights of others by using their powers in an arbitrary way. In particular in the digital world it is difficult to determine the boundaries of private life. The dimensions of interference in this sphere also vary widely. However, in spite of all these difficulties, contracting states should not allow their own authorities or others to violate this freedom. Furthermore, they have a duty to take effective measures to prevent infringements of these rights, as these are their negative and positive obligations. Of course, this right is not without restrictions. Any interference must have a legal basis, permission and comply with the principle of proportionality. Hence, in recent times the UN, ECtHR and EU mechanisms have brought in provisions (e.g. GDPR) as part of efforts to prevent arbitrary and unwarranted interference in this right. However, in spite of these developments, when considering that in today's world the personal data of one in ten people has been violated and more than 70 states have yet to introduce legal measures to safeguard this right, it is clear that sufficient remedies must be brought in as soon as possible at the international and national level.

As a result, Article 8 is not a right that can be solely interpreted in relation to the right to privacy. It plays a significant role in an individual's personal development. For instance, it relates to the enhancement of identity and personality.[126] This right is also connected to other rights and freedoms safeguarded by the Convention. It is consequently a very important and fundamental right and freedom. It is thus incumbent on states that have yet to enact legal provisions to introduce necessary and effective measures as soon as possible, an obligation they are required to fulfil in accordance with international mechanisms.

Notes

1. Ali Korkmaz, 'Insan Haklari Baglaminda Ozel Hayatin Gizliligi ve Korunmasi' [Right to Privacy and Its Protection in the Context of Human Rights], *KMU Sosyal ve Ekonomik Arastirmalar Dergisi* 16 (2014): 99.
2. C. T. Onions, G. W.S. Friedrichsen and R. W. Burchfield, *Oxford Dictionary of English Etymology* (Oxford: Oxford University Press1966), 711.
3. Yasar Salihpasaoglu, 'Ozel Hayatin Kapsami: Avrupa Insan Haklari Mahkemesi Ictihatlari Isiginda Bir Degerlendirme' [The Scope of Right to Privacy: An Evaluation in light of European Court of Human Rights' Case Law], *Gazi Universitesi Hukuk Fakultesi Dergisi* XVII (2013): 233.
4. Pal Fejos, *Ethonology of the Yagua* (New York: Viking Fund Publication, 1943); Barrington Moore, *Privacy: Studies in Social and Cultural History* (New York: Routledge, 1984); Also see Salihpasaoglu, pp. 228–229.
5. James R. Michael, *Privacy and Human Rughts: An International and Comparative Study, with Special Reference to Development in Inforation Technology* (Paris: UNESCO, 1994), p. 15; Also see Salihpasaoglu, p. 229.
6. Guclu Akyurek, *Ozel Hayatin Gizliligini Ihlal Suclari, Cesitli Hukuk Dallarinda Ozel Hayatin Gizliliginin Korunmasi [A Violation of Right to Privacy, The Protection of Right to Privacy in Various Law Branches]* (Ankara: Seckin Publication House, 2011), 105–8; Also see Korkmaz, 'Insan Haklari Baglaminda Ozel Hayatin Gizliligi ve Korunmasi', 100.
7. *Niemietz v. Germany*, 13710/88, 16.12.1992, para. 29.
8. Arthur Miller, *Assault on Privacy: Computers, Data Banks and Dossiers* (Michigan: The University of Michigan Press, 1971); Also see Salihpasaoglu, 'Ozel Hayatin Kapsami', 234.
9. Julie C. Innes, *Privacy, Intimacy and Isolation* (Oxford: Oxford University Press, 1992), 3; Also see Salihpasaoglu, 'Ozel Hayatin Kapsami', 234.
10. Ibid, 235–6.
11. Human Rights Council Resolution, A/HRC/RES/34/7.
12. Human Rights Council, 'Report of the Special Rapporteur on the right to privacy', A/HRC/37/62, 2018, p. 14.
13. Korkmaz, 'Insan Haklari Baglaminda Ozel Hayatin Gizliligi ve Korunmasi', 102.
14. *Costello-Roberts v. the United Kingdom*, 13134/87, 25.03.1993, para. 36.

15. *Niemietz v. Germany*, 13710/88, 16.12.1992, para. 29.
16. See Council of Europe, *Guide on Article 8 of the European Convention on Human Rights* (Strasbourg: Council of Europe, 2019); See also e.g. *Pretty v. the United Kingdom*, 2346/02, 29.04.2002; *Peck v the United Kingdom*, 44647/98, 28.01.2003; *Von Hannover v. Germany* (No. 2), 40660/08, 60641/08, 07/07/2012; *Barbulescu v. Romania (GC)*, 61496/08, 05.09.2017; *Satakunnan Markkinaporssi Oy and Satamedia Oy v. Finland (GC)*, 931/13, 27.06.2017.
17. Ursula Kilkelly, *The Right to Respect for Private and Family Life: A Guide to the Implementation of Article 8 of the European Convention on Human Rights* (Strasbourg: Council of Europe, 2003), 16.
18. *Johnston and others v. Ireland*, 9697/82, 18.12.1986.
19. *Berrehab v. the Netherlands*, 10730/84, 21.06.1998.
20. *X, Y and Z v. the United Kingdom (GC)*, 21830/93, 22.04.1997.
21. *Vallianatos and Others v. Greece [GC]*, 29381/09 and 32684/09, ECHR 2013, paras. 73-74; *X and Others v. Austria [GC]*, 19010/07, ECHR 2013, para. 95.
22. See Gulay Arslan Oncu, *Ozel Yasama ve Aile Yasamina Saygi Hakki [Right to Private and Family Life]* (Ankara: Anayasa Mahkemesi Yayinlari, 2019), 125.
23. *K. and T. v. Finland [GC]*, 25702/94, 12.07.2001, para. 150.
24. *Giacomelli v. Italy*, 59909/00, 02.11.2006, para. 76.
25. *Khatun and 180 others v. the United Kingdom*, 38387/97, EComHR Admissibility Decision, 01.07.1998, para. 1.
26. *Gillow v. the United Kingdom*, 9063/80, 24.11.1996, para. 46; *Khatun and 180 others v. the United Kingdom*, 38387/97, EComHR Admissibility Decision, 01.07.1998, para. 1.
27. *Niemietz v. Germany*, 13710/88, 16.12.1992, para. 29; *Chapman v. the United Kingdom [GC]*, 27238/95, 18.01.2001, para. 74; *Demades v. Turkey*, 16219/90, 31.07.2003, para. 45.
28. *O'Rouke v. the United Kingdom*, 39022/97, 26.06.2001, para. 3.
29. Kilkelly, *The Right to Respect for Private and Family Life*, 19.
30. *Copland v. the United Kingdom*, 62617/00, 03.04.2007, para. 41; *Margareta and Roger Andersson v. Sweden*, 12963/87, 25.02.1992, para. 72.
31. Oncu, *Ozel Yasama ve Aile Yasamina Saygi Hakki*, 34.
32. *Bernh Larsen Holding AS and Others v. Norway*, 24117/08, 14.03.2013, para. 106.
33. *Schönenberger and Durmaz v. Switzerland*, 11368/85, 20.06.1988.
34. Oncu, *Ozel Yasama ve Aile Yasamina Saygi Hakki*, 154.
35. Kilkelly, *The Right to Respect for Private and Family Life*, 25.
36. *Silver and Others v. the United Kingdom*, 5947/72; 6205/73; 7052/75; 7061/75; 7107/75; 7113/75; 7136/75, 25.03.1983, para. 90.
37. *Open Door Counsel- ling v. Ireland*, 14234/88, 29.10.1992.
38. Kilkelly, *The Right to Respect for Private and Family Life*, 30.
39. *Olsson v. Sweden*, 10465/83, 24.03.1988, para. 67.
40. *Coster v. the United Kingdom*, 24876/94, 18.01.2001, para. 104; *Jane Smith v. the United Kingdom*, 25154/94, [GC], 18.01.2001, para. 54.
41. *Handyside v. the United Kindgom*, 5493/72, 07.12.1976, para. 49.
42. Ibid., para. 48.
43. Ibid., 11.
44. *Olsson v. Sweden (No. 2)*, 13441/87, 30.10.1992, para. 91.
45. Kilkelly, *The Right to Respect for Private and Family Life*, 32.
46. Council of Europe, *Guide on Article 8 of the European Convention*, 8.
47. Kilkelly, *The Right to Respect for Private and Family Life*, 21.
48. *Beganovic v. Crotia*, 46423/96, 25.06.2009; *Storck v. Germany*, 61603/00, 16.06.2005.
49. *Von Hannover v. Germany* (no. 2) [GC], 40660/08 and 60641/08, 07.02.2012, para. 95.
50. Oncu, *Ozel Yasama ve Aile Yasamina Saygi Hakki*, 79.
51. *S. and Marper v. the United Kingdom* [GC], nos. 30562/04 and 30566/04, ECHR 2008.
52. Liz Heffernan, 'DNA and Fingerprint Data Retention: S and Marper v. United Kingdom', *European Law Review* 34, no. 3 (2009): 491–504.

53. R v. The Commissioner of Police of the Metropolis [2011] UKSC 21: See also GeneWatch UK, 'The Marper Case', http://www.genewatch.org/sub-563146 (accessed January 18, 2020).
54. *Klass and others v. Germany*, Series A no. 28, 06.09.1978.
55. See Salihpasaoglu, footnotes 104, 116, 117, 120.
56. Convention for the Protection of Individuals with regard to Automatic Processing of Personal Data, Strasbourg, 28.I.1981.
57. *Amann v. Switzerland [GC]*, 27798/95, 16.02.2000, para. 65.
58. *Z. v. Finland*, 22009/93, 25.02.1997, para. 95.
59. *Bernh Larsern Holding AS and Others v. Norway*, 24117/08, 08.07.2013, para. 107.
60. E.g. *M. S. v. Sweden*, 20837/92, 27.08.1997; *Gaskin v. the United Kingdom*, 10454/83, 07.07.1989; *Leander v. Sweden*, 9248/81, 26.03.1987; *Amann v. Switzerland*, [GC], 27798/95, 16.02.2000, para. 65; *S. and Marper v. the United Kingdom*, [GC], 30562/04 30566/04, 04.12.2008, para. 41; *Rotaru v. Romania*, [GC], 28341/95, 04.05.2000, para. 43.
61. E.g. *P.G. and J.H. v. the United Kingdom*, 44787/98, 25.09.2001; *Vetter v.France*, 59842/00, 31.05.2005; *Wisse v. France*, 71611/01, 20.12.2005; *L. H. v. Latvia*, 52019/07, 29.04.2014.
62. Salihpasaoglu, 'Ozel Hayatin Kapsami', 245.
63. *Von Hannover v. Germany (no. 2)*, paras. 108–113; Axel Springer AG v. Germany [GC], 39954/08, 07.02.2012, paras. 89–95; See also Council of Europe, *Guide on Article 8 of the European Convention*, 34.
64. Global Freedom of Expression, 'Von Hannover v. Germany (no. 2)', https://globalfreedomofexpression.columbia.edu/cases/von-hannover-v-germany-no-2/ (accessed January 18, 2020).
65. *Von Hannover v. Germany (no. 1)*, 59320/00, 24.06.2004, para. 72.
66. 5rb Media and Communications Law, 'Von Hannover v. Germany (no. 2)', https://www.5rb.com/case/von-hannover-v-germany-2/ (accessed January 18, 2020).
67. Kilkelly, *The Right to Respect for Private and Family Life*, 34.
68. *Friedl v. Austria*, Comm. Rep., 15225/89, 19.05.1994, p. 20.
69. Kilkelly, *The Right to Respect for Private and Family Life*, 35–7.
70. *McVeigh, O'Neill and Evans v. the United Kingdom*, 8022/77, 8025/77, 8027/77, 18.03.1981, DR 24, p. 15.
71. Edward Crysler, 'Brannigan and Mcbride v. U.K.: A New Direction on Article 15 Derogations Under the European Convention on Human Rights?' *Revue Belge De Droit International* 2 (1994): 609.
72. *Murray v. the United Kingdom*, 18731/91, 28.10.1994.
73. *Leander v. Sweden*, 9248/81, 26.03.1987, paras. 59-60.
74. Ibid., para. 62.
75. Ibid., para. 65.
76. *Gaskin v. the United Kingdom*, para. 49.
77. Ibid., para. 49.
78. Revolvy, 'Gaskin v. United Kingdom', https://www.revolvy.com/page/Gaskin-v-United-Kingdom (accessed January 18, 2020).
79. *Doorson v. the Netherlands*, 29.11.1993, DR 75, p. 231.
80. Kilkelly, *The Right to Respect for Private and Family Life*, 39.
81. A. Beijer, and A.M. van Hoorn, 'Report on Anonymous Witnesses in the Netherlands', https://webcache.googleusercontent.com/search?q=cache:IbmAGHVHRJIJ:https://dspace.library.uu.nl/bitstream/handle/1874/43921/b25.pdf%3Fsequence%3D1±&cd=8&hl=en&ct=clnk&gl=nl (accessed on January 18, 2020), 547.
82. Oncu, *Ozel Yasama ve Aile Yasamina Saygi Hakki*, 93–4.
83. *Tolstoy Miloslavsky v. the United Kingdom*, 18139/91, 13.07.1995.
84. *Jishkariani v. Georgia*, 18925/09, 20.09.2018, paras. 59-62.
85. *Egill Einarsson v. Iceland*, 24703/15, 07.11. 2017, para. 52; See also Council of Europe, p. 35.
86. *Tamiz v. the United Kingdom*, 3877/14, 19.09.2017, paras. 80-81.
87. Council of Europe, *Guide on Article 8 of the European Convention*, 36.

88. Global Freedom of Expression, 'Egill Einarsson v. Iceland', https://globalfreedomofexpression.columbia.edu/cases/einarsson-v-iceland/ (accessed January 18, 2020).
89. *Tamiz v. the United Kingdom*, paras. 83–84.
90. Case C-131/12, *Google Spain SL, Google Inc. v. Agencia Española de Protección de Datos (AEPD), Mario Costeja González*, Judgment of the Court (Grand Chamber), 13.05.2014, EU: C: 2014: 317
91. *Tamiz v. the United Kingdom*, para. 81.
92. Global Freedom of Expression, 'Tamiz v. United Kingdom', https://globalfreedomofexpression.columbia.edu/cases/tamiz-v-united-kingdom/ (accessed January 18, 2020).
93. *M.L. and W.W. v. Germany*, 60798/10 and 65599/10, 28.01.2018, paras. 91, 97, 116.
94. Global Freedom of Expression, 'M.L. and W.W. v. Germany', https://globalfreedomofexpression.columbia.edu/cases/m-l-w-w-v-germany/ (accessed January 18, 2020).
95. Oleg Soldatov, 'M.L. AND W.W. v. Germany: Recent Developments in Judicial Balancing of Privacy and Free Speech Online', 2018, https://www.rcmediafreedom.eu/Tools/Legal-Resources/M.L.-AND-W.W.-v.-Germany-Recent-Developments-in-Judicial-Balancing-of-Privacy-and-Free-Speech-Online (accessed January 18, 2020).
96. *Khadija Ismayilova v. Azerbaijan*, 65286/13 and 57270/14, 10.01.2019, paras. 142-150.
97. *J.S. v. the United Kingdom*, 445/10, 03.03.2015.
98. Council of Europe, *Guide on Article 8 of the European Convention*, 40.
99. *Satakunnan Markkinapörssi Oy and Satamedia Oy v. Finland*, 931/13, 27.06.2017.
100. Dirk Voorhoof, 'No journalism exception for massive exposure of personal taxation data', 2017, https://strasbourgobservers.com/2017/07/05/no-journalism-exception-for-massive-exposure-of-personal-taxation-data/#more-3801 (accessed January 18, 2020).
101. Global Freedom of Expression, 'Satakunnan Markkinapörssi Oy and Satamedia Oy v. Finland', https://globalfreedomofexpression.columbia.edu/cases/case-satakunnan-markkinaporssi-oy-satamedia-oy-v-finland/ (accessed January 18, 2020).
102. Ibid.
103. *Peck v. the United Kingdom*, para. 57–63.
104. 5rb Media and Communications Law, 'Peck v United Kingdom', https://www.5rb.com/case/peck-v-united-kingdom/ (accessed January 18, 2020).
105. *Murray v. the United Kingdom*, 14310/88, 28.10.1994, para. 93; *Segerstedt-Wiberg and others v. Sweden*, 62332/00, 06.09.2006, para. 88.
106. *Weber and Saravia v. Germany*, 54934/00, 29.06.2006, para. 49-50.
107. *Weber and Saravia v. Germany*, para. 42; *Rotaru v. Romania* [GC], 28341/95, 04.05.2000, para. 47; *Weber and Saravia v. Germany*, para. 78.
108. *Segerstedt-Wiberg and Others v. Sweden*, para. 88.
109. Global Freedom of Expression, 'Weber and Saravia v. Germany', https://globalfreedomofexpression.columbia.edu/cases/weber-saravia-v-germany/ (accessed January 18, 2020).
110. *Big Brother Watch and others v. the United Kingdom*, 58170/13, 62322/14 and 24960/15 [2018] ECHR 722.
111. Ibid, para. 347.
112. Reed Smith, 'ECtHR rules on UK mass surveillance under RIPA', https://www.lexology.com/library/detail.aspx?g=7a2e807c-ac9b-4fa9-b751-7deee591b6d9 (accessed January 18, 2020).
113. Council of Europe, *Guide on Article 8 of the European Convention*, 41.
114. Kilkelly, *The Right to Respect for Private and Family Life*, 39–40.
115. *Z v. Finland*, 22009/93, 25.02.1997, para. 96; See also Kilkelly, Ibid., 40.
116. Antonella Galetta and Paul de Hert, 'A European Perspective on Data Protection and the Right of Access', in *The Unaccountable State of Surveillance: Exercising Access Rights in Europe*, eds. Clive Norris and others (New York: Springer, 2017), 32.
117. *Mockutė v. Lithuania*, 66490/09, 27.02. 2018, para. 95.
118. *MV v. Sweden*, 20837/92, 27.08.1997.
119. *S. and Marper v. the United Kingdom* [GC], 30562/04 and 30566/04, 04.12.2008, para. 71-77; *Van der Velden v. the Netherlands* (dec.), no. 29514/05, ECHR 2006-XV; *W. v. the Netherlands* (dec.), no. 20689/08, 20.01.2009.

120. *Peruzzo and Martens v. Germany* (dec.), nos. 7841/08 and 57900/12, 04.06.2013, paras. 42 and 19.
121. *Kolyadenko and Others v. Russia*, 17423/05, 28.02.2012, para. 216.
122. *M. M. v. the United Kingdom*, 24029/07, 13.11.2012, para. 199.
123. *Aycaguer v. France*, 8806/12, 22.06.2017, paras. 34, 38, 44, 45.
124. *Haralambie v. Romania*, 21737/03, 27.10.2009.
125. Oncu, p. 85.
126. Sloot, Bart van der, 'Privacy as Personality Right: Why the ECtHR's Focus on Ulterior Interests Might Prove Indispensable in the Age of Big Data', *Utrecht Journal of International and European Law* 31, no. 25 (2015): 44.

Disclosure statement

No potential conflict of interest was reported by the author(s).

Informational privacy post GDR – end of the road or the start of a long journey?

Aysem Diker Vanberg

ABSTRACT

The General Data Protection Regulation (GDPR) is a far-reaching legal instrument that regulates the collection and use of personal data by private actors, individuals and by governments. In this respect, the GDPR is indeed a key legal instrument for protecting informational privacy. This article will analyse and discuss the impact of the GDPR on the right to privacy particularly in the context of data protection. It also explores whether the GDPR in itself is adequate to ensure the right to privacy in the European Union (EU) and whether the protection provided by the GDPR can be supplemented by other means. The article finds that while the GDPR is a significant step in the right direction to protect informational privacy, it is certainly not the end of the journey. It argues that on its own, the GDPR cannot fully address the imbalance of power between data subjects and data controllers. Hence, it needs to be complemented by other regulatory tools such as the ePrivacy Regulation, EU competition law and Consumer Protection rules. Furthermore, some provisions in the GDPR must be revisited in the near future to ensure they do not become obsolete.

1. Introduction

Sound data protection laws are crucial for protecting fundamental human rights including the right to privacy. Nevertheless, due to the advancement of technology coupled with the rise of data centric business models, the right to privacy is under threat. The General Data Protection Regulation (GDPR) a far-reaching legal instrument regulating the collection and use of personal data by private actors, individuals and by governments. In this respect, the GDPR is a key legal instrument for protecting informational privacy.[1]

This article will analyse and discuss the impact of the GDPR on the right to privacy, particularly in the context of data protection. It also aims to explore whether the GDPR in itself is adequate to ensure the right to privacy in the European Union (EU) and whether the protection provided by the GDPR can be supplemented by other means. There are a vast number of articles written on the GDPR and various aspects of it. However, there is no article in the literature that specifically analyses the impact of the GDPR on informational privacy. In this respect, the article fills this gap. The article highlights that GDPR is a significant step in the right direction to protect informational privacy, however it cannot fully address the imbalance of power between data subjects and data controllers. To deal with this shortcoming, the article suggests that the GDPR needs to be complemented by other regulatory tools such as the ePrivacy Regulation, EU competition law and other consumer protection laws.

In order to achieve its objective, the article will first discuss the origins of the right to privacy and the two systems in the EU that includes the European Convention on Human Rights (ECHR) and the EU System and the divergence and differences between these two systems. The article will then discuss the General Data Protection Regulation and the key provisions of the GDPR pertaining to informational privacy. Subsequent to this, the article will consider some of the issues pertaining to the GDPR and informational privacy. Finally, conclusions are drawn and recommendations made to ensure that the GDPR has teeth in achieving its desired goals, particularly in strengthening informational privacy.

2. The origins of the right to privacy and its development in Europe

The right to privacy is not a newly developed concept. As noted by Çınar from the earliest days of mankind, human beings have always shared public spaces with others whilst retaining a personal and private life, as encapsulated by the right to privacy.[2]

The right to privacy is a fundamental human right contained in the Universal Declaration of Human Rights and the International Covenant on Civil and Political Rights (ICCPR).[3] The main issue pertaining to the right to privacy is that there does not seem to be consensus on its limitations and what it entails. As stressed by Post,[4] 'privacy is a value so complex, so entangled in competing and contradictory dimensions, so engorged with various and distinct meanings, that I sometimes despair whether it can be usefully addressed at all'. Nevertheless, numerous prominent scholars attempted to find some common understanding as to what is meant by privacy.[5]

In their seminal article entitled Right to Privacy,[6] Warren and Brandeis articulate the right as the right to be let alone. In the digital age, everything a person does online generates or implicates data that can compromise their right to privacy. Hence, arguably the right to be left alone as articulated by Warren and Brandeis is difficult to ensure, particularly with the rise of online media and services that are financed via data-driven targeted advertising and rely on a business model of collecting data. According to Cornell,[7] the right to privacy involves several key components. These include territorial and bodily integrity, personal autonomy and private entity, such as within a private sphere for seeking information as well as making intimate and private decisions related to religion, sexuality and the protection of personal data.

Finally, the American privacy scholar Solove made an attempt to approximate the concept of privacy and refers to six main categories that can all be used when referring to privacy. According to Solove, the right to privacy entails: (1) the right to be left alone, (2) limited access to self, (3) secrecy, (4) control over personal information, (5) personhood – protection of identity and dignity, and (6) intimacy.[8]

In Europe, there are two systems in place, working in parallel, that safeguard the protection of fundamental human rights including the right to privacy and the protection of personal data. These systems are governed by the Council of Europe and by the EU.

3.1. The European convention on human rights

The first system that safeguards the right to privacy and data protection is the ECHR, an international agreement between the 47 States of the Council of Europe. There are also third states which are members of the ECHR such as Russia, Turkey, and the Switzerland. Complaints by individuals pertaining to alleged breaches of human rights, including the right to privacy is heard by the European Court of Human Rights (ECtHR) in Strasbourg. The ECHR had a significant impact in shaping the case law in the EU, as all the member states of the EU are members of the ECHR. Furthermore, both the General Court and the CJEU, from time to time, refer to Article 8 of ECHR in their judgments, which shows the ongoing influence of the ECHR on the EU legal system .[9]

Article 6 (2) TEU introduced by the Treaty of Lisbon concerns the accession of the EU to ECHR. It reads as follows:

> The Union shall accede to the [ECHR]. Such accession shall not affect the Union's competences as defined in the Treaties.

The draft Accession Agreement of the EU to the ECHR between the 47 Member States of the Council of Europe and the EU was finalised on 5 April 2013. Pursuant to Article 218 (11) of the Treaty on the Functioning of the EU (TFEU), the European Court of Justice (CJEU) were asked to give its opinion on the compatibility of the draft agreement with EU law. The CJEU has identified some problems in relation to the draft agreement. The Court delivered its opinion on 18 December 2014.[10] Referring to Protocol No 8 relating to Article 6(2) of the Treaty on European Union (TEU), the Court retracted that the accession agreement had to fulfil certain conditions to make provision for preserving the specific characteristics of the EU and of EU law, as well as to ensure that accession does not affect EU institutions' competences or the powers.[11] In that context, the Court concluded that accession to the ECHR was likely to upset the underlying balance of the EU and undermine the autonomy of EU law. The CJEU also noted that the advisory opinion mechanism foreseen by Protocol 16 to the ECHR would affect the autonomy and effectiveness of the preliminary ruling procedure provided for in the TFEU.[12]

For the time being no new accession agreement has been drafted. Nevertheless, the Parliament and the Commission still emphasise the need for EU accession to the ECHR.[13]

3.2. The European Union system

The second system that safeguards the protection of fundamental human rights including the right to privacy is the Court of Justice of the European Union (CJEU) based in Luxembourg, which is a EU institution. Respect of human rights is part of the constitutional principles of the EU.

In 2009, with the enactment of the Treaty of Lisbon, the Charter of Fundamental Rights of the European Union (the Charter) entered into force.[14] The fundamental human rights including the right to privacy and data protection are laid down in the Charter.

The Treaty of Lisbon provides a legal basis for data protection legislation covering all aspects of Union Law.[15] Article 16(2) TEU provides that EU legislature shall lay down the rules relating to the processing of personal data. Below the article will analyse the approaches to the right to privacy and the right to data protection under the ECHR and the EU.

3.3. Approaches to the right to privacy and the right to data protection

3.3.1. The ECHR approach

Both the ECHR and the Charter have a provision on privacy. Article 8 of the ECHR provides that:

(1) Everyone has the right to respect for his private and family life, his home and his correspondence.
(2) There shall be no interference by a public authority with the exercise of this right except such as is in accordance with the law and is necessary in a democratic society in the interests of national security, public safety or the economic well-being of the country, for the prevention of disorder or crime, for the protection of health or morals, or for the protection of the rights and freedoms of others.

The ECtHR has interpreted the above provision in a fairly flexible way more than a purely negative obligation of the 'right to be let alone' as envisaged by Warren and Brandeis[16]. The ECtHR has interpreted the interests protected by Article 8(1) dynamically. Article 8 encompasses a wide variety of information such as traffic data on telephone calls,[17] video surveillance images[18] and e-mails sent from work,[19] which were all seen to fall within the scope of private life.

In order to establish the existence of an interference with protected interest under Article 8(1) ECHR, the Court takes into consideration several factual circumstances. The mere storage of data relating to private life of an individual may amount to violation of Article 8(1) ECHR. In Leander,[20] the storage of data concerning the applicant's private life in police files, the fact that they were shared with his employer, and consequently the refusal to allow the applicant to contest that data, amounted to an interference with the right to privacy. This position was reaffirmed in S. and Marper[21] when the Court held that mere retention and storage of personal data by public authorities has a direct impact on the private life of the individual concerned and cannot be justified by its future use. When examining whether there has been an interference with Article 8(1) the Court considers whether the use of information goes beyond which was reasonably foreseeable by the applicant. In Perry v UK, a security camera covertly filmed the applicant, after he refused to take part in an identification parade[22].

Article 8(1) ECHR sets out the general principle and Article 8(2) ECHR allows interference with the right to respect for private and family life, home and correspondence as long as it is compliant with the law and is necessary in a democratic society.

The scope of the right is determined by taking into consideration whether there is a reasonable expectation of privacy. Expectation of privacy can be slightly lower when the person in question is a public figure. In Bohlen v Germany, the applicant, a famous German musician and artistic producer, complained of Germany's failure to protect him against the use of his first name by a tobacco company in an advertisement campaign without his consent. The court concluded that the applicant was a public figure who could not claim the same degree of protection of his private life as an individual not in the public eye[23]. This however does not entail that well known figures do not have the right to privacy[24]. The right to privacy is not an absolute right and there might be clashes between Article 8 and other Convention rights such as the freedom of expression incorporated under Article 10 of the ECHR. When balancing Article 8 of the ECHR and the freedom of expression protected by Article 10, the ECHR applies several criteria. They include whether sharing the information (interference with the right) contribute to a debate of general interest; how well known the person concerned is, the method of obtaining the information, the reliability of the information, the content, form and consequences of the publication and the severity of the sanction imposed[25]. In other words, if there is a general interest in disclosing information coupled with other factors, freedom of expression may be given priority over the right to privacy.

3.3.2. The European Union approach

Article 7 of the Charter states that 'Everyone has the right to respect for his or her private and family life, home and communications'. According to both the ECtHR and the CJEU the term private life needs to be interpreted broadly.[26]

The right to respect for private life had been and continues to be significant principle of EU law.[27]

Article 8 of the Charter concerns the fundamental right to the protection of personal data. Article 8 of the Charter asserts that:

(1) Everyone has the right to the protection of personal data concerning him or her.
(2) Such data must be processed fairly for specified purposes and on the basis of the consent of the person concerned or some other legitimate basis laid down by law. Everyone has the right of access to data which has been collected concerning him or her, and the right to have it rectified.
(3) Compliance with these rules shall be subject to control by an independent authority.

Case law of the CJEU that concerns Article 7 and Article 8 of the Charter offer valuable insight.

In one of its early decisions, in Rundfunk,[28] the CJEU noted that 'the mere recording by an employer of data by name relating to the remuneration paid to employees cannot constitute an interference with private life' under Article 8 ECHR. The Court suggested that such recording would constitute personal data processing and fall under the data protection rules. It is worth noting that in this case CJEU explicitly made reference to Article 8 ECHR.

Article 52(1) of the Charter accepts that limitations may be imposed on Charter rights, as long as they are provided by law, respect the essence of those rights and are proportionate (necessary and genuinely meet objectives of general interest recognised by the EU or the need to protect the rights and freedoms of others.).

Bavarian Lager[29] concerns the conflict between the right of access to documents and data protection law. Bavarian Lager was created to import bottled German beer for public houses and bars in the UK. However, the company could not sell their products easily because most of those establishments in the UK were bound by exclusive purchasing contracts with certain breweries. UK regulations required British breweries to allow public house managers to buy beer from another brewery if the beer was cask-conditioned ('Guest Beer Provision' (GBP)). However, most beers produced outside the UK, like the applicant's, were sold in bottles.[30]

Bavarian Lager lodged a complaint with the Commission in regard to the restriction on imports and claimed that the UK is in violation of EU law. Subsequent to this complaint, the European Commission initiated infringement proceedings against the UK. Nevertheless, following a meeting attended by Commission officials, UK government officials and some industry representatives, these proceedings were dropped. Bavarian Lager was informed of this. Bavarian Lager made several requests under Regulation No 1049/2001 (Access to Documents Regulation) to the Commission for access to documents placed on the file, including full minutes of the meeting with British authorities, including the names of the industry participants.[31] The Commission agreed to disclose the minutes of the meeting but blanked out some names. The Commission held that the applicant had not demonstrated the need for such disclosure as required under Article 8 of the Regulation No 1045/2001 (the former Personal Data Protection Regulation) and argued that Article 4(1) (b) privacy and integrity of the individual exception of Regulation No 1049/2001 (Access to Documents Regulation) applied. The applicant appealed the Commission's decision before the General Court. The General Court asserted that, even though professional activities are excluded from the scope of Article 8 of the ECHR, the mere fact that a document contains personal data does not mean that the privacy or the integrity of the persons is affected.[32] The Court stated that the attendees were at the meeting as representatives of an industry association and the opinions they expressed in the meeting were not attributable to them personally.[33] Hence, the disclosure of the names of the participants would not undermine the protection of their private life and their integrity pursuant to Article 4 (1) (b).[34] The Commission appealed the judgment of the General Court. In the appeal, the CJEU concluded that the General Court erred in limiting the application of the exception in Article 4 (1) (b) to situations in which the privacy or the integrity of the individual would be infringed for the purposes of Article 8 of the ECHR and the ECtHR. In reaching this conclusion, the CJEU relied on the recital 15 of the Personal Data Regulation, which states that Article 6 TEU (which captures Article 8 of the ECHR) applies to processing activities falling outside the scope of Personal Data Regulation. In other words, according to the CJEU, if an activity falls under the Personal Data Regulation, Article 8 of the ECHR is not applicable. Therefore, the CJEU asserted that, where a document requested pursuant to Regulation 1049 contains personal data, the provisions of the Personal Data Regulation become applicable in its entirety.[35] In the light of above, the CJEU held that the Commission was right to require the applicant to demonstrate the necessity of the data disclosure under Article 8 of the Personal Data Regulation and if the applicant failed to do so, the Commission did not have disclose the name of attendees.

In Schecke,[36] the CJEU concluded that by imposing a legal obligation to publish personal data relating to each natural person who was a beneficiary of aid from certain agricultural funds, the Council and the Commission had exceeded the limits imposed by the principle of proportionality. The CJEU found that the requirement breached Art. 8(1) Charter on right to protection of personal data and Art. 7 on right to respect for private life. While the measures were legal and pursued an objective of general interest, and enhanced transparency regarding the use of Community funds the measures could not meet the proportionality criterion. The objective of transparency could not automatically take priority over the right to protection of personal data. According to the CJEU, this balancing act had not been performed.

Another seminal EU case that concerns Article 7 and Article 8 of the Charter is the Digital Rights Ireland case.[37] The Irish law implemented Directive 2006/24/EC (the Data Retention Directive) concerning the retention of data relating to electronic communications, obliging Member States to retain data relating, among other things, to data necessary to trace and identify the source of communication, data necessary to identify the destination of a communication, data necessary to identify the type of communication, and data necessary to identify the location of mobile communication equipment. The Irish High Court referred a question to the CJEU asking whether the Data Retention Directive violated Art. 5(4) TFEU requiring proportionality as well as the right to privacy, the right to protection of personal data, and the right to freedom of expression, established by 7, 8, and 11 of the Charter of Fundamental Rights respectively.

The CJEU concluded that the EU legislature exceeded the limits on it imposed by the principle of proportionality in light of Arts. 7, 8, and 52(1) of the Charter.[38] According to the CJEU, the obligation to retain data relating to a person's private life constituted an interference with the right to privacy guaranteed by Art.7 of the Charter. Moreover, the processing of personal data constitutes an interference with the rights under Art. 8 of the Charter. As noted earlier, Article 52(1) of the Charter provides that any limitation on the exercise of the rights and freedoms laid down by the Charter must be provided for by law, respect their essence and, subject to the principle of proportionality. The Data Retention Directive covered all people using electronic communications without exception. It applied to individuals for whom there is no evidence capable of suggesting that their conduct may have a link with a serious crime.[39] While the retention of data allowed authorities to have access pursued a genuine objective of general interest, it was disproportionate. Where interferences with fundamental rights were at stake, the EU legislature's discretion may be limited, depending on a number of factors, including the area concerned, the nature of the right at issue, the nature and seriousness of the interference and the object pursued by the interference.[40]

CJEU concluded that the protection of personal data and the respect of private life were so significant that the EU legislature's discretion had been reduced, and any interference to rights contained under Article 7 and Article 8 of the Charter had to be limited to what is strictly necessary.[41] Subsequent to this case, the Data Retention Directive was annulled.

Article 8 of the Charter distinguishes data protection from the right to privacy and lays down some specific guarantees such as that personal data must be processed fairly for specified purposes and on the basis of consent. Under Article 8 of the Charter, the right to data protection is identified as a distinct right to the right to privacy. This is very significant and very specific to the EU legal order, as data protection is not included in other international human rights documents such as the ICCPR,[42] a multilateral Treaty adopted by the United Nations General Assembly Resolution 2200A (XXI) which entered into force on 23 March 1976, and it is legally binding all Member States who ratify it. This Treaty makes reference to a variety of important civil and political rights such as the right to life, right to privacy, freedom of religion, freedom of speech, freedom of assembly, electoral rights and rights to due process and a fair trial. Nevertheless, it does not make any reference to data protection.

In the same vein, there is no corresponding provision in the ECHR that deals specifically with the protection of personal data. However, the ECtHR frequently applies, Article 8 of the ECHR that concerns the right to privacy, to give rise to data protection as well.[43]

As discussed above, the ECtHR stated in S. and Marper v the United Kingdom that the gathering and holding of personal data, even if it is not used, constitutes violation of the ECHR Article 8.[44] In other words, the lack of a specific provision pertaining to data protection in the ECHR does not mean that data protection is not an important concern for the ECHR system. It is merely covered by Article 8 of the ECHR.

The most prominent view in academic literature is that data protection is a facet of the right to privacy.[45] In other words, privacy law is capable of encompassing aspects of data protection. Accordingly, it could be argued that data protection is the most recent evolution of the right to privacy.[46] Solove argues that privacy evolved in this way because of the proliferation of digital dossiers that created new informational privacy problems.[47] In our digitally connected era, vast amounts of information are collected, stored and analysed. This has created data centric business models, in which companies collect data and use this data for targeted advertising. On a daily basis companies such as Google, Amazon, Facebook collects an unprecedented amount of data from their users, which may have adverse implications on their userś privacy. For instance, Amazon knows not only about our shopping habits but also has sensitive data on us such as our health and sexual preferences, based on the products we purchase. If this data is hacked or passed on to third parties such as one's employer without the consent of the user, this can have grave consequences.

Some scholars do not concur with the above-mentioned prominent view and suggest that data protection is a separate right in itself as it serves a number of purposes that privacy does not and vice versa.[48] According to these scholars, data protection overlaps with the right to privacy, as they both ensure informational data privacy, but it is important to note that broader privacy concepts cannot be used to explain data protection principles such as purpose limitation, data minimisation, data quality and data security.

Despite the academic debate in relation to whether the right to data protection and privacy and whether they are separate rights, the overlap and common grounds between data protection and privacy are irrefutable. More importantly, the jurisprudence of the ECtHR and the CJEU demonstrates that the right to privacy is a very important element of personal data protection and vice versa.[49] In this respect, it can be deduced that strong data protection laws such as the GDPR are significant instruments to protect informational privacy.

The following section will discuss the General Data Protection and the ePrivacy Regulation with a view to analyse important aspects of therein.

4. The GDPR and the ePrivacy Regulation

4.1. The GDPR

25 January 2012, the European Commission proposed a reform of the EU's data protection rules by drafting the General Data Protection Regulation (GDPR)[50] in order to strengthen online data protection rights and boost Europe's digital economy. It was also done to adapt to technological advancements that had taken place in the previous decade, following the introduction of the Data Protection Directive.[51] The reactions to the GDPR have been mixed. Some scholars[52] saw it as a welcome development as it introduces stringent set of rules in terms of safeguarding the rights of data subjects and aims to empower

individuals against the misuse of their personal data. On the other hand, some scholars were more sceptical of the GDPR, as it might lead to red tape, extra costs for data controllers/ data processors as well being incompatible with the fast-paced nature of technology markets.[53]

The GDPR was published in the Official Journal of the EU on 4 May 2016. It came into force 25 May 2018. It replaced the EU Data Protection Directive 95/46/EC.[54] There are several key differences between the Directive 95/46 and the GDPR. First, the GDPR adopts a much wider definition of personal data as it reflects the changes in technology and the way organisations collect data about people. Under Directive 95/46/ EC, Article 2, personal data was defined as any information relating to an identified or identifiable natural person ('data subject'); directly or indirectly, in particular by reference to an identification number or to one or more factors specific to his physical, physiological, mental, economic, cultural or social identity. In other words, according to the Directive personal data included names, photos, email addresses, phone numbers, addresses, and personal identification numbers. Under the GDPR 4(1) personal data is defined as any information that could be used, on its own or in conjunction with other data, to identify an individual directly or indirectly, in particular by reference to an identifier such as a name, an identification number, location data, an online identifier or to one or more factors specific to the physical, physiological, genetic, mental, economic, cultural or social identity of that natural person. Under the GDPR, personal data includes IP address, geo location data and biometric data such as fingerprint scans, and retina scans, which is much wider than envisaged in the Directive. Second, the GDPR places a significant emphasis on consent. The GDPR requires explicit opt- in for the processing of any personal data. This gives more control to users as to how their data is used. Pursuant to Article 7(2) of the GDPR, if the data subject's consent is given in the context of a written declaration which also concerns other matters, the request for consent shall be presented in a manner which is clearly distinguishable from the other matters, in an intelligible and easily accessible form, using clear and plain language. In other words, the GDPR aims to put an end to long-drawn user agreements with complex language that users hardly read. Any description of data in user agreements use must be short and to the point. A third key difference between the Directive and the GDPR is that under the GDPR both data controllers and processors will be jointly responsible for complying with the data protection rules, meaning if an organisation outsources data entry or analysis to another organisation, both parties will be liable for GDPR violations. Finally, the GDPR introduces some new data subject rights, such as the right to data portability, which did not exist under the Directive. Data subject rights under the GDPR will be analysed below.

In contrast to Directive 95/46/EC, the GDPR applies directly in all Member States. It is supplemented by the national legislation of EU member states. In other words, countries within Europe were given the ability to make their own changes to suit their own needs such as introducing new laws.[55]

Article 5 of the GDPR comprises seven key principles, which has been introduced to guide how personal data can be handled. These seven principles are: (1) lawfulness, (2) fairness, (3) transparency, (4) purpose limitation, (5) integrity, (6) security and (7) accountability.

The GDPR strengthens the rights of individuals with regard to the protection of their personal data and imposes stringent obligations on those processing personal data. It also introduces hefty fines of up to €20 million or 4 per cent of global turnover for those who do not comply .The GDPR is extraterritorial in its scope, which means that it will apply to data processors even when they are not based in the EU, as long as they offer goods and services to individuals and/or monitor the behaviour of individuals such as collecting personal data in the EU. This includes large US digital platforms such as Google, Facebook, Amazon that process the personal data of EU citizens. This is significant as it demonstrates that the GDPR is a key legal instrument not only for the EU but also for the whole world.

Article 4 of the GDPR provides the key definitions. Under Article 4(1) of the GDPR personal data is defined broadly to encompass 'any information relating to an identified or an identifiable person'. This means that even where the data does not directly identify a specific person, if the identity of the person can be deduced from the data; it is still considered personal data. According to the GDPR 4(1) the data subject is the identified or identifiable person whose data is being collected, stored and used. As defined under Article 4 of the GDPR, the data controller is the person or company that decides why and how personal data will be processed. The data processor is an individual or company that processes personal data on behalf of the data controller and can be same as the data controller. Under GDPR data processing is defined broadly to include any activity such as collecting, storing, using and sharing data.

Article 4 (11) of the GDRP provides the definition of consent, which is one of the requirements for processing data legally. Accordingly, 'consent' of the data subject means any freely given, specific, informed and unambiguous indication of the data subject's wishes by which he or she, by a statement or by a clear affirmative action, signifies agreement to the processing of personal data relating to him or her'.

Under Article 6 of the GDPR, companies must ask for consent before collecting or using a data subject's data. Under Art. 6(1) (a) of the GDPR the request for consent must be clearly distinguishable, in an intelligible and easily accessible form, and use clear and plain language.

Another important concept included in the GDPR is privacy by design. Privacy by design is an approach to systems engineering developed by Ann Cavouikan and formalised in a joint report in 1995.[56] As mentioned by Romanou, privacy by design can be articulated as the implementation of several privacy principles in the process of designing technological systems, in a way that privacy rules will be engrained in the operation and management of the processing of the data.[57] The principle is incorporated under Recital 78 and Article 25 of the GDPR. Article 25(1) and Article 25(2) of the GDPR provides that:

(1) Taking into account the state of the art, the cost of implementation and the nature, scope, context and purposes of processing as well as the risks of varying likelihood and severity for rights and freedoms of natural persons posed by the processing, the controller shall, both at the time of the determination of the means for processing and at the time of the processing itself, implement appropriate technical and organisational measures, such pseudonymisation, which are designed to implement data-protection principles, such as data minimisation, in an effective manner and to

integrate the necessary safeguards into the processing in order to meet the requirements of this Regulation and protect the rights of data subjects.

(2) The controller shall implement appropriate technical and organisational measures for ensuring that, by default, only personal data which is necessary for each specific purpose of the processing is processed. That obligation applies to the amount of personal data collected, the extent of their processing, the period of their storage and their accessibility. In particular, such measures shall ensure that by default personal data is not made accessible without the individual's intervention to an indefinite number of natural persons.

Although privacy by design is a well-known concept, the GDPR does something novel by converting a well-known theoretical concept into a legal obligation for all controllers.[58] This crucially means privacy by design is now a legal requirement rather than an optional consideration. As such this is a big step in terms of making data controllers take privacy by design seriously. Privacy by design comprises two key concepts; data protection by design and data protection by default. Data protection by design will entail efforts such as the use pseudonymisation (replacing personally identifiable material with artificial identifiers) and encryption. Data protection by default necessitates providers to have at the onset the most privacy friendly settings. For example, social media platforms like Facebook should be encouraged to set users' profile settings in the most privacy-friendly setting by, for example, by limiting from the start the accessibility of the users' profile so that the users accounts are not accessible by default to everyone. Privacy by design is crucial to ensure that data controllers and companies design their ecosystems with privacy in mind at the onset rather than thinking privacy and data protection when things go wrong. In this respect, the successful enforcement of this provision is crucial for ensuring informational privacy in the online sphere.

Chapter 3 of the GDPR lays out the data privacy rights and principles that all 'natural persons' are guaranteed under EU law.

The articles that concern the right of data subjects are encompassed in articles 12, 13, 14, 15, 16, 17, 18, 19 and 20 of the GDPR.

Under Article 12 of the GDPR data processors need to explain how they process data process data in 'a concise, transparent, intelligible and easily accessible form, using clear and plain language'.

Under Articles 13 & 14 of the GDPR, when collecting personal data, the data processor needs to communicate specific information to data subjects. This entails:

i the identity and the contact details of the controller and, where applicable, of the controller's representative;
ii the contact details of the data protection officer in an organisation;
iii the purpose of the data processing;
iv the categories of personal data concerned;
v the recipients or categories of recipients of the personal data, if any;
vi Finally, if the personal data is transferred to a third country or international organisation, the existence or absence of an adequacy decision by the Commission, or any appropriate or suitable safeguards and the means as to how to obtain a copy of this information.

Article 15 of the GDPR articulates the right of access. Accordingly, data subjects have the right to know certain information about the processing activities of a data controller. This information includes the source of their personal data, the purpose of processing, and the length of time the data will be held, among other items. Most importantly, data subjects have a right to be provided with the personal data of theirs that a data processor is processing. Accordingly, a data subject can ask a data processor what data they hold of them.

Article 16 of the GDPR concerns accuracy. Data processors need to ensure that the data they hold is accurate and complete and according to this principle data subjects have a right to correct inaccurate or incomplete personal data.

Article 17 of the GDRP is about the right to erasure. This right is often referred to as the right to be forgotten. As noted by Rosen[59] in theory this right addresses an important problem in the digital age, as every photo, status update and tweet an individual post stays online for an unlimited time and it becomes very difficult to escape one's past. Perhaps this is the most renowned data subject right, as there have been several legal cases pertaining to this right, and it has generated a lot of media attention. Two cases will be discussed below.

According to Article 17 of the GDPR, data subjects may ask data processors to delete any information about them that a processor may have. There are certain exemptions to this right, which is included in the GDPR. The right to erasure, or right to be forgotten was first affirmed by the CJEU prior to the GDPR in Google v Spain.[60] In 2010, Mario Costeja González filed a complaint with the Agencia Española de Protección de Datos (AEDP), the Spanish Data Protection Agency, against a local newspaper and Google Spain for claims relating to auction notices, showing that Gonzalez failed to pay his social security debts in 1998. Gonzalez argued that the proceedings against him had been resolved and the reference to them was not relevant. He asked the local newspaper, La Vanguardia, to remove the pages or alter them so his personal information was no longer displayed. He also sought for Google Inc. to remove the links to the articles in question so that information pertaining to him did not appear in Google's search results.

The AEDP dismissed González's claims against the newspaper, but allowed those against Google. Google appealed to Spain's high court, which in turn referred three questions to the ECJ:

(a) Whether EU rules apply to search engines if they have a branch or subsidiary in a Member State;
(b) Whether the Directive 95/46/EC applies to search engines; and
(c) Whether a person has the right to request that their personal data be removed from search results (i.e. the 'right to be forgotten')?

Google asserted that as a search engine it should not be regarded as a data processor. Hence it is not subject to the Directive provisions. Nevertheless, paragraph 41 of the Google judgment states that 'the activity of a search engine consisting in finding information published or placed on the internet by third parties, indexing it automatically, storing it temporarily and, finally, making it available to internet users according to a particular order of preference must be classified as 'processing of personal data'. Furthermore, under Paragraph 94 of the ruling the CJEU concluded that:

> following a request by the data subject [...] that the inclusion in the list of results displayed following a search made on the basis of his name of the links to web pages [...] to be inadequate, irrelevant or no longer relevant, or excessive [...] the information and links concerned in the list of results must be erased.

In other words, the Court concluded that as a data processor, Google is subject to data protection rules and it is required to remove links from search results, which consists of information, which may no longer be relevant.[61] However, the above landmark decision left some questions unanswered such as whether Google would be required to delete such data only in the EU or globally. Subsequent to this case, the right to erasure was incorporated into the GDPR.

In a case brought by Google against the French data protection authority, the CJEU was asked to clarify the geographical scope of the right to erasure.[62] The case concerned a dispute between the French data protection authority, Commission Nationale de l'informatique et des libertés (CNIL) and Google. On May, 2015, the President of the CNIL served a formal notice on Google that, when granting a request from a natural person for links to web pages to be removed from the list of search results (de-referencing request), it must apply that removal to all its search engine's domain name extensions.[63] In other words, Google was asked to remove information from its search engines not only in a specific member state but globally. Google refused to comply with this request and continued to limit removal of links only on search results conducted in the versions of its search engines in the Member States.[64] In addition, instead of complying with CNIL's order Google proposed to use geo-blocking, whereby internet users would be prevented from accessing the search results at issue from an IP (Internet Protocol) address deemed to be located in the State of residence of a data subject no matter which version of the search engine they used.[65] The CNIL regarded Google's geo blocking proposal insufficient. By an adjudication of 10 March 2016, CNIL imposed a penalty of EUR 100,000 to Google for violation of the GDPR.[66]

Google contended that CNIL only had the power to request and deal with deletion (de orders on the google.fr domain but not for other countries).

In its ruling the Court concluded that the right to erasure should be applied to all domain names from the EU, but it does not extend outside the EU.[67] The Court also noted that the right to be forgotten is not an unlimited right and may be limited by EU member states in order to protect freedom of information. This ruling is arguably problematic as it paves the way for divergent approaches across the EU. This could undermine the unifying effect of the GDPR. Furthermore, by allowing Google not to delete certain information for all domain names this judgment arguably reduces the scope of the right to erasure.

Article 18 and Article 19 of the GDPR concerns the right to restrict processing. Pursuant to this article, data subjects can request processors to temporarily change the way their data is processed. In addition, the data subject has the right to simply object to their data being processed.

Article 20 of the GDPR concerns the right to data portability. This is a novel data subject right which did not exist in the Data Protection Directive 95/46/EC. The right to data portability in the GDPR will require businesses to ensure that they can hand over the personal data provided by a data subject himself/herself in a usable and transferable format. In other words, this right will enable users to transfer their personal information from one provider to another. For instance, this right will enable a user to transfer all their personal data from Facebook to another social network. The preamble of the GDPR demonstrates that the right to data portability is not just limited to social networking sites but will also be applicable to cloud computing, web services, smartphone systems and other automated data processing systems.[68] The right to data portability will apply to a wide range of areas such as social media, search engines, photo storage, email or online shops. It will be equally applicable to banks, pharmaceutical companies, energy providers, airlines – even small businesses like pizza shops or tailors if they are data controllers.

According to this article data processors need to store users' personal data in a format that can be easily shared with others and understood. Hence, if a data subject asks the data controller to send their data to a designated third party, the data controller is required to do this, if this is technically feasible. Arguably the notion of technical feasibility can undermine the scope of this right as data controllers may suggest that transferring data to a designated third party is not technically feasible due to lack of certain standards.[69] The notion of technical feasibility could have implications for the practical application of this right, as what is technically feasible for one controller may not be technically feasible to another, potentially making widespread controller to controller data transfer unrealistic in practice.

Article 21 of the GDPR concerns the right to object. Data subjects have the right to object to their data being processed by others. Their objection can only be overridden if there is a legitimate basis for processing their data.

The data subject rights included under the GDPR are quite significant rights which aim to give data subjects control over how their data is processed, stored, kept and used. However, other than the right to erasure and the right to access,[70] at time of writing there is limited precedence pertaining to the rights of data subjects, making it difficult to determine whether the users are aware of and are making good use of data subject rights such as the right to data portability.

4.2. The ePrivacy regulation

The ePrivacy Regulation[71] is a proposal for the regulation of several privacy-related topics, particularly in relation to electronic communications within the EU. When it comes to into force it will replace the Privacy and Electronic Communications Directive.[72] The Regulation is primarily aimed at companies operating in the digital economy such as Amazon and Facebook, and specifies additional requirements in relation to the processing of personal data. The ePrivacy Regulation was intended to come into force on 25 May 2018, at the same time as the GDPR, but due to disagreements between Member states concerning its scope it did not.

According to the EU Commission, the key features of the ePrivacy Regulation will be[73]:

i Privacy rules will apply to new players such as Facebook, Messenger and Skype so that these services ensure the same level of confidentiality as traditional telecommunication operators,

ii Stronger rules which will grant the same level of protection in relation to electronic communications for both individuals and businesses,
iii Privacy will be guaranteed for communications and metadata such as the time and the location of a call,
iv More business opportunities will be available for traditional telecommunication operators once consent is given for data,
v The rules on cookies, which has created a dramatic amount of consent requests for internet users, will be streamlined, simplified and it will be made more user-friendly,
vi The new rules will ban unsolicited electronic communications by e-mails, SMS and automated calling machines.
vii Finally, the enforcement of the confidentiality rules in the Regulation will be the responsibility of data protection authorities in the member states, which will make enforcement of these rules more effective.

Arguably, the ePrivacy Regulation is a significant contribution to the strengthening of informational privacy particularly in two ways. First, it will ensure that digital companies such as Facebook, Zoom, WhatsApp are expected to adhere to the same stringent standards as traditional telecommunication operators whilst providing their services. Second, the ePrivacy Regulation is expected to strengthen enforcement of the confidentiality rules, which means that any unlawful interception of online communications data such as listening or tapping will be subject to penalties and that these will be followed up vigorously by the relevant data protection authority in a Member State.

As noted by Voss, while the GDPR ensures the protection of personal data, the ePrivacy Regulation ensures the confidentiality of communications, which may also contain other forms of data including non-personal data (for instance friends data) and data related to a legal person, which is not protected by the GDPR.[74] ePrivacy Regulation will extend the scope of data protection as it will cover data that is currently not protected by the GDPR. Furthermore, whilst the GDPR only concerns protection of data under Article 8 of the Charter, ePrivacy Regulation is concerned about Article 7 of the Charter as it deals with the right to private life and communications. Hence, the ePrivacy Regulation is an important regulatory tool in complementing the GDPR, in particular in relation to communications data.

5. Issues pertaining to the GDPR and informational privacy

5.1. Enforcement issues and potential divergence between member states

As noted above, the GDPR introduced hefty fines for those who do not comply with its principles. As an example, if an organisation does not process an individual's data without consent, it can be fined. Also, if an organisation has a security breach and does not deal with it as required by the GDPR it can be fined.

Before the GDPR was implemented there was growing concern that some companies/organisations could be adversely impacted due to excessive fines. One of the biggest fines under the GDPR was issued against Google. On 21 January 2019, the French data protection regulator (CNIL) fined Google €50 million for not providing enough information to users about how it uses the data that it gets from different services as well as not obtaining proper consent for processing user data.[75] The case was initiated on May 2018 as CNIL received complaints from the associations None of Your Business (NOYB) and La Quadrature du Net (LQDN). In the two complaints the associations stated that Google did not have a valid basis to process the personal data of its users of its services, particularly for advertisement personalisation purposes. CNIL carried out inspections and concluded that there were two types of breaches of the GDPR. First, CNIL observed that essential information such as data processing purposes, the data storage periods and how personal data will be used for ads personalisation was not easily accessible for users and the information provided by Google was neither clear nor comprehensive.[76] Second, CNIL observed for processing personal data for advertising personalisation, userś consent was not sufficiently informed and the collected consent neither specific nor unambiguous.[77] For instance, before creating an account, the user is asked to tick the boxes 'I agree to Google's Terms of Service' and 'I agree to the processing of my information as described above and further explained in the privacy policy' in order to create an account. Therefore, the user gives his/her consent in full, for all the processing operations carried out by Google based on this consent. This contradicts Article 4(11) of the GDPR, as consent is specific only if it is given distinctly for each purpose.

In Germany, the Federal Commissioner for Data Protection and Freedom of Information (BfDI) imposed a fine of EUR 9,550,000 on the telecommunications service provider 1&1 Telecom GmbH, as the company had not taken sufficient technical and organisational measures to prevent unauthorised persons from being able to obtain customer information.[78]

In the case of 1&1 Telecom GmbH, the BfDI was informed that anyone calling the company's customer service could obtain extensive personal customer data by providing a customer's name and date of birth.[79] The BfDI concluded that this authentication procedure was in breach of Article 32 of the GDPR and asked the company to take appropriate technical and organisational measures to protect the processing of personal data.[80]

In the UK, the Data Protection Agency, the Information Commissioner's Office (ICO) has issued a notice of intent to British Airways. Following an investigation, on July 2019, the ICO has issued a notice of its intention to fine British Airways £183.39 million for violation of the GDPR.[81] The proposed fine related to a cyber incident which involved user traffic to British Airway's website being diverted to a fraudulent website. As a result of this security breach, the personal data of 500,000 British Airways customers was compromised, it is believed to have started in June 2018.[82] The breach is held to be caused by the poor security arrangements of British Airways.

According to DLA Piper's GDPR Data Breach Survey dated January 2020, data protection authorities in the EU have imposed EUR 114 million in fines under the GDPR regime for a wide range of GDPR infringements, from the period of January 2019 to January 2020.[83] Amongst all member states France, Germany and Austria are the member states which have imposed the highest total amount of fines. France has imposed fines of just over EUR 51 million, Germany EUR 24.5 million and Austria EUR 18 million respectively.[84]

In the light of above, it may be argued that there is a need to strengthen the enforcement of the GDPR across all member states. Current cases suggest that larger member states such as France, Germany may be more likely to enforce the GDPR than smaller member states, perhaps due to lack of resources. Also, some member states might be more lenient towards violation of the GDPR. This in the long run may lead to deviations between Member states which could be detrimental to informational privacy as it can lead to forum shopping, where data subjects can bring their case before an EU member state that is more likely to render a decision in their favour.

5.2. Ambiguity with regards to data subject rights may undermine the enforcement of the GDPR

As noted above, Chapter 3 of the GDPR contains several key data subject rights such as the right to data portability. Following an open public consultation that continued until the end of January 2017, on 5 April 2017, the Article 29 Working Party[85] approved a revised and substantive guidance clarifying some of the ambiguities with regards to the right to data portability.[86] In other words, due to some uncertainties surrounding the right to data portability, Article 29 Working Party issued guidance clarifying the extent and scope of the right to data portability. As of 25 May 2018, the Article 29 Working Party was replaced by the European Data Protection Board (EDPB). EDPB has also issued guidance on issues including but not limited to automated decision-making, profiling, consent and data breach notifications.

Nevertheless, the lack of case law and precedent particularly with regards to some data subject rights (with the exception of the right to erasure and the right to access) begs the question as to whether there is a need for further guidance and clarity with regards to some data subject rights. As mentioned above, the right to erasure under Article 17 of the GDPR seems to be a right which is regularly utilised by data subjects. The Google Spain case analysed above demonstrates that data subjects are utilising this right and regularly taking action to have inaccurate or out-dated information deleted from a search engine or a website. However, since the inception of the GDPR, there seems to be no other cases in relation to the rights of data subjects. Perhaps it is a bit premature to expect cases pertaining to data subject rights, 2 years after GDPR's inception. Nevertheless, it must be noted that if data subjects are better informed of their rights, they might be in a better position to take up their rights, which may lead to efficient enforcement of the GDPR and perhaps more precedent in this area. This currently this does not seem to be the case.

5.3. The GDPR does not fully address the imbalance of power between the data subjects and the data controllers and may need to supplemented by other laws

As discussed above the GDPR gives data subjects several important rights, such as the right to data portability. Nevertheless, the GDPR does not and cannot fully address the imbalance of power between data subjects and data controllers. For instance, when signing up to use the services of a company such as Google or Facebook, the users have the option of not consenting to the terms and conditions offered by that company. Nevertheless, this may result in them not being able to use the services offered by that company, which may be essential for them in order to communicate with others or receive/share information. The GDPR gives the users some power by raising the standards for acquiring consent. However, due to the significant market power of digital giants such as Google and

Facebook, data subjects often have very limited choice when it comes to giving consent. This may push them to consent to data collection practices they would not otherwise have consented to. As pointed out by Lynskey, the validity of consent can be questioned when these power and informational asymmetries exist.[87] For example, in its complaint to the Irish Data Protection Commissioner the group Europe v Facebook contended that Facebook has become a standard form of communication and the validity of consent given to a monopoly such as Facebook is questionable, as it is not an informed, unambiguous and specific consent .[88] This view was also shared by the Article 29 Working Party in its opinion WP187 [89]: 'Considering the importance that some social networks have acquired, some categories of users (such as teenagers) will accept the receipt of behavioural advertising in order to avoid the risk of being partially excluded from social interactions'.

In other words, even if the data subjects know that a company's terms and conditions are not respecting their informational privacy, in practice they do not have much bargaining power particularly when the company that provides the services has a near monopoly position. This suggests that the GDPR itself cannot tackle all the problems associated with the imbalance of power between the data subjects and the data controllers. Arguably, in the case of digital monopolies such as Google and Facebook, the imbalance of power and indirectly informational privacy issues created by unfair terms and conditions can be dealt with by the relevant competition authorities. If a competition authority finds that a dominant undertaking abuses its market power by imposing unfair terms and conditions, which harms competition or other competitors, this undertaking can be subject to proceedings under Article 102 of the Treaty on the Functioning of the European Union. Art 102 TFEU prohibits any exclusionary or exploitative abuse by one or more undertakings in a dominant position. The provision can also be used to tackle large platforms with questionable data collection practices, if there is a clear harm to consumers and to the competitive process. In this regard, it is worth mentioning the recent case against Facebook. On 6 February 2019, the Bundeskartellamt (the German Federal Cartel Office) concluded its three-year investigation into Facebook. The investigation concerned Facebook's data collection practices and the interplay between data protection and competition law. The Bundeskartellamt asserted that Facebook is dominant in the German market for social networks for private users.[90] Furthermore, according to Bundeskartellamt, Facebook made the use of its social networking service conditional upon users granting excessive permission to collect and process their personal data. It also failed to make its users aware that it collected users' personal data from third party websites and other Facebook owned platforms (such as WhatsApp and Instagram) and merged them with data gathered on its own platform, which enabled it to profile users.[91] As elaborated by Colangelo, if a third-party website has embedded Facebook products such as the 'like' button or use analytical services such as Facebook Analytics, the users' data will be transferred to Facebook via application programming interfaces (API's) when they visit that third party's website.[92] As a result, through API's, even if a user visits other website than Facebook his/ her data is collected and processed by Facebook. To summarise, according to Bundeskartellamt Facebook's terms of service, which enabled excessive data collection, was contrary to the General Data Protection Regulation. This allegedly amounted to an exploitative abuse under ARC § 19(1) (the German equivalent of Article 102 TFEU that concerns abuse of a dominant position) in violation of competition law. As a remedy, the Bundeskartellamt ordered Facebook to change its terms of service and to refrain from collecting data from third party websites and other Facebook owned platforms.

Facebook applied for the suspension of this judgement before the Higher Regional Court of Düsseldorf (OLG). On 26 August 2019, the OLG suspended the Bundeskartelamt's decision, questioning its legal basis.[93] With regard to the alleged exploitative conduct, the OLG held that FCO did not carry out sufficient investigation into ' as if competition' (the counterfactual situation[94]) and as a result did not provide any meaningful findings on the issue of which conditions of use would have been formed under competitive conditions.[95] In other words, since the Bundeskartellamt did not assess the counterfactual and how the situation would have developed in the absence of Facebook's alleged conduct, it had no evidence to show that Facebook's terms and conditions deviated from the behaviour of a company in a competitive market.[96] The OLG stated that the Bundeskartellamt's decision failed to explain why the data collected by Facebook was excessive.[97] The OLG noted that the use of Facebook is conditional on the consent of the users to the processing of their data, however the users remained free to use or not use Facebook depending on their values and preferences.[98] According to OLG, the FCO was merely discussing a data protection issue, which is not a competition problem. OLG contended that, even if Facebook's terms and conditions were contrary to data protection rules, not every legal violation is sufficient to give rise to an abuse of a dominant position.[99] Both German law (Section 19GWB) and EU Competition law (Article 102 TFEU) require a harm to competition, which was arguably not proved in the instant case. Subsequent to this decision, the Bundeskartellamt has lodged an appeal with the Federal Court if Justice. At the time of writing, the case is pending.

This case demonstrates that in the near future more competition authorities in different member states may take action against digital companies with questionable data collection practices, if there is a clear link between dominance and abusive conduct and they can prove that there is harm to competition. Hence, issues that are not addressed by the GDPR, such as imbalance of power between data controllers and data subjects, can be resolved by competition laws and other laws such as the Consumer Protection Law and Contract Law.

5.4. It may be too early to assess the impact of the GDPR on the right to privacy

In a 2020 study, Linden et al investigated the impact of the GDPR on privacy policies. Linden et al concluded that overall, the GDPR has made a positive impact on the incorporation of privacy rights and information and indeed the GDPR had a more pronounced impact in the EU.[100] However, it must be noted that the GDPR is a relatively new instrument and it may be premature to assess its impact. Perhaps assessing its impact in the next 5–10 years perspective will be more useful in terms of getting a fuller picture. Furthermore, further research needs to be undertaken to evaluate the impact of the GDPR outside of the EU due to its extraterritorial impact.

5.5. Technological advancements may make some provisions of the GDPR redundant

The GDPR has many provisions that are drafted taking into consideration the current state of technology. For this reason, certain provisions in it might be obsolete in a few years due to technological advancements. As an example, as mentioned under Section 2.2, Article 20(2) of the GDPR suggests that data subjects can ask their data to be transmitted directly from one controller to another where technically feasible. For the time being, certain data transfers may not be technically feasible for data controllers, nevertheless in 10 years time, particularly with the adoption of common standards in different industries, it may not be possible for a data controller to say that data transfer is not technically feasible. In other words, wording in certain provisions in the GDPR may need to adopted/ amended taking in to consideration technical developments. It would be particularly useful to conduct further research as to the specific parameters of and criteria for technically feasibility within and across industries, to determine when the term 'feasible' needs to be revisited. This may be applicable to other provisions of the GDPR as well.

5.6. Even the strongest data protection laws are not sufficient to resolve all privacy issues

As pointed out by Bruschi, even the strongest data protection laws such as the GDPR will not suffice to protect users and companies from cyber-attacks and security breaches, and ultimately there will always be data breaches undermining individuaĺs privacy.[101] Although the GDPR introduces strong data protection measures, hackers and computer attacks will remain a constant threat to useŕs informational privacy as evidenced in the recent Facebook Cambridge Analytica scandal. The scandal came to surface in 2018, when it became evident that Cambridge Analytica gained access to the personal data of 87 million Facebook users without their consent and used this data for political advertising and for manipulating voters both in the US elections and for the Brexit referendum in the UK.[102] Hence, data protection laws are indeed welcome instruments in protecting privacy in the online sphere, but they cannot be sufficient on their own without vigilant and well-informed consumers as well as companies/organisations who are constantly reviewing and improving the security of user data.[103]

5.7. Privacy by design is still far from unfolding its full potential

As noted above, Article 25 GDPR and Recital 78 of the GDPR incorporates the privacy by design principle which is a significant step for enhancing informational privacy. However, as noted by the European Data Protection Supervisor (EDPS), Gioavanni Butarelli, in 2018, privacy by design is far from unfolding its full potential.[104] In its report the EDPS made some useful recommendations to the European Institutions. According to the EDPS, in order to make privacy by design achieve its desired impact, the EU needs to;

i ensure strong privacy protection, including privacy by design, in the on-going legislative process for the ePrivacy Regulation,
ii support privacy when adapting or creating legal frameworks which influence the
iii design of technology, by increasing incentives and substantiating obligations including liability rules,
iv foster the roll-out and adoption of privacy by design approaches and Privacy enhancing technologies in the EU and at the Member State level through appropriate implementing measures and policy initiatives;

v ensure continuous availability of competence and resources for research and analysis on privacy engineering and privacy enhancing technologies at EU level,

vi support the development of new practices and business models through the research and technology development instruments of the EU, with a special focus on emerging technologies such as artificial intelligence, machine learning and blockchain;

vii support policy initiatives for EU institutions and national public administrations to lead by example and to integrate appropriate privacy by design requirements in public procurement,

viii support an inventory and observatory of the 'state of the art' of privacy engineering and Privacy Enhancing Technologies (PETs) and their advancement to raise awareness on the subject.[105]

In general, all the above-mentioned measures will contribute to the adoption of privacy friendly technologies and ensure that privacy is considered at the design phase, rather than at the end.

In the light of above, it can be said that there are quite a few efforts that the EU needs to undertake to ensure that privacy by design becomes a reality rather than a theoretical obligation drafted under the GDPR. First, the ePrivacy Regulation should come into force as soon as possible. Second, all EU institutions should instigate dialogue with key stakeholders such as IT companies to ensure that privacy is taken into consideration at the time of planning a processing system. Finally, the EU should incentivise privacy by design by developing policy initiatives and by rewarding efforts of industry players who are working towards solutions that respect and enforce informational privacy. This could take the form of financial incentives such as grants or tax reliefs, or leveraging the power of the public sector through solution requirements in public tenders.

6. Conclusion

Data protection regulation such as GDPR is one piece of a larger puzzle. GDPR has been a significant step in the right direction to protect the right to privacy particularly in the online sphere. Nevertheless, it must be noted that the GDPR is not a complete revolution as it builds on existing EU law on data protection and the right to data privacy such as Directive 95/46/EC. A very important aspect of the GDPR is to empower data subjects against exploitation and potential misuse of their data and in this respect, it is a crucial instrument for informational privacy. Having said that GDPR merely as a legal instrument is not sufficient to strengthen data protection and enforce informational privacy in the online sphere. As discussed above even the strongest privacy laws cannot such as the GDPR cannot stop data breaches which are caused by poor online security and evolving online attacks.

In the light of above, it must be noted that GDPR is a right step in direction in terms of protecting informational privacy but there is still a long way to go in terms of achieving informational privacy.

The following observations can be made to ensure that the GDPR has teeth and achieves its full potential.

First, the enforcement of the GDPR needs to be vigorous, companies and all relevant stakeholders including public and private actors that exploit and misuse personal data need to be subjected to strong penalties.

Second, the EDPB should monitor divergent practices in Member States. If the EDPB finds that some member states issue less fines and there has been relatively less enforcement activity in a particular member state, the underlying reasons behind these needs to be thoroughly investigated to ensure consistent implementation of the GDPR in all Member states.

Third, as noted above in order to take full advantage of data subject rights under Chapter 3 of the GDPR, data subjects and data processors who are faced with data subject requests need to better informed. As noted above, the Article 29 Working Party and the now the EDPB has issued various guidance with the aim of clarifying certain ambiguities in the GDPR. The efforts of the EDPB is invaluable, however Member states should also take active steps to ensure that the public and data processors are aware of the content and limitation of these rights. As noted above, the lack of case law post GDPR particularly pertaining to data subject rights is concerning as it may indicate that there is still a level of ambiguity surrounding these rights.

Fourth, as discussed above GDPR does not fully address the power imbalance between data controllers and data subjects. This power imbalance can be rectified by other laws such as competition law, when there is a clear harm to competition and consumers. In this respect data protection authorities in member states should develop good working relations with other regulatory bodies and collaborate on issues pertaining to informational privacy.

Fifth, as mentioned under Section 3.7, the GDPR Article 25 incorporates privacy by design, which is very significant step for enhancing informational privacy. Nevertheless, as pointed out by the EDPS, privacy by design is still far from unfolding its full potential.[106] In this respect, the EDPB should continue to promote privacy by design alongside with other European data protection authorities and provide guidance to controllers on the appropriate implementation of the principle. As noted earlier, there is a pressing need to ensure that the ePrivacy Regulation comes into force as soon as possible, as it will be very useful in complementing the GDPR particularly in relation to the protection of online personal communications. Furthermore, European policymakers should implement, encourage and develop frameworks and facilitate dialogue with key stakeholders such as engineering companies, to make privacy by design a reality rather than a theoretical legal provision.

Ultimately, it must be noted that the GDPR is not an end in itself to protect and promote informational privacy; it is just the start of a journey with perhaps no end destination. As noted under Section 3.5, the use of certain terminology and provisions in the GDPR must be revisited due to the pace of technological advancement to ensure provisions do not become obsolete. Protecting informational privacy is neither a simple task that can be left to the EU alone, nor to a single piece of legislation such as the GDPR. Hence, not only the EU, but all developed/developing countries and international organisations including the European Council and the United Nations should work towards policy aimed at establishing common ground rules for protecting privacy in the online sphere.

Notes

1. This article will concentrate on informational privacy. In this article, the term 'informational privacy' is used to describe the relationship between the collection and dissemination of data, technology, the public expectation of privacy, legal and political issues surrounding them.
2. Özgür H. Çinar, 'The Right to Privacy in International Human Rights Law', *Journal of Information Systems & Operations Management* 13, no. 1 (2019): 33.
3. International Covenant on Civil and Political Rights adopted 16 December 1966 entered into force 23 March 1976 999 UNTS 171, Art 17.
4. Robert C. Post, 'Three Concepts of Privacy', *The Georgetown Law Journal* 89, no. 6 (2001): 2087–98.
5. See for instance, Post, 'Three Concepts of Privacy', 2087–98; Samuel Warren and Louis Brandeis, ' Right to Privacy', *Harvard Law Review* 4, no. 5 (1890): 193–220.
6. Samuel Warren and Louis Brandeis, ' Right to Privacy', *Harvard Law Review* 4, no. 5 (1890): 193–220.
7. Anna Jonsson Cornel, 'Right to Privacy' *Oxford Constitutional Law* (2015), https://oxcon.ouplaw.com/view/10.1093/law:mpeccol/law-mpeccol-e156?print=pdf (accessed June 15, 2020).
8. J. Solove, 'Understanding Privacy', *Harvard University Press GWU Legal Studies Research Paper* GWU Law School Public Law Research Paper, no. 420 (2008), https://ssrn.com/abstract=1127888 (accessed June 15, 2020).
9. See for instance; Case T-194/04 the Bavarian Lager Co Ltd v Commission [2007] ECR II-04523, where the General Court expressly makes reference to ECHR Article 8.
10. Opinion 2/313 pursuant to Article 218(11) TFEU 18 December 2014 ECLI: EU: C: 2014:2454.
11. Ibid.
12. Ibid.
13. European Parliament Briefing ' EU Accession to the European Convention on Human Rights (2017) https://www.europarl.europa.eu/RegData/etudes/BRIE/2017/607298/EPRS_BRI(2017)607298_EN.pdf (accessed June 15, 2020).
14. Charter of Fundamental Rights of the European Union OJ C 326, 26.10.2012 :391–407.
15. Hielke Hijmans, and Alfonso Scirocco, 'Shortcomings in EU Data Protection in the Third and the Second Pillars. Can the Lisbon Treaty be Expected to Help?' *Common Market Law Review* 46 (2009): 1485–525.
16. Orla Lynskey, *The Foundations of EU Data Protection Law* (Oxford: Oxford University Press, 2015), 106.
17. *Gaskin v United Kingdom* (1989) 12 EHRR 36.
18. *Perry v United Kingdom* (2004) 39 EHHR 3.
19. *Copland v United Kingdom* (2007) 45 EHRR 37.
20. *Leander v Sweden* (1987) 9 EHRR 433.
21. *S. and Marper v. the United Kingdom* (2009) 48 EHRR 50 para 121.
22. *Perry v United Kingdom* (2004) 39 EHRR 3, para 42.
23. *Bohlen v Germany* [2015] ECHR 194.
24. For example, see *Von Hannover v Germany (59320/00) [2004]* E.M.L.R. 21; *(2005) 40* E.H.R.R. 1 *and Editions Plon v France (58148/00) (2006)* 42 E.H.R.R. 36.
25. European Court of Human Rights, Guide on Article 8 of the European Convention on Human Rights Right to respect for private and family life, home and correspondence (2019) para 115, https://www.echr.coe.int/Documents/Guide_Art_8_ENG.pdf (accessed June 15, 2020).
26. Juliane Kokott and Christoph Sobotta, 'The Distinction between Privacy and Data Protection in the Jurisprudence of the CJEU and the ECtHR', *International Data Privacy Law* 3, no. 4 (2013): 222.
27. See for instance; Case C-62/90 *Commission v Germany* [1992] ECR I-2575, para 23.
28. Case C-139/01 *Oesterreicher Rundfunk and Others* [2003] ECR I- 4989.
29. Case T-194/04 the Bavarian Lager Co Ltd v Commission [2007] ECR II-04523.

30. Ibid., para 15–17.
31. Ibid., para 23–36.
32. Ibid., para 123.
33. Ibid., para 124.
34. Ibid., para 125.
35. Ibid., para 63.
36. Joined Cases C-92/09 and C-93/09 *Volker und Markus Schecke GbR* (C-92/09) and *Hartmut Eifert (C-93/09) v Land Hessen* [2010] ECR I-11063.
37. Joined Cases C-293/12 and C- 594/12 *Digital Rights Ireland Ltd v Minister for Communications, Marine and Natural Resources and Others and Kärntner Landesregierung and Others* [2014].
38. Ibid., para 69.
39. Ibid, para 64 and 65.
40. Joined Cases C-293/12 and C- 594/12 Digital Rights Ireland Ltd v Minister for Communications, Marine and Natural Resources and Others and Kärntner Landesregierung and Others [2014] para 47.
41. Ibid., para 52.
42. International Covenant on Civil and Political Rights adopted 16 December 1966 entered into force 23 March 1976 999 UNTS 171 (ICCPR).
43. See, e.g., *Amann v Switzerland*, no 27798/95, ECHR 2000-II, para 65 and *Rotaru v Romania* [GC] App no 28341/95, ECHR 200-V, para 43.
44. *S. and Marper v. the United Kingdom* (2009) 48 EHRR 50.
45. For example Westin describes privacy as ‘ the claim of individuals, groups, or institutions to determine for themselves when, how and to what extent information about them is shared with others’ Alan Westin, *Privacy and Freedom* (Athenaeum, 1967), 158; Daniel Solove, *The Digital Person: Technology and Privacy in the Information Age* (New York : New York University Press, 2004); Yves Poullet, ‘ Data Protection Legislation: What is at Stake for our Society and Democracy) *Computer Law and Security Review* 25, no. 3 (2009): 211–26.
46. For instance in the American context Solove argues that ‘ the right to information privacy has emerged in the courts as a spin-off of the regular constitutional right to privacy’. Daniel Solove, *The Digital Person: Technology and Privacy in the Information Age* (New York : New York University Press, 2004), 75.
47. Solove, *The Digital Person*, 8.
48. See e.g.; Juliane Kokott and Christoph Sobotta ‘ The Distinction between Privacy and Data Protection in the Jurisprudence of the CJEU and the ECtHR’, *International Data Privacy Law* 3, no. 4 (2013): 223; Maria Tzanou, ‘Data Protection as Fundamental Right Next to Privacy? “ Reconstructing” a Not So New Right’, *International Data Privacy Law* 3 (2013): 88; Orla Lynskey, *The Foundations of EU Data Protection Law* (Oxford: Oxford University Press, 2015), 104.
49. Kokott and Sobotta, 223.
50. Regulation (EU) 2016/679 of the European Parliament and of the Council of 27 April on the protection of natural persons with regard to processing of personal data and on the free movement of such data, and repealing Directive 95/46/EC [2016] OJ L 119/1.
51. Directive 95/46/EC of the European Parliament and of the Council of 24 October 1995 on the protection of individuals with regard to processing of personal data and on the free movement of such data [1995] OJ L 281/31.
52. For example see; Amy Kristin Sanders, ‘The GDPR One Year Later: Protecting Privacy or Preventing Access to Information’, *Tulane Law Review* 93, no. 5 (May 2019): 1229–54; Simon Davies, ‘The Data Protection Regulation: A Triumph of Pragmatism over Principle’, *European Data Protection Law Review* 2, no. 3 (2016): 290–6.
53. See for instance, Tal Z. Zarsky, ‘Incompatible: The GDPR in the Age of Big Data’, *Seton Hall Law Review* 47, no. 4 (2017): 995–1020; Eduardo Ustaran, ‘EU General Data Protection Regulation: Things You Should Know’, *Privacy and Data Protection Journal* 16, no. 3 (2016): 3; and see also Francoise Gilbert, ‘European Data Protection 2.0: New Compliance

Requirements in Sight – What the Proposed EU Data Protection Regulation Means for U.S. Companies', 28 *Santa Clara Computer & High Tech. Law Journal* 815 (2012): 848–49.

54. Directive 95/46/EC of the European Parliament and of the Council of 24 October 1995 on the protection of individuals with regard to processing of personal data and on the free movement of such data [1995] OJ L 281/31.
55. It is worth noting that different member states have different legal traditions, which has an influence on their data protection law. For instance, German data protection law is anchored to the notion of human dignity; French data protection prioritises the concept of individual liberty; whilst Belgian data protection law places emphasis on privacy. On this see Evelien Brouwer, *Digital Border and Real Rights: Effective Remedies for Their Country Nationals in the Schengen Information System* (The Hague: Martinius Nijhoff Publishers, 2008), 198.
56. Ronald Hes and John Borking 'Privacy-Enhancing Technologies: The Path to Anonymity Volume 1 (1995), https://collections.ola.org/mon/10000/184530.pdf (accessed June 15, 2020).
57. Anna Romanou, 'The Necessity of the Implementation of Privacy by Design in Sectors Where Data Protection Concerns Arise', Computer Law & Security Review 34 (2018): 99–110.
58. Ibid.
59. Jeffrey Rosen, 'The Right to Be Forgotten' Stanford Law Review 64 (2012) https://www.stanfordlawreview.org/online/privacy-paradox-the-right-to-be-forgotten/ (accessed June 15, 2020).
60. *Google Spain SL and Google Inc. v Agencia Española de Protección de Datos (AEPD) and Mario Costeja González, Case C- 131/12,* ECLI: EU: C:2014:317, ILEC 060 (CJEU 2014) 13,05.2014.
61. Ibid.
62. Case C-507/17 Judgment of the Court (Grand Chamber) of 24 September 2019. Google LLC, successor in law to Google Inc. v Commission Nationale De L'informatique Et Des Libertés (CNIL) ECLI: EU: C: 2019: 772
63. Ibid, para 30.
64. Ibid, para 31.
65. Ibid, para 32.
66. Ibid, para 33.
67. Ibid, para 6 and 65.
68. Gabriela Zanfir, 'The Right to Data Portability in the Context of Data Protection Reform', *International Data Privacy Law* 2, no. 3 (2012): 149.
69. For a comprehensive discussion of the right to data portability see Aysem Diker Vanberg and Mehmet Bilal Ünver, 'The Right to Data Portability in the GDPR and EU Competition Law: Odd Couple or Dynamic Duo? *European Journal of Law and Technology* 8, no. 1 (2017), http://ejlt.org/article/view/546/727 (accessed June 15, 2020).
70. It is worth noting that there have been several cases prior to the GDPR that concerns the right to access such as the Bavarian Lager C-28-08P and Egan& Hackett v Parliament T-190/10. Bavarian Lager case has been discussed in this article.
71. Regulation of The European Parliament and of the Council concerning the Respect for Private Life and for the Protection of Personal Data in Electronic Communications within the European Union.
72. Directive 2002/58/EC e European Parliament and of the Council of 12 July 2002 concerning the processing of personal data and the protection of privacy in the electronic communications sector (Directive on privacy and electronic communications) OJ L 201, 31.7.2002, p. 37–47.
73. European Commission, Proposal for an Eprivacy Regulation, https://ec.europa.eu/digital-single-market/en/proposal-eprivacy-regulation (accessed June 15,2020).
74. W Gregory Voss, 'First the GDPR Now the Proposed ePrivacy Regulation', *Journal of Internet Law* 21, no. 1 (2017): 3–11.

75. The CNIL's restricted committee imposes a financial penalty of 50 Million euros against GOOGLE LLC, https://www.cnil.fr/en/cnils-restricted-committee-imposes-financial-penalty-50-million-euros-against-google-llc (accessed June 15, 2020).
76. Ibid.
77. Ibid.
78. European Data Protection Board 'BfDI imposes fines on telecommunications service providers' (20, https://edpb.europa.eu/news/national-news/2019/bfdi-imposes-fines-telecommunications-service-providers_en (accessed June 15, 2020).
79. Ibid.
80. Ibid.
81. Information Commissioner's Office, 'Intention to fine British Airways £183.39m under GDPR for data breach' (2019) https://ico.org.uk/about-the-ico/news-and-events/news-and-blogs/2019/07/ico-announces-intention-to-fine-british-airways/ (accessed May 2, 2020).
82. Ibid.
83. DLA Piper Data Breach Survey, January 2020, https://sweden.dlapiper.com/sites/default/files/node/field_download/DLA%20Piper_Data%20Breach%20Report%202020.pdf (accessed June 15, 2020).
84. Ibid.
85. It should be noted that as of 25 May 2018, the Article 29 Working Party ceased to exist and it has been replaced by the European Data Protection Board (EDPB).
86. Guidelines on the right to data portability, Article 29 Working Party, [2017] 16/EN WP 242 rev. 01 adopted on April 5, 2017.
87. Orla Lynskey, *The Foundations of EU Data Protection Law* (Oxford: Oxford University Press, 2015), 189.
88. Europe v Facebook, ' Response to the Audit' by the Irish Office of Data Protection Commissioner on "Facebook Ireland Ltd"', Vienna, 4 December 2012, 42: < http://www.europe-v-facebook.org/report.pdf> (accessed June 15, 2020).
89. Article 29 Data Protection Working Party, Opinion 15/2011 on the definition of consent 01197/11/EN WP187 adopted on 13 July 2011 available < https://ec.europa.eu/justice/article-29/documentation/opinion-recommendation/files/2011/wp187_en.pdf> (accessed June 15, 2020).
90. Case summary, "Facebook, Exploitative business terms pursuant to Section 19(1) GWB for inadequate data processing" 2019, https://www.bundeskartellamt.de/SharedDocs/Entscheidung/EN/Fallberichte/Missbrauchsaufsicht/2019/B6-22-16.pdf?__blob=publicationFile&v=3> p. 5, 2019 (accessed June 15, 2020).
91. Ibid.
92. Guiseppe Colangelo, ' Facebook and the Bundeskartellamt's; Winter of Discontent' (2019) https://www.competitionpolicyinternational.com/facebook-and-bundeskartellamts-winter-of-discontent/ (accessed June 10, 2020).
93. OLG Düsseldorf, August 26, 2019, Case VI-Kart 1/19 (V).
94. Counterfactuals in competition law analysis can be used to assess the effects of an event and how the situation would have developed in the absence of that event.
95. OLG Düsseldorf, para 27 and 47.
96. Colangelo, supra note 92.
97. OLG Düsseldorf, para 32.
98. Ibid, para 71, 76 and 77.
99. Ibid, para 44, 46 and 71.
100. Thomas Linden et al., 'The Privacy Policy Landscape after the GDPR, Proceedings on Privacy Enhancing Technologies', *Proceedings on Privacy Enhancing Technologies* 1 (2020): 47–64.
101. Danilo Bruschi, 'Information Privacy: Not just GDPR', in *Computer Ethics - Philosophical Enquiry (CEPE) Proceedings*, ed. D. Wittkower (2019), 9 https://digitalcommons.odu.edu/cepe_proceedings/vol2019/iss1/9 (accessed June 15, 2020).
102. Jim Isaak and Mina J. Hanna, 'User Data Privacy: Facebook, Cambridge Analytica, and Privacy Protection', *Computer* 51, no. 8 (2018): 56–9.

103. John Thornhill, 'GDPR is a Start but not Enough to Protect Privacy on its Own', *Financial Times* https://www.ft.com/content/624f813e-5f5e-11e8-9334-2218e7146b04 (accessed June 15, 2020).
104. Opinion 5/2018 Preliminary Opinion on Privacy by Design by European Data Protection Supervisor, para 22, p. 5 https://edps.europa.eu/sites/edp/files/publication/18-05-31_preliminary_opinion_on_privacy_by_design_en_0.pdf (accessed June 15, 2020).
105. Ibid., p. 21.
106. Ibid., p. 5.

Disclosure statement

No potential conflict of interest was reported by the author(s).

ORCID

Aysem Diker Vanberg http://orcid.org/0000-0002-0614-1707

Playing catch up – privacy regimes in South Asia

Smitha Krishna Prasad and Sharngan Aravindakshan

ABSTRACT
This article is an attempt to examine the growing consolidation and harmonisation of privacy and surveillance laws in the major SAARC member nations, as well as to take stock of South Asia's emerging privacy jurisprudence. Driven by reactions to increasingly frequent data collection and profiling attempts by the government, as well as the side effects of growing digital markets, the privacy discourse in South Asia is evolving with a heightened awareness of privacy as a core fundamental right. At the same time, some governments in the region are also keen to explore the benefits of the digital economy, and are increasingly developing economic policies that focus on the use of data as a 'resource' for the State and the industry. Apart from outlining these developments, the article delves into and identifies the source of privacy rights in these countries, whether derived from the constitutions of the respective countries or otherwise provided for through specific legislation. The article traces and examines the legal architectures of privacy and surveillance in the region, including national profiling databases. It then zooms out to pinpoint possible trends and influences.

1. Introduction

The landscape of privacy laws, like most other laws in South Asia, is fragmented. The region consists of India, Pakistan, Sri Lanka, Nepal, Bhutan, Bangladesh, Maldives and Afghanistan, which together constitute the South Asian Association for Regional Cooperation (SAARC), the primary regional body in South Asia.

The SAARC nations have not remained immune to the increased focus on privacy and data protection the world over, and have begun their own processes of formulating and/or shoring up their privacy regimes. The mandate of the SAARC does not specifically refer to harmonisation of laws or legal policies, examining their legal regimes. However, it is still a worthwhile exercise to undertake a comparative study of legal regimes in the region, given many of its members share common colonial pasts (India, Sri Lanka, Maldives), have similarities in ethnicities, culture and experiences of their peoples (India, Pakistan, Nepal, Bangladesh, Sri Lanka) and even have common origins (India, Pakistan and Bangladesh all having been part of a larger pre-independence India).

The gaping digital divide, coupled with the perception that privacy is only an elitist concern, meant that privacy as a legal and policy issue was not high in the priority list for most governments in the region, resulting in little focus on the development of a comprehensive legislative framework or architecture for privacy.[1] In fact, most countries in South Asia, notably even India, which has the largest economy in the region, are still engaged in massive digitisation drives to ensure digital penetration and access to all sections of their population. For instance, 'Digital India', the flagship digital outreach programme of the Government of India which aims *inter alia* to 'bring digital infrastructure as a core utility to every citizen',[2] is still ongoing.

Despite the perception of low levels of privacy concern, measures such as the establishment of nation-wide identity databases with minimum protection,[3] and expanding communications surveillance,[4] led to strong reactions and a call for greater restraints on government surveillance.[5] This in turn forced an examination of the content and contours of the right to privacy in some countries in the region. While several countries in South Asia expressly recognise a constitutional right to privacy, including Nepal[6] and Bangladesh[7] and a limited form of the right is recognised in Pakistan's constitution,[8] the constitutions of other countries such as India and Sri Lanka do not provide for such rights in writing. These government-led measures, such as the national identity databases, provided citizens an opportunity to approach the courts, and in India this resulted in a unanimous judicial recognition of privacy as a constitutional right.[9] A similar challenge is reportedly pending in Sri Lanka's Supreme Court.[10]

Along with privacy concerns, governments were also simultaneously faced with burgeoning urban digital economies. The South Asian population with its median age of 27 has proved a highly attractive market for digital driven players including global giants such as Uber, Google and Facebook, all of whom have bottomless appetites for data. Soon, this brought to light several problems with corporate data aggregation and monetisation, requiring rules on collection, processing, use, and dissemination of personal data. In the Indian sub-continent, remedying these problems was only made more urgent by the inception of the European Union's General Data Protection Regulation (GDPR) with its adequacy status requirements[11] and its potential impact on trade in the region.[12]

In this background, South Asian countries seem to have discovered that they can no longer hold off on establishing strong privacy protection frameworks. Having realised that this is also the best way to harness the full benefits of the digital economy, they have begun framing new laws, as well as updating and harmonising existing laws on privacy, personal data and surveillance, unique to their experiences as part of the global south.

By examining both the constitutional and legislative frameworks of privacy rights across Bangladesh, India, Nepal, Pakistan, Sri Lanka and Bhutan, this article attempts to identify existing trends and influences in these regimes across the SAARC countries region. These countries have all either taken real and tangible steps towards establishing elaborate privacy regimes or are seriously considering legislative action relating to privacy in the immediate future. Relevant legislations in these countries, including pending bills, have been examined. Maldives and Afghanistan, despite being part of the region, are not dealt with in detail given there exists no substantial privacy legislation in these countries, with little indicating any change soon.

The second part of the article traces and illustrates the existing laws relevant to privacy and surveillance across the countries identified above. This part of the article looks at constitutional rights to privacy, and specific privacy or data protection legislations. The other set of laws discussed in the article, which may not typically fit within the realm of privacy law, are the right to information laws in these countries. In many of these countries, enacted well before any other meaningful privacy legislation or regulations, these laws typically contain provisions on balancing the right to information with the right to privacy of individual persons by public sector bodies.

The article also discusses national identity systems, which are prevalent across the region. Although these systems may be governed by separate laws, and regulators, (or possibly no law or regulatory authority at all) they raise many questions regarding both the protection of personal data and the potential for surveillance. The third part of this article takes a preliminary look into the national identity systems present in South Asian countries.

The fourth part of the article threads together the similarities in the region and attempts to examine whether evolving a region-specific standard for the Indian sub-continent is possible, or if the privacy and data protection regimes are developing in tune with each country's experiences.

2. Privacy and surveillance frameworks in South Asia

2.1. Bangladesh

2.1.1. Constitutional Guarantee

Bangladesh ensures constitutional protection to privacy in the form of Article 43 of its Constitution which provides citizens the right to be secured in their home against search and seizure, as well as the privacy of correspondence and other means of communication.[13] This right is not unqualified as it is subject to reasonable restrictions imposed by law in the interests of the security of the State, public order, public morality or public health.[14]

Separately, Article 32 of Bangladesh's Constitution states that no person shall be deprived of life or personal liberty save in accordance with law. The language of Article 32 is identical to Article 21 of the Indian Constitution and given the lack of case law on this issue in Bangladesh, it may be helpful to look to Indian caselaw on the same subject.

Although neither constitutional provisions expressly recognise a right to privacy, the Indian Supreme Court has relied on Article 21 of the Indian Constitution to provide protection from state surveillance since the 1960s. The first such instance was in *Kharak Singh v. The State of Uttar Pradesh*. In this case, the Indian Supreme Court struck down a provision in the Uttar Pradesh Police Regulations, which allowed police to carry out 'domiciliary visits', in other words, home visits, as part of a larger surveillance mechanism of alleged criminals. The Court found such police actions to be in violation of the right to 'personal liberty' guaranteed under Article 21 of India's Constitution.[15] Scholars have pointed to this judgement as support for the proposition that Article 32 of Bangladesh's Constitution can be similarly interpreted to include a broader form of protection from state surveillance.[16]

2.1.2. Personal data protection laws

There is currently no comprehensive data protection law in Bangladesh other than the Information and Communications Technology Act 2006 (Bangladesh ICT Act). The

Bangladesh ICT Act is largely based on or similar to India's Information Technology Act, 2000, with several provisions having been reproduced from the Indian legislation.[17] Certain provisions under the Bangladesh ICT Act could be used for data protection, such as Section 54, which prohibits unauthorised interference with computer systems by third parties.[18] However, no meaningful data protection classification such as data controllers, data processors or data subjects exists. The Bangladesh ICT Act also envisages a Cyber Tribunal and Cyber Appellate Tribunal for adjudication and enforcement.[19]

2.1.3. Legal framework for surveillance by security and law enforcement agencies

(a) Telegraph Act, 1885

The Telegraph Act of 1885 is a legacy legislation from the times of colonial rule, that remains in force in Bangladesh. Section 5 of the Telegraph Act, 1885 permits the government to take temporary possession of licensed telegraphs and to order interception of messages.[20] At the same time, the government also has the power to frame rules to prevent improper interception or disclosure of messages.[21] Unlawfully attempting to learn the contents of messages is also penalised, both for governmental[22] and non-governmental persons.[23]

(b) Bangladesh Telecommunication Act, 2001

This law was enacted essentially for regulation of the telecommunications sector, consisting of public and private mobile and other service operators such as TeleTalk, Robi etc. With rising internet connectivity within Bangladesh, this sector has been touted as crucial to making Bangladesh a middle income country.[24] Under the law, unlawful interference with or interception and divulgence of radio communications without consent or approval is penalised,[25] along with intentional eavesdropping on telephone conversations.[26] However, the government has the power to take over any telecommunication system in public interest, as well as continue engaging the operator who is required to comply with its directions.[27] The government also has a preferential right to the use of such equipment in the case of war, internal rebellion, disorder, defence, other security or state affair of Bangladesh.[28]

(c) Digital Security Act 2018

The Digital Security Act 2018 was brought in to regulate digital security as part of national security as well as to deal with cyber crimes generally.[29] Significantly, it was also introduced to assuage concerns regarding the widespread misuse of the draconian Section 57 of the Bangladesh ICT Act. This provision allowed prosecution of any person who published in electronic form material that was fake, defamatory, obscene, hurt religious sentiments or prejudices the image of the state or person.[30] It was reportedly widely abused by the government to suppress dissent and criticism.[31] However, critics note that the Digital Security Act did nothing to reign in the excesses complained of.[32]

This law gives the government powers to remove or block information in case it threatens digital security.[33] The same power is given to the government in broadly worded exceptions available on the grounds of 'national unity, financial activities, security, defense, religious values, public discipline or incites racism and hatred ... '[34]

The law also gives free reign to law enforcement agencies to take into custody computer systems, collect data including traffic data and even enlist 'experts' in this task,[35] without any prior warrant requirements at the investigation stage. Search and seizure powers for traffic data and computer systems are subject to a warrant by a judge,[36] but broad provisions have been made for these powers without requiring a warrant as well, leaving much to the discretion of the law enforcement official.[37] Directions can be issued to retain and preserve the data, for a total of 180 days.[38] Service providers can be called upon to assist/provide information in investigations and are obligated to comply.[39]

Offences under the Digital Security Act 2018 are also expansively worded and include illegal entrance in critical information infrastructure,[40] unauthorised entry into computers or computer networks,[41] and damage to computer systems,[42] damage to source code[43] and digital forgery.[44] Importantly, collecting and using 'identity information' without permission,[45] cyber-terrorism[46] and illegal transferring and saving of government data-information without authorisation[47] are all also offences under the Digital Security Act, 2018.

2.1.4. Other laws

Bangladesh's Right to Information Act, 2009 does impose some privacy obligations on its public sector. In an inclusive definition, Section 2(b) captures within the Act's ambit all organisations established under the Constitution, private bodies running on government aid as well as organisations carrying out sovereign functions under contract with the government.[48] The Act also exempts from disclosure any information that offends the privacy of the personal life of an individual[49] as well as any information given to law enforcement agencies in confidence.[50] Even though the Act exempts from its ambit organisations involved in state security and intelligence,[51] it overrides other laws such as the Digital Security Act 2018, in case of conflict.[52]

An Information Commission is established under the Act for inquiring into and disposing of complaints[53] as well as for performing other functions under the Act generally.

2.2. Nepal

2.2.1. Constitutional Guarantee

In Nepal, the right to privacy is constitutionally guaranteed as a fundamental right, both in the Interim Constitution of 2007[54] as well as the Constitution adopted in 2015[55] ('2015 Nepal Constitution') currently in force. Article 28 of the Nepal's 2015 Constitution provides that '*the privacy of any person, his or her residence, property, document, data, correspondence and matters relating to his or her character shall, except in accordance with law, be inviolable*'.[56]

This constitutional right to privacy has also been robustly enforced by the Supreme Court of Nepal in the context of homosexual and transgender rights. In *Sunil Babu Pant and Others v. Nepal Government and Others*, several organisations representing LGBTQ persons, among others, filed a writ petition in the Supreme Court seeking recognition of transgenders as a third gender and prohibition on discrimination on the basis of sexual orientation and gender identity. Upholding their rights, the Supreme Court viewed sexual activity through the prism of privacy, expressly stating that the right to privacy was 'a fundamental right of an individual' and that the 'issue of sexual activity falls under the definition of privacy'.[57]

The Supreme Court of Nepal has also upheld the right to privacy in other contexts. In the year 2007, in *Advocate Sapana Pradhan Malla v. Prime-minister, Nepal Government and Office of the Council of Ministers and Ors.*, a petition was filed by several rights organisations, among others, specifically seeking protection of the privacy of victims of sexual crimes, juvenile criminal cases and HIV/AIDS infected persons. Significantly, the Supreme Court not only upheld their right to non-disclosure of their 'personal introductory information', but also invoked Article 107(2) of the Interim Constitution of Nepal, 2007 which granted it extraordinary jurisdiction to settle legal disputes, to lay down interim guidelines to secure their privacy.[58]

These guidelines, titled 'The Procedural Guidelines for Protecting the Privacy of the Parties in the Proceedings of Special Types of Cases, 2064 (2007)' ('Guidelines') are applicable to cases with women victims of sexual crimes, children in juvenile criminal cases and cases with HIV/AIDS infected persons.[59] The Guidelines define 'personal introductory information' as all related description regarding disclosure of identity including name, family title, address, etc.[60] The Guidelines, apart from prohibiting the disclosure of personal introductory information by all bodies including investigating bodies, body trying the case and the verdict implementing body, also require these bodies to protect the privacy of the persons appearing in these cases.[61] They also lay down the method for protecting privacy, such as keeping the confidential information in sealed envelopes and attaching it separately to the case file, and so on.[62] The guidelines specify that any violation will be considered contempt of court and also invite disciplinary action.[63]

While this was certainly a welcome step, the guidelines were more a form of makeshift protection of the person's privacy than a concrete privacy law would have afforded. Rule 4 of the Guidelines permits disclosure of the confidential information by the officer responsible for its secrecy if he or she deemed it legally fit for disclosure, subjecting the persons' privacy to the whims of the authorities. Moreover, Rule 4(2) allows disclosure if 'it looks necessary for the protection of fair judicial hearing'. The deciding authority for this ground is not specified, although it is presumably the court itself.

In any case, given their interim nature, with the enactment of the Privacy Act, 2018, these guidelines are likely no longer applicable.

2.2.2. Personal data protection law

In order to give effect to the right to privacy in Article 28 of Nepal's latest Constitution (2015), Nepal has also recently enacted the Privacy Act, 2018 (Nepal Privacy Act). Described as 'an Act made to provide for Privacy', it is a legislation to ensure the right to privacy in certain identified spheres of privacy, i.e. the body, residence, property, document, data, correspondence and character of every person.[64] The Nepal Privacy Act uses an exhaustive list (as opposed to the inclusive definitions we see in the European Union and some other jurisdictions) to define 'personal information'. Personal information includes as information relating to caste, ethnicity, religion, colour, marital status, educational qualifications, address and contact details, biometric information, passport, national identity card number, license number or any information related to such identity documents, academic qualifications and details of criminal background, if any, as well as private communications that mention personal information and professional or expert opinions expressed by a person in relation to any decision.[65]

Collection, processing and storage are prohibited without the consent of the individual.[66] The information can also only be used for the use specified at the time of collection,[67] and third party sharing is limited.[68]

Nepal's Privacy Act deviates from many typical data protection frameworks in that the Privacy Act does not appear to classify relevant stakeholders. Terms such as 'data controllers' and 'data subjects' as in the GDPR or OECD Guidelines, or India's proposed trifurcation of data principals, data fiduciaries and data processors, are missing in the Privacy Act. There is also no designated regulating body for enforcement of these rights such as a Data Protection Authority, as this falls to the 'concerned District Court'.[69]

The Nepal Privacy Act does not limit itself to only data protection or data privacy provisions, and also deals with larger issues of privacy, such as physical and mental privacy[70] (particularly in the context of health), reproductive health related privacy,[71] familial privacy,[72] and search and seizure in the context of the person and the home,[73] among others.

2.2.3. Legal framework for surveillance by security and law enforcement agencies

Despite the numerous protections offered by Nepal's Privacy Act, there is not yet any legal framework governing interception and surveillance by government authorities in Nepal.[74] Greenleaf, while quoting a report by Privacy International, has noted that telecommunications interception is rampant and widespread, with participation from telecommunications companies.[75]

The government has recently proposed a controversial Information Technology Management Bill which reportedly gives broad powers to authorities to carry out surveillance, restrict free speech as well as mandatorily require social media companies to register in Nepal.[76] [77] It was tabled in Nepal's Parliament in December 2019 and is currently pending consideration.[78]

2.2.4. Other laws that affect privacy

(a) Electronic Transactions Act 2008

While primarily concerning itself with the record keeping and authenticity of electronic records, this legislation also penalises acts such as altering or destroying source codes in *mala fides*,[79] unauthorised access to computer materials,[80] unauthorizedly divulging confidential information otherwise protected under the law[81] and computer fraud.[82] The law also penalises offences under the Electronic Transactions Act committed by persons outside Nepal, but involving computer systems located within Nepal.[83]

(b) Right to Information Act, 2007

Nepal's Right to Information Act is primarily meant to provide a means to obtain information from public bodies thereby fostering public accountability and an informed citizenry. However, many of its provisions also serve basic data protection functions and posit obligations on public bodies to protect personal data that is entrusted to them.[84]

Section 3(3)(c) of the Nepal RTI Act prohibits the dissemination of information held by a public body in case of interference with 'individual privacy and security of body, life, property or health of a person'.[85] Information with the public bodies is subject to a right of correction by the concerned person if 'the information in a Public Body on a particular matter is wrong' and 'necessary evidence' is provided to correct it.[86] Other basic data protection functions in the Nepal RTI Act include protection of accessed personal information from misuse by third parties,[87] restrictions on use and disclosure of personal information by public bodies,[88] and even compensation for losses occurred on account of public bodies providing wrong or partially wrong information, destruction of information and so on.[89]

(c) Criminal Code Act 2017[90]

Nepal has recently begun revamping its historical legal code, the *Muluki Ain*, and has enacted the Criminal Code Act 2017 ('Criminal Code') as part of this effort. The Criminal Code also serves to protect privacy – it penalises unauthorised tapping of a voice conversation, breach of confidentiality, taking and editing photos of a person without consent, breach of privacy of information in electronic media, unauthorised search of body or belongings of person, and trespassing.[91] However, under the Criminal Code, these offences are considered private offences and need to be pursued privately, as opposed to prosecution by the state.[92] The victims are also entitled to compensation.[93]

2.3. Pakistan

2.3.1. Constitutional guarantee

A form of domestic or household privacy finds place in Pakistan's Constitution ('Constitution of Pakistan') in Article 14(1) which provides that the dignity of man and, subject to law, the privacy of home, shall be inviolable.[94] Along with this, Article 8 of the Constitution declares void any law inconsistent with fundamental rights.[95] However, this protection is immediately diluted by an exception to Article 8 which exempts laws relating to armed forces or the police charged with the maintenance of public order or the discharge of their duties.[96]

Digital Rights Foundation notes that Pakistani courts are yet to develop a coherent doctrine of privacy, perhaps on account of the limited protection given to privacy in the constitution.[97] Despite this, there are instances of courts espousing broader privacy rights, such as the Lahore High Court in *Tahir v. State Bank* striking down a directive issued by the State Bank of Pakistan mandating the collection of its clients' private information and handing them over to the tax authorities.[98] In *Tahir* (supra), the petitioner challenged a circular issued by the State Bank of Pakistan to banks seeking classified information about depositors whose annual profit was Rs.10,000 or more.[99] The State Bank of Pakistan contended that it was merely collecting the information for the tax department to bring more people into the tax net and that this was in the 'best public interest'.[100] The Lahore High Court ruled that the taking of private information without any allegation of wrongdoing of ordinary people is an extraordinary invasion of this fundamental right of privacy.[101]

2.3.2. Personal data protection law

In 2018, the Cabinet in the Government of Pakistan approved the 'Digital Pakistan Policy 2017' which proposed to 'promulgate necessary policy frameworks, laws and rules to enable creation of a sustainable IT environment including enactment of data protection law'.[102]

This prompted the Pakistan Government to introduce its primary data protection legislation, i.e. the Personal Data Protection Bill 2018 ('Bill') which, like in India, is still in bill form.[103] The Bill was proposed by the Ministry of Information Technology and Telecommunication in Pakistan.[104] The Bill defines 'personal data' along GDPR lines, as information relating to data subjects who are identifiable from such information including sensitive personal data and expression of opinion.[105] Anonymized, encrypted or pseudonymized data incapable of identifying a data subject does not amount to personal data.[106] Sensitive personal data has been defined as consisting of information revealing race, ethnicity, religious beliefs, membership in political parties, trade unions, biometric or genetic data, criminal proceedings and financial or other personal data as may be notified.[107]

The proposed legislation also adopts the data subject[108]; data controller[109]; data processor[110] triumvirate. Processing by government entities is exempted from the purview of the bill if it is solely for the purposes and to the extent provided under the applicable legislation.[111] It is also subject to ensuring security, secrecy and confidentiality of the personal data.[112] However, processing of personal data for commercial purposes by the government still falls within the scope of the legislation.[113]

Processing of personal data is conditional on consent[114] and is restricted to the standard principles of lawfulness, necessity and proportionality.[115] Exemptions from the consent requirement are somewhat broad – if it is necessary for performance of contract, compliance of legal obligations, for legitimate interests of the data controller, or for the exercise of any functions conferred by law.[116] Interestingly, consent is also not required in case processing is necessary to 'protect the vital interests of the data subject'.[117] The Bill also defines 'vital interests' as matters relating to life, death or security of a data subject.[118] This particular exemption is found neither in the GDPR nor the proposed Indian legislation.

Other general principles include non-disclosure of personal data,[119] data retention (not longer than necessary and destruction of data after),[120] access to data & data correction rights[121] and notice to the data subject.[122] Strangely, notwithstanding the obligation of non-disclosure, the data controllers can disclose personal data in cases, apart from when there is consent, where the data controller reasonably believed that he had the right to disclose or reasonably believed that the data subject would have given consent had he known of the disclosure.[123] This provision gives great leeway to data controllers to freely disclose personal data without bothering with consent.

The Bill also prohibits the transfer of personal data to unauthorised persons or systems as well as to countries without an equivalent data protection system.[124] Data controllers are also required to notify the Commission of personal data breaches within 72 hours of knowledge.[125]

Data subjects' rights include right of access to personal data,[126] right to correct the personal data[127] and the right of consent withdrawal.[128] The Bill also provides a right to erasure[129] together with the right to prevent processing likely to cause damage or distress,[130] together constituting a form of the right to be forgotten, which also finds place in the equivalent proposed Indian legislation.[131]

Exemptions from the legislation are broad and include processing for prevention or investigation of crimes,[132] apprehending of criminals[133] and discharge of regulatory functions should they be prejudiced by the application of these provisions.[134] Significantly, the Government reserves the right to make further exemptions as well as impose any terms or conditions for such exemption.[135]

The Bill also establishes a Commission for Personal Data Protection as a regulator to enforce and implement the legislation.[136] Processing, disclosure or dissemination of personal data in contravention of the Bill,[137] failure to adopt appropriate data security measures[138] and failure to comply with orders[139] are all made punishable offences.

2.3.3. Legal framework for surveillance by security and law enforcement agencies

Pakistan has an extensive surveillance system in place, involving constant and widespread monitoring of data of its citizens and foreigners. Project Hotel Eye is one such system requiring software based registration in hotels and aimed at keeping an eye on travellers, both foreign and local. Linked with the government-issued National Identity Card, the hotel is able to record the criminal data of the visitor, if any, which is then shared with the police.[140] According to Privacy International, the Inter-Services Intelligence ('ISI'), Pakistan's premier intelligence agency, also had plans to tap international undersea cables in southern Pakistan for a mass surveillance system with massive reach and impact.[141]

The legislative framework for such a surveillance system is detailed below.

(a) Pakistan Telecommunication (Re-organization) Act, 1996

This legislation was intended to provide for the reorganisation and regulation of Pakistan's telecommunication system.[142] Section 54 of this Act permits the Federal Government to authorise any person to intercept calls and messages or to trace calls through any telecommunication system in the interest of national security or in the apprehension of any offence.[143] The Federal Government also has the power to make rules regarding lawful interception.[144] The relevant authority under this Act, the Pakistan Telecommunication Authority, also reportedly prohibited unpermitted use of encryption and VPN 'which conceal communication to the extent that prohibits monitoring', ostensibly for reducing revenue losses on account of increasing grey traffic.[145]

(b) The Investigation for Fair Trial Act, 2013

This Act grants broad surveillance and interception powers to designated government bodies and legitimises the use of the collected material as evidence.[146] It allows the grant of a warrant authorising interception and recording of telephonic communication, video recordings of persons, electronic transactions including SMS, e-mails, etc., as well as taking over of equipment including telephones, mobiles and electronic databases.[147] Such warrants can also authorise collection of evidence, use of human intelligence, covert surveillance and property interference as well as any related information or data in any form, or any other form of surveillance or interception the federal government may notify.[148]

Despite authorisation being restricted by the requirement for approval by Minister[149] followed by a judicial warrant by a Magistrate,[150] these broad provisions are considered a legitimate threat to privacy,[151] seeing as how they are not circumscribed by standard principles such as necessity and proportionality.

(c) Prevention of Electronic Crimes Act, 2016

Under this Act, warrants can authorise investigation agencies to access data,[152] search and seize data and information systems[153] and access content data.[154] The Act also authorises removal or blocking of access to information under certain specified grounds.[155]

Significantly, real time collection and recording of information is also authorised for criminal investigation, subject to a court issued warrant, for up to seven days and extendable thereafter by the court.[156] The Federal government can also forward information obtained from its own investigations to foreign governments and their agencies.[157] The Pakistani government is known to have shared information (including that of its own citizens) with the United Kingdom and the United States.[158] According to Privacy International, the Pakistani government is the largest known recipient of NSA funds.[159]

Pakistan's relationship with the NSA for surveillance is extensive. According to the documents leaked by Edward Snowden, Pakistan (among other countries) is an approved third party SIGINT Partner, which can also entitle it to 'technical solutions (e.g. hardware or software) and/or access to related technology'.[160] The Guardian has reported that under the NSA's 'Boundless Informant' programme, in which the NSA collected 'pieces of intelligence' from any part of the world, Pakistan had the second highest amount of intelligence or information collected.[161] Privacy International has also alleged that the NSA, through its SKYNET programme, harvests call data from Pakistani telecommunications providers (though it does not specify how) and that 55 million phone records were fed into an NSA analysis system for an analysis exercise.[162]

2.3.4. Other laws that affect privacy

Pakistan's RTI equivalent, i.e. the Freedom of Information Ordinance, 2002, also has certain privacy-relevant provisions for the public sector. Originally promulgated in 2002 by President Musharaff, the Freedom of Information Ordinance became permanent after an amendment to the Constitution which legitimised all of President Musharaff's orders/ordinances.[163]

Information will not be disclosed if they pertain to privacy and personal information.[164] Similarly, records relating to the personal privacy of the individual[165] and private documents furnished to a public body on an implied or express condition of non-disclosure[166] are also excluded from the ambit of disclosure.

While not having a direct impact on privacy or data protection, the Electronic Transactions Ordinance, 2002 was promulgated to give legal recognition of electronic records,[167] as well as to establish a Certification Council to monitor accreditation and research cryptography services.[168]

2.4. Sri Lanka

2.4.1. Constitutional guarantees

There is no right to privacy expressly guaranteed in the Constitution of Sri Lanka, 1978 ('Sri Lankan Constitution'). Courts have made references to privacy, but in the context of adjudicating the extent of other rights, such as the right to freedom of expression.[169] For instance, in *Sinha Rathnathunge v. The State,*[170] the editor of the Sunday Times, who had been indicted for defaming the President of Sri Lanka, challenged his indictment. The Court of Appeal observed as follows –

> The press should not think they are free to invade the privacy of individuals in the exercise of their constitutional right to freedom of speech and expression, merely because the right to privacy is not declared a fundamental right of the individual[171] ... The press should not seek under the cover of exercising its freedom of speech and expression make unwarranted intrusions into the private domain of individuals and thereby destroy his right to privacy. Public figures are no exception. Even a public figure is entitled to a reasonable measure of privacy. Therefore, Her Excellency the President even though she is a public figure is entitled to a reasonable measure of privacy to be left alone when she is not engaged in the performance of any public functions. That is a no entry zone which the press must not trespass.[172]

Scholars opine that this judgement located a right to privacy in the realm of tort law. In the absence of a constitutionally protected right to privacy, this judgment opens remedies to privacy breaches in the form of tort action in Sri Lanka's common law,[173] which is a mix of Roman Dutch civil law, English common law and Jaffna Tamil customary law.[174]

2.4.2. Personal data protection law

A personal data protection legislative framework is currently pending consideration in the Sri Lankan Parliament. The Sri Lankan Ministry of Digital Infrastructure and Information Technology introduced the Personal Data Protection Bill first in June 2019[175] and then again in September 2019 after making changes.[176] The definitions of 'personal data'[177] (information that can identify a data subject directly or indirectly), and 'special categories of personal data'[178] (data revealing *inter alia* racial or ethnic origin, financial data, genetic data, data concerning sex life or sexual orientation) conform to the EU GDPR standard. The Bill adopts the GDPR classification of data subjects, data controllers and data processors.[179] It also proposes adoption of data protection standards such as processing in a lawful manner,[180] ensuring that processing is for specified, explicit and legitimate purposes[181] and period of retention to be limited,[182] similar to the GDPR.

Data subjects' rights include chiefly the right to withdraw consent and object to processing,[183] right to access to personal data,[184] right to rectification or completion[185] and the right to erasure.[186] The Bill also mandates carrying out personal data protection impact assessments by controllers where the processing is likely to result in high risk to the rights and freedoms of data subjects.[187] A Data Protection Authority is also envisaged for implementing and ensuring compliance with the legislation.[188]

The Bill also separately deals with the use of data to disseminate unsolicited messages with a general proscription on dissemination without consent[189] and elaborating the exceptions to the prohibition.[190]

2.4.3. Legal framework for surveillance by security and law enforcement agencies

(a) Computer Crimes Act, 2007

The primarily legislation enabling surveillance in Sri Lanka is the Computer Crimes Act, 2007. Section 18 of the said Act empowers an expert or a police officer in an investigation to obtain information including subscriber information and traffic data from service providers, as well as intercept any wire or electronic communications at any stage of the communication.[191] Although the provision requires a warrant issued by a Magistrate,[192] this requirement can be dispensed with in the case of (a) urgency, (b) likelihood of evidence being destroyed or damaged and (c) need to maintain confidentiality.[193] Section 24(2) also requires service providers to maintain confidentiality of requests from law enforcement.[194]

Section 19 allows an expert or a police officer to require the preservation of information not exceeding 7 days, further extendable up to 90 days.[195]

2.4.4. Other laws that affect privacy

(a) Sri Lanka Telecommunications Act, 1991

The Sri Lanka Telecommunications Act, 1991 proscribes intrusion into message contents,[196] wilful interception of telecommunication transmission,[197] interception and disclosure of message contents by the telecommunication officer,[198] and the possession, custody or control of telecommunication wires.[199] Although no exception has been made for law enforcement agencies, it appears that these provisions do not impact the operation of law enforcement agencies under the subsequently enacted Computer Crimes Act, 2007.

(b) Payment Devices Frauds Act, 2006

With the objective being to prevent the possession and use of unauthorised or counterfeit payment devices, the Payment Devices Frauds Act, 2006 penalises unlawful tampering of payment devices or implanting foreign objects for recording transaction data[200] and uses without lawful authority a phone listening device or other similar device or the purpose of capturing authorisation data passing through the acquirer's point of sale networks or automated teller machine network,[201] among other offences. However, for purposes of investigation, the Act enables access to any information system related to the fraud,[202] as well as require any person to produce any information/document and traffic data without any requirement for a warrant.[203]

(c) Right to Information Act, 2016

The 19th Amendment to the Sri Lankan Constitution in 2015 resulted in the insertion of Article 14A which provides for the right of access to information.[204] Privacy is specified as one of the grounds under which the right can be restricted.[205]

In line with the constitutional right, the Right to Information Act, 2016 ('Sri Lanka RTI Act') was enacted and came into force in 2017.[206] Section 5 of the Sri Lanka RTI Act ensures that information will not be disclosed should it constitute an 'unwarranted invasion of the privacy of the individual'.[207] Other privacy related grounds for non-disclosure in Section 5 includes the disclosure of medical information without consent,[208] information required to be kept confidential on account of the existence of a fiduciary relationship[209] as well as information supplied 'in confidence' to the public authority by a third party and such third party does not consent.[210] Persons who disclose information in violation of the prohibitions under the Sri Lanka RTI Act are liable for a fine or imprisonment up to two years or both.[211]

The definition of 'public authority' under the Act is also wide, including all government bodies, companies in which the government or a public sector corporation has at least 25% shareholding, private bodies that are under government contracts or perform sovereign functions, etc.[212] The Sri Lanka RTI Act also provides for the establishment of a Commission to regulate and ensure performance of the obligations therein by the authorities concerned.[213]

(d) Miscellaneous Laws

Sri Lanka has other laws that are meant to promote, regulate and foster digitisation. The Information and Communication Technology Act, 2003 mandate the framing of national policies for ICT[214] and establishes the Information and Communication Technology Agency for implementing the policy and other directions or regulations framed under the Act.[215] The Electronic Transactions Act No. 19 of 2006 is mainly an e-governance legislation[216] and aims to regulate electronic transactions in the country as well as lay down requirements for admissibility of electronic documents.[217] The Cyber Security Bill, 2019 which provides for the implementation of Sri Lanka's national cyber security strategy,[218] establish a cyber security agency[219] and flesh out protection measures for critical infrastructure,[220] among other things, is currently pending consideration.

2.5. India

2.5.1. Constitutional guarantee

The right to privacy is recognised as a fundamental right under the Indian Constitution. While the right is not explicitly provided for in writing, in the Constitution, it has been recognised as a fundamental right by the Supreme Court of India (SCOI) in several cases since the 1960s.

In early cases, the SCOI looked at the right to privacy primarily from the lens of the rights under the Fourth Amendment of the American Constitution (U.S. Fourth Amendment).[221] In *MP Sharma v. Satish Chandra* (1954), an 8-judge bench decided a case involving a challenge to searches and seizures by the government against members of a group of companies.[222] In its judgement, the SCOI stated that there was no need to import a right to privacy analogous to that under the U.S. Fourth Amendment, since the power to search and seize was an overriding power of the State which was also regulated by law and that the drafters of the Constitution had thought it fit not to subject such regulation to a fundamental right of privacy.[223] In *Kharak Singh v. State of UP* (1962) (also discussed in the Bangladesh section), the SCOI struck down Regulation 236(b) of the Uttar Pradesh Police Regulations which permitted domiciliary visits by the police as a surveillance measure on the basis of the right to 'personal liberty' under Article 21 of the Indian Constitution. The Court acknowledged that there is no right to privacy equivalent to the U.S. Fourth Amendment under the Indian Constitution, but adopted the common law maxim '*Every man's house is his castle*' and held that an unlawful intrusion into a person's home was violative of personal liberty.[224] The minority view, on the other hand, clearly recognised privacy as a fundamental right and opined that the entirety of Regulation 236, which apart from domiciliary visits also included secret picketing and reporting and verification of movements and absence from home.[225] This case was decided by a 6-judge bench of the SCOI.

The SCOI has subsequently expressly recognised the right to privacy as a fundamental right in numerous other cases.[226] Some of these are briefly discussed here. In *Govind v. State of Madhya Pradesh and Another* (1975), the Court recognised that privacy-dignity claims deserve examination under fundamental rights jurisprudence in India. The Court assumed that the rights to personal liberty, the right to move freely throughout India and the freedom of speech create an independent right to privacy, in a judgment that read down a series of police regulations in the state of Madhya Pradesh permitting excessive surveillance of criminals.[227] Then, in *R. Rajagopal v. State of Tamil Nadu* (1994), the SCOI stated that the right to privacy has 'acquired constitutional status' in recent times and contextualised it as a 'right to be let alone', while dealing with a dispute involving the publication of private details of one of the parties.[228] Again, in *People's Union for Civil Liberties v. Union of India* (1996), the SCOI held that telephone tapping was 'a serious violation of an individual's privacy' and located it in the broader right to life and personal liberty under Article 21 of the Indian Constitution.[229] Importantly, the SCOI in this case also noted India's obligations under international law, such as Article 17 of the International Covenant for Civil and Political Rights (ratified by India) and held that where municipal law and international law could be harmoniously interpreted, it must be so interpreted by the Court.[230] Another significant case where the SCOI upheld the right to privacy was in *Selvi v. State of Karnataka*, in which the court ruled that involuntarily subjecting a person to certain interrogation techniques such as narcoanalysis, polygraph examination and the Brain Electrical Activation Profile (BEAP) test for investigative purposes, violated the prescribed boundaries of privacy.[231] Interestingly, the Court in this case distinguished between physical and mental privacy, holding that while there were certain accepted police practices such as extraction of bodily substances (hair, physical), the same logic could not be extended to police methods to force testimony (mental). In this manner, the Court connected the right to privacy with the right against self-incrimination in Article 20(3) of the Indian Constitution.[232]

While the decisions discussed immediately above do declare and treat the right to privacy as a constitutional and fundamental right, the respondents in *Puttaswamy I*, argued that the right to privacy was not in fact a fundamental right under the Indian Constitution.[233] These arguments were based on the SCOI's refusal to read a right to privacy analogous to the U.S. Fourth Amendment into the Indian Constitutional framework in the *MP Sharma* (supra) and *Kharak Singh* (supra) decisions. These decisions were issued by benches of higher strength, than the subsequent judgments discussed above, being rendered by 8-judge and 6-judge benches of the SCOI respectively. It was argued that these decisions set binding precedents on future benches of the SCOI as well as all other courts in India, as opposed to the other decisions listed above, all of which were rendered by smaller benches of the SCOI. These arguments were made in the context of a petition challenging a biometric based national identity system implemented by the State.

The SCOI decided to constitute of a 9-judge bench in *Justice KS Puttaswamy and Ors v. Union of India and Ors* (2017) (*Puttaswamy I*),[234] to separately decide the question of whether the Indian Constitution envisaged a fundamental right to privacy. The Union of

India argued the right to privacy is more of a common law right, or a right to be legislated for, rather than a fundamental, inalienable right guaranteed under the Constitution.[235] It was also argued that the decisions post *MP Sharma* (supra) and *Kharak Singh* (supra) were incorrect since they were all rendered by smaller which were bound by the precedent established by these two decisions.[236] The SCOI, by overruling *MP Sharma* and the *Kharak Singh* cases,[237] upheld the right as a fundamental right under the Indian Constitution and laid this issue to rest.[238]

Puttaswamy I is a landmark judgement which brings together the extensive privacy jurisprudence in India. It recognises that the right to privacy while primarily derived from the right to life and personal liberty (Article 21 of the Constitution), can be found within all of the fundamental rights under Chapter III of the Indian Constitution. Privacy is essential to the autonomy and dignity of an individual, which are core to the fundamental freedoms protected by the Constitution. *Puttaswamy I* also recognises the many facets of the right to privacy, including informational/data privacy, and recommends that the State enact legislation to protect these aspects of privacy.

2.5.2. Personal data protection laws

Not unlike other nations within the region, India has a chequered history of legislating and rule-making for data protection. The current legal framework on data protection, comes from the Information Technology Act 2000 (Indian IT Act), and the amendments made to this law in 2008. Data protection rules have been framed under this law and are currently in effect.

At the time of writing, there is also an ongoing discussion on a new data protection framework for India – stemming from arguments made during the hearings in *Puttaswamy I*, as well as the judgment itself. In this section, the both will be discussed, and also will be briefly looked at the law-making process itself.

(a) Information Technology Act 2000

In the 1990s, the growth of e-commerce and electronic transactions in the world prompted many countries to pass laws acknowledging, authenticating and regulating these transactions. The United Nations Commission on International Trade Law (UNCITRAL) also drafted a model law on e-commerce, which the UN General Assembly called upon its member nations to refer to while passing their own laws.[239]

Following in its footsteps, India also drafted the E-Commerce Bill, 1998 via the Ministry of Commerce. This was subsequently renamed as the Information Technology Act 2000 (Indian IT Act) and was originally mainly meant to provide for legal recognition of electronic transactions.[240]

The Indian IT Act is the primary law governing digital technology and communications in India. In 2008, this law was amended significantly, and among other things, Section 43A which provides compensation for wrongful gain or loss caused due to negligence in the processing of personal data, was added. In 2011, rules were framed under this provision to guide the collection and processing of personal data (Indian Data Protection Rules).

Section 43A is only applicable only to data processors that are body corporates,[241] which are required to implement reasonable security practices and procedures, as notified under the rules.

The Indian IT Act identifies 2 categories of data in this context – personal information and sensitive personal data or information. Personal information means 'any information that relates to a natural person, which, either directly or indirectly, in combination with other information available or likely to be available with a body corporate, is capable of identifying such person'.[242] 'Sensitive personal data or information' (SPDI) is defined[243] in the form of an exhaustive list of information, and includes –

> any personal information which consists of information relating to: (i) passwords; (ii) financial information such as bank account or credit card or debit card or other payment instrument details; (iii) physical, physiological and mental health condition; (iv) sexual orientation; (v) medical records and history; (vi) biometric information; and (vii) any details of information relating to the above that are provided to a body corporate for obtaining services, or received by a body corporate.[244]

The Indian Data Protection Rules incorporate the principles of notice, consent, and purpose limitation,[245] to a limited extent, and limit data retention to such time periods as required for the processing of data for such purpose.[246] In addition, there are limitations on the disclosure or transfer of SPDI. Data subjects are also provided with the rights to access, review and correct their data, and opt out of collection or withdraw consent. The Indian Data Protection Rules provide that a data controller or data processor must institute a grievance redressal mechanism[247]; and ensure that reasonable security practices and procedures (as may be notified by the Government) are used for the protection of such data.[248]

While the Indian Data Protection Rules do touch upon a number of traditionally accepted data protection principles, the drafting of the rules has often been criticised as inconsistent and ambiguous.[249] Several academic experts, members of civil society, and government appointed expert groups[250] have indicated that there is a need for improvement over these rules if personal information is to be protected adequately in India. The next section discusses current efforts to tackle this issue.

(b) Indian Personal Data Protection Bill, 2019

There have been several discussions about the need for a comprehensive data protection legislation in India, over the past decade, and multiple drafts of Bills have been circulated on this subject. In 2012 a Group of Experts on Privacy, constituted by the Indian government submitted a report recognising the need for a new law.[251] The judgment in *Puttaswamy I* sped the conversation up significantly. *Puttaswamy I* recognised the horizontal applicability of privacy, i.e. it could be enforced both against the State as well as against private actors. This necessitated the enactment of legislation that would ensure safeguards in the collection, use and dissemination of data by both the state as well as private companies. In July 2017, an expert committee was set up by the government of India, to recommend a data protection framework and bill to the government. This committee published its report and recommendations along with a draft bill (Draft Bill 2018) in August 2018.[252] After open and closed consultations on the report and draft bill, a revised Personal Data Protection Bill 2019 (PDP Bill), was published and introduced in Parliament in December 2019. At the time of writing, a Joint Committee of the Houses (of Parliament) has been appointed to discuss the bill and issue recommendations.[253]

While several bills have been drafted and published over the past decade (some by civil society members, some by members of parliament), this is the farthest the country has gone in terms of introducing comprehensive legislation on the subject.

The PDP Bill identifies both the State and private entities as data processors or data controllers (or rather 'data fiduciaries' as the bill identifies controllers), and protects all personal information collected and processed in India or by an Indian entity, or related to any individual in India.[254] It also identifies other categories of data such as sensitive personal information[255] and critical personal information,[256] that will be provided additional protections. The PDP Bill consists of several mechanisms to ensure protection of personal information, including detailed processes for notice, consent, collection limitation, purpose limitation, data minimisation and other data protection principles.[257] It also affords data principals more rights in the way of access, correction, data portability, erasure of personal information and the right to be forgotten. Additional compliances, such as data protection impact assessments and audits are required in the case of certain data fiduciaries depending on the volume, sensitivity etc. of data they process.[258]

In order to govern and enforce the implementation of the law, the PDP Bill calls for a data protection authority to be set up, and provides the authority with both regulatory and adjudicatory powers.[259]

While the PDP Bill definitely signifies a step forward in terms of data protection legislation in India, there remain a number of provisions that call for criticism and concern. Chief among these are the exceptions and exemptions granted to the State, in terms of obtaining consent for the collection and processing of personal information, as well as the use of personal information for law enforcement or security purposes.[260] The exemptions for surveillance are discussed in greater detail below.

The independence of the regulatory authority under the current provisions in the PDP Bill is also questionable, leading to more cause for concern where the State is acting as a regulator, adjudicator and a data fiduciary. The PDP Bill provides that the members of the authority will be appointed by 3 members of the executive, the Cabinet Secretary and the Secretaries of the Ministry of Law & Justice (Legal Affairs) and Electronics and Information Technology. This provision is a much criticised departure from the Draft Bill 2018, as well as established standards for appointment of officials of regulatory authorities in India. In the Draft Bill 2018, the selection committee for the data protection authority consisted of the Chief Justice of India or a judge of the Supreme Court nominated by the Chief Justice, the Cabinet Secretary and an independent expert to be nominated by the Chief Justice in consultation with the Cabinet Secretary.[261] Similarly, most other regulatory authorities require members to be appointed by a mix of executive and judicial authorities, and often also require independent experts to be consulted/involved in the process.[262] The Supreme Court has also specified that where administrative authorities play an adjudicatory role, they can be considered quasi-legal bodies.[263] In such cases, there is a need to ensure that the executive does not have full control over judicial or quasi-judicial appointments.[264] In light of these concerns, it is possible that the provisions giving executive control over the appointment of the Data Protection Authority may be challenged in court on the ground of separation of powers, if they are incorporated as is in the final legislation.

Much of this concern is also drawn from experiences over the past decade in the implementation of the Indian government's controversial biometric based national identity number system – Aadhaar, and the lack of meaningful legislative and judicial oversight in India's State surveillance architecture.

2.5.3. Legal framework for surveillance by security and law enforcement agencies

The primary laws that govern surveillance efforts by security and law enforcement agencies in India are the Indian Telegraph Act, 1885 (Indian Telegraph Act), the Indian IT Act, and the Code of Criminal Procedure, 1973 (Indian CrPC). The Indian Telegraph Act provides for the interception of post, telegraph and telephone communications, the Indian IT Act for access to information in computer systems, and interception of electronic communications, and the Indian CrPC provides for targeted access to documents, information or communications by law enforcement agencies.

The Indian Telegraph Act provides that the State may authorise interception of communications where there is a public emergency or in the interest of public safety, and the authorising official is satisfied that this interception is necessary in the interests of the sovereignty and integrity of India, the security of the state, friendly relations with foreign states or public order or for preventing incitement to the commission of an offence.[265] In 2007, procedural rules were put in place for the implementation of this process, after the Supreme Court directed, in 1997, that while interception may be permitted, procedural safeguards must be in place to ensure that the exercise of such powers is just and reasonable.[266]

The Indian IT Act, while applicable in the context of electronic communications, largely follows the same process, however, there are some notable expansions in the powers of the State under Section 69 of the Indian IT Act, and the rules issued under this provision. First, the State is allowed to authorise interception, monitoring and decryption of communications.[267] This may be done so long as such action is necessary in the interests of the sovereignty and integrity of India, the security of the state, friendly relations with foreign states or public order or for preventing incitement to the commission of an offence, and *for the defence of India and the investigation of any offence*. The preconditions of 'public emergency' or 'public safety interests' are not present here.

While the inclusion of detailed rules and procedural safeguards in these processes post 1997 is a step forward, these frameworks require improvement in order to meet both Indian constitutional standards[268] and international human rights standards.[269] This is exacerbated by the fact that in practice, the legal basis for many surveillance activities is unclear. For instance, Indian laws presently only provide for targeted surveillance, however, reports suggest that mass surveillance systems are being put in place in the country.[270] Another issue of concern is the fact that many of the intelligence agencies in India have not been established under law, and there is no legislative oversight for the functioning of these authorities.[271]

In *Puttaswamy I*, the Court acknowledged that the right to privacy is not absolute and exceptions may be required in the case of national security and other concerns.[272] The Court elaborated on the tests that any such exceptions need to meet – requiring action to be taken under law (legality test), for a legitimate state aim, and in a proportional manner.[273] In order for the various surveillance systems in place in India to meet these tests, the legal framework governing surveillance in India requires significant reform, and it was expected that the new data protection laws may act as the precursor to such reform. However, the provisions in both the Draft Bill 2018, and the PDP Bill (2019) that has been introduced in Parliament have been widely criticised.[274] The provisions exempting the government from compliance with the obligations in the bill on grounds of 'security of state'[275] and prevention, detection, investigation and prosecution of offences,[276] have been widely criticised for being too broad. These exemptions read with the provisions of the Draft Bill 2018 that require mandatory data localisation provisions requiring the storing of at least one copy of personal data by data fiduciaries within India were cause for additional concern regarding the lack of oversight in India's surveillance architecture.[277] However, whereas the Draft Bill 2018 required the enactment of a law authorising these activities for the exemption to be applicable, the current PDP Bill gives the government an even longer leash by way of exemptions from data protection obligations. Under the PDP Bill, the Central Government can exempt any agency of the government from data protection obligations if it is 'satisfied that it is necessary or expedient' in the interest of 'sovereignty and integrity of India, the security of the State, friendly relations with foreign States, public order', or for 'preventing incitement to the commission of any cognisable offence relating to' any of the above.[278] Such exemption can be provided by executive order. The PDP Bill does provide that these exemptions may be subject to procedural safeguards, but does not require such procedural safeguards to be put in place. Apart from this, as discussed in preceding sections, the PDP Bill has also enabled the possibility of executive control over the data protection authority, thereby endangering separation of powers.[279]

At the time of writing this article, there is a challenge against the constitutionality of the legal framework governing surveillance systems in India pending before the SCOI.[280] Reports indicate however, that the instances of State surveillance in India are only increasing, with the State also attempting to adopt more technologically savvy means of surveillance. These means range from wide-scale social media monitoring efforts, to allegations of the Indian government's involvement in the recently reported instances of the hacking of communication services used by a number of human rights activists in India.[281]

2.5.4. Other laws that affect privacy

In the absence of a comprehensive privacy or data protection law, there are several laws that affect privacy and particularly data privacy in India, including in many cases sectoral laws. Like other South Asian countries, India also has a strong freedom of information law – the Right to Information Act 2005. This law provides that an exception may be made from the sharing of public information, where the personal details of individuals are involved, and their privacy maybe infringed. The balance between the right to information and the right to privacy has been discussed by the courts in India in several cases, including most recently in *Central Public Information Officer, Supreme Court of India v. Subhash Chandra Agarwal*. In this case, the applicant had sought information regarding the assets of the Chief Justice of the SCOI, as well as a 1997 resolution passed by the Full Court of the SCOI in which every judge of the Supreme Court had to disclose their assets to the Chief Justice. While the relevant Central Public Information Officer (CPIO) provided the information pertaining to the resolution, information regarding the assets of the Chief Justice was denied on the basis that this information was not in the possession of the Registry. After various appeals, this case reached the division bench of the High Court of Delhi, where the CPIO argued that disclosure would result in an unwarranted intrusion of the judges' privacy. The High Court of Delhi made a distinction between privacy expectations of public servants and private persons and ruled that in case of public servants, the degree of privacy protection was lower, directing disclosure of the information sought.[282] This order was again challenged before the SCOI. The SCOI looked at whether the office of the Chief Justice of the Court would be considered a public authority required to furnish information under the law. The Court found that the Office of the Chief Justice was indeed a public authority, and also noted that the right to privacy and right to information are on an equal footing, and could be balanced using the test of proportionality set out in *Puttaswamy I*.[283]

The impact of the right to privacy, as upheld specifically in *Puttaswamy I*, is also seen in personal and criminal laws in India, with the SCOI striking down Section 377 of the Indian Penal Code, 1860 which criminalised 'carnal intercourse against the order of nature' – interpreted to mean sexual intercourse between individuals of the same sex.[284] The provision was struck down as far as it relates to consensual sexual intercourse between adults.

There are also several sector specific laws and regulations in India that have a privacy impact. The financial and health sector both have frameworks that dictate how customers and patients' personal information are to be dealt with. These regulations are often simplistic, and consist of vague provisions requiring 'confidentiality' of information, rather than detailed processes aimed to fully protect data. On the other hand, regulations or even licensing documents in sensitive sectors such as the telecommunications and financial sector, do often consist of requirements to maintain records, and transfer data as may be required to the regulatory authorities.

Post the Court's judgment in *Puttaswamy I*, and if a new data protection law comes into place, these regulations will need to either be amended, or overwritten altogether to adequately protect privacy.

2.6. Bhutan

2.6.1. Constitutional guarantee

Article 19 of the Constitution of Bhutan provides for a fundamental right to privacy, articulated in a similar manner as Article 17 of the ICCPR. The Constitution of Bhutan provides that: A person shall not be subjected to arbitrary or unlawful interference with his or her privacy, family, home or correspondence nor to unlawful attacks on the person's honour and reputation.

Privacy law in Bhutan is still at a nascent stage with no significant interventions by courts. clear.

2.6.2. Personal data protection laws

The Bhutan Information, Communications and Media Act of 2018 ('BICMA 2018') appears to be the primary legislation that protects the right to privacy, and guides the processing of personal data in Bhutan. Enacted to revamp the earlier version of this Act (BICMA 2006), it is reportedly aimed at reducing the administrative burden on the government and regulators, as well as promote cyber security and streamline licensing.[285] This law, which has been in the works for a few years now, is an extensive legislation, providing the framework for licensing of communications systems, including telecommunications, internet, media, and broadcasting, and the use of these systems.[286] While privacy and data protection provisions are peppered across this law, two chapters in this legislation deal directly with the subject.

Chapter 17 contains provisions for the protection of privacy, both offline and online, requiring all ICT/media service providers and vendors to respect the privacy of their users/consumers. This chapter largely incorporates the principles of notice, collection limitation, and purpose limitation in relation to personal data and sensitive personal data. Restrictions are placed on the disclosure and transfer of personal data and sensitive personal data, and maintenance of minimum-security standards is prescribed.

Chapter 21 consists of the data protection framework, providing a framework for consent, limitations to the disclosure of personal data,[287] and requirements for the deletion of data once such data is obsolete. This law adopts a unique definition of personal data, defined to mean 'any data or information which relates to a person who can be identified from that data or that data or other information, which is in the possession of, or is likely to come into the possession of' a service provider. This includes expressions of opinion about the person, and indications of the intention of the service provider in relation to the person.

Apart from these specific provisions, there is an obligation on broadcasters licensed under the act to respect the privacy of individuals.[288] Under a relatively progressive provision (as compared to other jurisdictions in the region), government agencies are required to conduct privacy impact assessments, and ensure privacy protections are in place, in relation to e-governance programmes.[289]

2.6.3. Legal framework for surveillance by security and law enforcement agencies

Under the Information, Communications and Media Act of Bhutan 2018, the government has the powers to direct that public access to any information or service is blocked, or any information that is generated, transmitted, received or stored in an ICT system is blocked, intercepted, monitored or decrypted.[290] Such directions can be issued with a warrant from the court, if they are found necessary or expedient in the interest of

> the sovereignty, security, harmony and defence of Bhutan or friendly relations with foreign States; in the interest of public order; for preventing incitement to the commission of any cognizable offence; for the investigation of any offence under the Information, Communications and Media Act of Bhutan 2018.

The government also has the power to authorise the monitoring or collection of any data or information, by a warrant of the court, in order to enhance cyber security and for identification, analysis and prevention of intrusion or spread of computer contaminant.[291]

The provisions in the law governing these actions are very similar to the provisions under the older Indian IT Act. The government also has the powers to prescribe the actual process as well as the safeguards under these provisions. It is not clear whether any such rules have been issued yet.

3. Other countries in South Asia

Apart from the countries discussed above, Maldives and Afghanistan also fall under South Asia. However, unlike the rest, they do not exhibit any major steps towards consolidating or establishing privacy laws, let alone set up comprehensive data protection regimes.

While both countries have strongly worded constitutional protections for privacy, this has not necessarily translated to extra-constitutional legislative action. In any case, the existing privacy protections in both these countries is briefly discussed below.

The Constitution of Maldives (2008) guarantees a right to privacy to all citizens of Maldives. Article 24 provides that 'Everyone has the right to respect for his private and family life, his home and his private communications'.[292] As Greenleaf has noted, this right could be considered a horizontal right, given the additional requirement that 'every person must respect these rights with respect to others'.[293] This argument is also supported by the general provision under Article 16 of the Constitution of Maldives that provides that the obligation to establish that any limitation to a fundamental right is a reasonable limitation as prescribed under the Constitution falls upon 'the State or the person asserting the limitation of the right or freedom'.[294] Importantly, all fundamental rights are guaranteed by the Constitution, only so long as they are not contrary to any tenet of Islam.[295]

It is also not clear if there is any other legal framework that governs privacy, data protection or surveillance in place in the Maldives, although there are some suggestions that there is interest in such laws.[296]

The Constitution of Afghanistan (2004), which established Afghanistan as an Islamic Republic, provides a limited right to privacy in the form of a right to 'freedom and confidentiality of correspondence'.[297] Article 37 of the Constitution provides that any correspondence or communication between individuals will be secure from intrusion.[298] The State cannot inspect personal communications, unless authorised by law.[299]

There is little information available about other legal frameworks governing privacy, data protection or surveillance in Afghanistan, and given its political situation, it is not clear whether and to what extent these existing constitutional rights are protected in Afghanistan.

Further, at the time of writing, neither Maldives nor Afghanistan has any landmark caselaw on these issues.

4. National identity systems

Irrespective of the nature or existence even, of privacy protections under law, every country in the region has some version of a national identity number system, typically introduced with the aim of facilitating social protection mechanisms and government services. This phenomenon is not limited to South Asia, and national ID systems are being developed across the world. Where older national ID systems exist, many countries are now 'modernizing' their ID databases to include biometric identifiers that authenticate or verify identity based on physical characteristics such as fingerprints, iris, face and palm prints, gait, voice and DNA.[300] These systems are often put in place as part of digital governance schemes, leading to the establishment of 'digital welfare states', as reportedly described by United Nations Special Rapporteur on extreme poverty and human rights, Philip Alston.[301] Other reasons used to justify national ID systems include the need for information in criminal investigations, or multi-purpose/one-stop IDs for all citizens of a country. Sustainable Development Goal 16.9, which aims to ensure that every person should have a legal identity, is also often cited as a driver for these schemes.[302]

Privacy and security of the personal data that individuals must provide while registering for these national ID numbers is of increasing concern. In many cases multiple stakeholders including government agencies, law enforcement and national security agencies, and private sector actors have access to this information, often with weak frameworks, if any governing the use of such data.

In South Asia, the most notable of these systems are the national identity systems in place in India and Pakistan.

4.1. India

In India, biometric based national identity system – the Aadhaar project, was first implemented in 2009 on executive order with no legislative oversight.[303] A voluntary ID system, the project was implemented with the purpose of improving welfare delivery, by increasing efficiency, and savings in a corrupt system. The other motivation for this new ID system was to provide a legal ID for those without documents, and enable such individuals to obtain welfare benefits they were entitled to.

In 2016, the Aadhaar (Targeted Delivery of Financial and Other Subsidies, Benefits and Services) Act 2016[304] (Aadhaar Act), was implemented, to govern this project, and among other things, provide for data privacy protections. The Aadhaar Act states that consent must be obtained for the collection of personal information, including biometric information. It requires minimum security measures to be put in place for the protection of Aadhaar related personal information, to protect against unauthorised access, use and disclosure of such information.

However, both the system itself and the law were criticised for lacking adequate safeguards on this front, and a petition was filed before the SCOI challenging the constitutional validity of this system. Among other things, the discussions around privacy and security concerns with the Aadhaar system catalysed the discussion on privacy and data protection in India, leading to the SCOI's judgment in *Puttaswamy I*, and the subsequent developments discussed separately in this article.

In 2018, the Court upheld the validity of the Aadhaar system, noting that any infringement of privacy under this system would be a reasonable restriction to the constitutional right.[305] The Court also recommended some additional safeguards to improve privacy and security measures under the Aadhaar Act, to meet constitutional standards – specifically recommending judicial oversight for the disclosure of personal information to the State in the interests of national security. Privacy scholars have long called for judicial oversight in the context of surveillance by law enforcement and intelligence agencies in India, and this was commended as a big step in Indian privacy jurisprudence. This argument was also previously noted by the SCOI as well in the *PUCL* (supra) case where, in the context of telephone tapping under the Telegraph Act, 1885, the petitioner argued that the only way to safeguard the right of privacy of an individual was for there to be prior judicial scrutiny before any order for telephone-tapping.[306] In this case, the SCOI while criticising the Central Government for not having framed any rules to control improper interception or disclosure of messages, also noted that in the absence of any provision in the statute, it could not import a requirement for judicial oversight.[307] However, despite the recommendations of the SCOI, the subsequent amendment to the Aadhaar Act in 2019 did not incorporate a requirement for judicial oversight, only revising the provision to require oversight by a higher ranking officer.[308]

At the time of writing, although enrolment for the Aadhaar ID continues to remain voluntary, the requirement to link this ID number while filing income taxes has rendered such 'voluntariness' mostly ineffective.[309]

4.2. Pakistan

Established by ordinance as long back as in the year 2000, National Database and Registration Authority ('NADRA') is one of the world's largest citizen registration regimes.[310] National identity cards are issued by the government[311] and registration is mandatory for all citizens (18 years and above),[312] These cards are now required to be produced to avail of any government service, including obtaining a passport, voting, opening a bank account, and cellular phone services (SIM cards).[313]

NADRA's functions include establishing and maintenance of a 'Citizen Database' by 'collection and collation of multi-faceted data regarding citizens'.[314] For this purpose, NADRA can access information across government agencies.[315] Based on the data from the Citizen Database, as well as other registries and databases, the National Data Warehouse is established.[316] Access to the National Data Warehouse is available to all government agencies, as well as semi-government and private agencies specified by regulations.[317] The Ordinance also permits the NADRA to demand information from users and other agencies who are required to comply with such requests.[318]

Recently, the NADRA began issuing Smart NICs with biometric information and security features.[319] NADRA is also tasked with ensuring the security, protection and confidentiality of the data in the data warehouses.[320] Civil society and other groups have raised privacy and security concerns with the management of the biometric databases.[321]

One of the concerning developments in the context of these controversial and extensive biometric based ID systems in India and Pakistan has been the export of these systems to other developing and least developed countries, often backed by international organisations such as the World Bank.[322] This may be done by way of knowledge sharing initiatives between different governments, or even through the use of common service providers across different jurisdictions.

4.3. Other SAARC countries

The Sri Lankan experience in the context of national ID systems is also relevant. The Registration of Persons Department in Sri Lanka is currently engaged in a project involving the digitisation of the National Identity Card (NIC) issued to Sri Lankans. The bid for the project was won by Pakistan's NADRA[323] and not only involves digitising existing identity paperwork, but also collecting biometric data.[324] The objectives of the e-NIC project include collecting personal and family tree data to establish a National Persons Registry and a central database, to issue an e-NIC to all Sri Lankan citizens above 15 years as well as to facilitate economic development and national security.[325] The Commissioner General for the Register of Persons also has the power to requisition data from any authority who are obligated to furnish such data.[326] This project has raised various privacy and security alarms, not least of which is the involvement of the Pakistani NADRA.[327]

In Bangladesh, a national identity number has been introduced with an objective to facilitate social inclusion by providing identity cards to those who did not previously possess one. Introduced under the National Identity Registration Act, 2010, the national identity number is registered and cards that contain other personal information, including biometric data are issued.[328] This number is now required for major and vital services including obtaining passports, driver's licenses, voting, opening bank accounts as well as sim registration.[329]

Nepal is also developing a national identity database, with governing legislation currently pending approval.[330] The proposed National ID card will also have biometric information, along with other personal information.[331] Apart from reports that the ID is intended to be multi-purpose and facilitate access to government services, it is also worryingly meant to assist in criminal investigation.[332]

Bhutan, Maldives and Afghanistan reportedly have national ID systems as well. In Bhutan, a citizenship number is allocated at birth, and a national ID card (which contains encoded data) issued at the age of 15.[333] Some concerns have been reported regarding the accuracy of the data recorded in relation to this citizenship number.[334]

The Maldives government introduced a biometric based national ID card in 2017 – which acts as an electronic passport, driver's license, a health card, an insurance document, and a payment card.[335] The card is designed to contain biometric fingerprint data, in order to be compatible with passport screening systems. While little other information is available on how the card functions, and the legal frameworks it is governed by, reports suggest that the card is seen as an innovative push towards interoperability,[336] and that the Maldives government is open to sharing its technology with other governments that are interested in similar systems.[337]

Afghanistan first introduced a new national ID card system in 2013. The chip based electronic national ID card (eNID) was introduced for the purpose of addressing voter fraud and promoting national unity. However, the card was quite controversial because of the manner in which details of ethnicity were to be described and stored on these cards.[338] It has been reported that the eNID cards were finally issued in 2018 – however, the controversy around the card had not been resolved at the time.[339]

5. Conclusion

While the South Asian privacy landscape is generally marred by loosely regulated surveillance and weak safeguards against personal data exploitation, there is a definite increase of consolidation of laws governing privacy in the past decade. Comprehensive data protection legislations are pending in at least three major states (India, Sri Lanka and Pakistan), and existing regulations are either being revamped or updated, which is a welcome trend.

However, all the five nations discussed above have set up national identity databases which, though at various stages of progress and are ostensibly for facilitating access to governmental services, also present data security risks, as well as tremendous potential for abuse and increased state surveillance. Given the high illiteracy rate in South Asian countries, home to almost 49% of the world's illiterate population,[340] there is still insufficient awareness of the significance of privacy as a basic human right, making it easier for governments to abuse their powers and ramp up the scope of surveillance.

Further, as the experience of Pakistan and Bangladesh shows, express constitutional protection to the right to privacy has not necessarily translated to strong on-ground protection from either the state or industry players exploiting personal data. As a review of their existing frameworks makes evident, Pakistan still has over-broad and extensive surveillance mechanisms in place with limited overview, with Bangladesh not far behind. While there is some judicial oversight in these countries, most provisions do not adhere to basic principles of necessity and proportionality. While in terms of legislation and practice, India does not currently do much better, the conclusive reading of the right to privacy in the Indian Constitution by the Supreme Court of India in *Puttaswamy I* certainly gave a much-needed fillip to privacy protection in India.

Also guaranteeing privacy as a constitutional right, Nepal has appeared to develop its own privacy framework. Unlike the popular personal data protection models, Nepal's Privacy Act has treated privacy as a core right consisting of several sub-rights, such as the right to bodily privacy, right to mental privacy, right to reproductive privacy and so on. Whether or not this model will be amended or a new law brought in to make it more along the lines of data protection models across the world, is not yet clear.

Common trends can also be identified in policy and legislative efforts. For instance, similar language is often used in information technology related laws and rules in different South Asian countries. Most of the countries in the region have also expressly recognised the importance of supporting the digital economy – Sri Lanka has proposed a National Digital Policy,[341] and both Pakistan and India have Digital Pakistan[342] and Digital India schemes, respectively, in place. While these documents do typically note that the protection of privacy and personal data is important in the context of the digital economy, we will have to wait to see how (if at all) a proper balance is achieved between individual rights, and the State's economic policies. In India for instance, some of the economic policies that centre on technology and particularly the use of (personal) data, have been criticised for not taking privacy rights into consideration in an adequate manner.[343] In terms of data protection frameworks, most countries in the region seem to be adopting comprehensive, sector and technology agnostic laws – following the European/GDPR approach in what is often seen as a clash between US and EU styles. However, given that most of these frameworks are in early stages, it is yet to be seen whether the GDPR will have further impact on law making in the South Asian countries. In the Indian context, the report of the expert committee tasked with recommending a law, specifically identifies three different global perspectives on data protection law making – the US, EU and Chinese approaches. The report suggests that India should draw best practices from different jurisdictions and craft a fourth/middle path to data protection law making.[344]

These common trends however, do not seem to be suggestive of coherent policy or law making at the regional level, especially given the geopolitical issues at play in the region. But to the extent that privacy is to be recognised as a fundamental right, and steps taken to actively protect this right, an increased common awareness across the region, followed by the principles laid down in *Puttaswamy I*, can serve as a lighthouse for the course of future regulation in the region.

Notes

1. Malavika Jayaram, 'Aadhaar Debate: Privacy is not An Elitist Concern – It's the Only Way to Secure Equality', *Scroll*, August 15, 2015, https://scroll.in/article/748043/aadhaar-debate-privacy-is-not-an-elitist-concern-its-the-only-way-to-secure-equality.
2. Government of India, Ministry of Electronics & Information Technology, Digital India (Vision and Vision Areas), https://digitalindia.gov.in/content/vision-and-vision-areas.
3. Nilesh Christopher, 'Security Experts Say Need to Secure Aadhaar Ecosystem, Warn about Third Party Leaks', *Economic Times*, March 26, 2018, https://economictimes.indiatimes.com/news/politics-and-nation/there-is-a-need-to-secure-full-aadhaar-ecosystem-experts/articleshow/63459367.cms.
4. Anurag Kotoky, 'India Quietly Expands Surveillance System to Tap Phone Calls, Email', *Livemint*, June 27, 2013, https://www.livemint.com/Politics/J1jxvQ5Su9Su4pGLHDCepM/India-sets-up-new-surveillance-system-to-tap-phone-calls-em.html.x.
5. Satpathy and others, 'Are India's Laws On Surveillance A Threat To Privacy?' *The Hindu*, December 28, 2018, https://www.thehindu.com/opinion/op-ed/are-indias-laws-on-surveillance-a-threat-to-privacy/article25844250.ece.
6. Article 28 of the Constitution of Nepal 2015 (2072).
7. Article 43 of the Constitution of the People's Republic of Bangladesh, 1972.
8. Article 14(1) of The Constitution of the Islamic Republic of Pakistan, 1973.
9. *Justice (Retd.) K. S Puttaswamy v. Union of India*, 2017 (10) SCALE 1 (Supreme Court of India).
10. Staff Reporter, 'Sri Lanka Supreme Court Petitioned on Invasion of Privacy, Central Database Profiling', *economynext*, October 10, 2017, https://economynext.com/sri-lanka-supreme-court-petitioned-on-invasion-of-privacy-central-database-profiling-8526/.
11. Article 45 of the General Data Protection Regulation (2018).
12. The European Union's country-wise share of trade in the region is 12.9% for India, 12.9% for Pakistan, 31% for Sri Lanka and 24% for Bangladesh. For more details on the economic relationship between the European Union and the listed countries, please see https://ec.europa.eu/trade/policy/countries-and-regions/. The European Union's share of Nepal's trade in the region is 13%. For more details on the economic relationship between the European Union and Nepal, please see https://mofa.gov.np/nepal-european-union-relations/.
13. Article 43 of the Constitution of the People's Republic of Bangladesh.
14. Ibid.
15. *Kharak Singh v. State of Uttar Pradesh*, AIR 1963 SC 1295, ¶20 (Majority Judgement). *Kharak Singh v. State of Uttar Pradesh* was decided by a bench of five judges. The majority view (consisting of three judges) was that the right to privacy was not a constitutionally guaranteed right, however, the provision enabling domiciliary visits by the police, i.e. Regulation 236(b) of the Uttar Pradesh Police Regulations, was a violation of the right to personal liberty guaranteed under Article 21 of the Constitution. The minority view (consisting of two dissenting judges) stated instead that Regulation 236 in its entirety, (including secret picketing, domiciliary visits, periodical inquiries into repute, habits, etc., reporting and verification of movements and absence from home as well as collection and recording of all information bearing on conduct) was in violation of the right to personal liberty under Article 21 as well as the right to move freely within India under Article 19 of the Indian Constitution. The minority view also more or less recognised a right to privacy.
16. Ershad Karim, 'Citizen's Right to Privacy: Reflection in the International Instruments and National Laws', *Bangladesh Journal of Law* 9, no. 1 and 2 (April 9, 2005): 43–44.
17. Graham Greenleaf, 'Privacy in the Other Seven South Asian (SAARC) States', in *Asian Data Privacy Laws: Trade and Human Rights Perspectives* (Oxford University Press, 2014), 11.
18. Ibid.
19. Section 686 of the Information and Communications Technology Act, 2006 (Bangladesh).
20. Section 5 of the Telegraph Act, 1885 (Bangladesh).
21. Section 7(1)(b) of the Telegraph Act, 1885 (Bangladesh).

22. Section 26 of the Telegraph Act, 1885 (Bangladesh).
23. Section 24 of the Telegraph Act, 1885 (Bangladesh); Section 23 of the Telegraph Act, 1885 (Bangladesh).
24. Muhammad Zahidul Islam, 'Telecom Sector's Revenue to Cross $5bn by 2023', *The Daily Star*, December 15, 2019, https://ww.thedailystar.net/business/news/telecom-sectors-revenue-cross-5b-2023-1840516.
25. Section 67 of the Bangladesh Telecommunication Act, 2001.
26. Section 71 of the Bangladesh Telecommunication Act, 2001.
27. Section 96(1) of the Bangladesh Telecommunication Act, 2001; Section 96(2) of the Bangladesh Telecommunication Act, 2001.
28. Section 97 of the Bangladesh Telecommunication Act, 2001.
29. Preamble to the Digital Security Act, 2018 (Bangladesh).
30. Section 57 of the Bangladesh Information and Communications Technology Act, 2006.
31. Rahul Krishna, 'How Dissent is Prosecuted in Bangladesh', *Observer Research Foundation*, October 5, 2019, https://www.orfonline.org/expert-speak/how-dissent-prosecuted-in-bangladesh-56190/.
32. Ibid. See also 'Bangladesh: Protect Freedom of Expression', *Human Rights Watch*, May 9, 2018, https://www.hrw.org/news/2018/05/10/bangladesh-protect-freedom-expression.
33. Section 8(1) of the Digital Security Act, 2018 (Bangladesh).
34. Section 8(2) of the Digital Security Act, 2018 (Bangladesh).
35. Section 41 of the Digital Security Act, 2018 (Bangladesh).
36. Section 42 of the Digital Security Act, 2018 (Bangladesh).
37. Section 43 of the Digital Security Act, 2018 (Bangladesh).
38. Section 44 of the Digital Security Act, 2018 (Bangladesh).
39. Section 46 of the Digital Security Act, 2018 (Bangladesh).
40. Section 17 of the Digital Security Act, 2018 (Bangladesh).
41. Section 18 of the Digital Security Act, 2018 (Bangladesh).
42. Section 19 of the Digital Security Act, 2018 (Bangladesh).
43. Section 20 of the Digital Security Act, 2018 (Bangladesh).
44. Section 22 of the Digital Security Act, 2018 (Bangladesh).
45. Section 26 of the Digital Security Act, 2018 (Bangladesh).
46. Section 27 of the Digital Security Act, 2018 (Bangladesh).
47. Section 33 of the Digital Security Act, 2018 (Bangladesh).
48. Section 2(b) of the Right to Information Act, 2009 (Bangladesh).
49. Section 7(h) of the Right to Information Act, 2009 (Bangladesh).
50. Section 7(j) of the Right to Information Act, 2009 (Bangladesh).
51. Section 32(1) of the Right to Information Act, 2009 (Bangladesh).
52. Section 3 of the Digital Security Act, 2018 (Bangladesh).
53. Section 11 of the Right to Information Act, 2009 (Bangladesh).
54. Article 28 of the Interim Constitution of Nepal 2063 (2007).
55. Article 28 of the Constitution of Nepal 2015 (2072).
56. Ibid.
57. *Sunil Babu Pant v. Government of Nepal,* Writ No. 917 of the Year 2064 BS (2007 AD).
58. *Advocate Sapana Pradhan Malla v. Prime-minister, Nepal Government and Office of the Council of Ministers and Ors.*, Writ No. 3561 of the year 2063 (2006 AD).
59. Rule 2(a) of the Procedural Guidelines for Protecting the Privacy of the Parties in the Proceedings of Special Types of Cases, 2064 (2007).
60. Rule 2(b) of the Procedural Guidelines for Protecting the Privacy of the Parties in the Proceedings of Special Types of Cases, 2064 (2007).
61. Rule 3 of the Procedural Guidelines for Protecting the Privacy of the Parties in the Proceedings of Special Types of Cases, 2064 (2007).
62. Rule 5 of the Procedural Guidelines for Protecting the Privacy of the Parties in the Proceedings of Special Types of Cases, 2064 (2007).

63. Rule 9 of the Procedural Guidelines for Protecting the Privacy of the Parties in the Proceedings of Special Types of Cases, 2064 (2007).
64. Chapters 2–8 of the Privacy Act 2075 (2018) (Nepal).
65. Section 2(c) of the Privacy Act 2075 (2018) (Nepal).
66. Section 12 of the Privacy Act 2075 (2018) (Nepal).
67. Section 12(3) of the Privacy Act 2075 (2018) (Nepal).
68. Section 12(4) of the Privacy Act 2075 (2018) (Nepal).
69. Section 30 of the Privacy Act 2075 (2018) (Nepal).
70. Section 3(1) of the Privacy Act 2075 (2018) (Nepal).
71. Section 6 of the Privacy Act 2075 (2018) (Nepal).
72. Section 4 of the Privacy Act 2075 (2018) (Nepal).
73. Section 5 of the Privacy Act 2075 (2018) (Nepal).
74. 'Privacy in the Developing World: A Global Research Agenda',*Privacy International* (blog), July 13, 2012, https://privacyinternational.org/blog/1456/privacy-developing-world-global-research-agenda.
75. Greenleaf, 'Privacy in the Other Seven South Asian (SAARC) States', 4.
76. Bhrikuti Rai, 'Everything You Need to Know about the Nepal Government's New IT Bill', *The Kathmandu Post*, February 22, 2019, https://kathmandupost.com/2/2019/02/22/everything-you-need-to-know-about-the-governments-new-it-bill; Rojita Adhikari, 'No Debate, No Democracy: Journalists in Nepal Fight New Threat to Press Freedom', *The Guardian*, January 13, 2020, https://www.theguardian.com/global-development/2020/jan/13/journalists-in-nepal-fight-new-threat-to-press-freedom.
77. The authors have been unable to find an accessible English translation of the Information Technology Management Bill, and have relied on secondary sources of information for the purpose of this section of the article.
78. Bhrikuti Rai, 'Everything You Need to Know about the Nepal Government's New IT bill', *The Kathmandu Post*, March 3, 2020, https://kathmandupost.com/national/2019/02/22/everything-you-need-to-know-about-the-governments-new-it-bill.
79. Section 44 of the Nepal Electronic Transactions Act, 2008.
80. Section 45 of the Nepal Electronic Transactions Act, 2008.
81. Section 48 of the Nepal Electronic Transactions Act, 2008.
82. Section 52 of the Nepal Electronic Transactions Act, 2008.
83. Section 55 of the Nepal Electronic Transactions Act, 2008.
84. Graham Greenleaf, 'Nepal's Unknown Data Privacy Law: No Shangri-La, But a First for South Asia', *International Data Privacy Law* 3, no. 4 (2013): 1, https://papers.ssrn.com/sol3/papers.cfm?abstract_id=2326799.
85. Section 3(3)(c) of the Nepal Right to Information Act, 2064 (2007).
86. Section 35 of the Nepal Right to Information Act, 2064 (2007).
87. Section 31 of the Nepal Right to Information Act, 2064 (2007).
88. Section 28 of the Nepal Right to Information Act, 2064 (2007).
89. Section 33 of the Nepal Right to Information Act, 2064 (2007).
90. The authors have been unable to find an accessible English translation of the Criminal Code, and have relied on secondary sources of information for the purpose of this section of the article.
91. 'Nepal: An Introduction to the Individual Privacy Act 2018', *OneTrust Data Guidance*, January 2019, https://platform.dataguidance.com/opinion/nepal-introduction-individual-privacy-act-2018; 'Introduction to the Privacy Act, 2018', *Neupane Law Associates*, February 18, 2019, https://www.neupanelegal.com/news-detail/introduction-to-the-privacy-act-2018.html; Binod Ghimire, '15 Things in the New National Law Every Nepali Should Know about', *The Kathmandu Post*, August 17, 2018, https://kathmandupost.com/national/2018/08/17/15-things-in-the-new-national-law-every-nepali-should-know-about.
92. Ibid.
93. Ibid.
94. Article 14(1) of the Constitution of the Islamic Republic of Pakistan, 1973.

95. Article 8 of the Constitution of the Islamic Republic of Pakistan, 1973.
96. Article 8(3) of the Constitution of the Islamic Republic of Pakistan, 1973.
97. 'A Data Protection Law in Pakistan: Policy Recommendations by Digital Rights Foundation' (Digital Rights Foundation, n.d.), 4, https://digitalrightsfoundation.pk/wp-content/uploads/2017/10/Policy-Brief-for-MOIT.pdf.
98. *M. D. Tahir v. State Bank*, 2004 CLC 1680 (Lahore High Court).
99. Staff Reporter, 'Detailed Order in SPB Case', *Dawn*, June 29, 2005, https://www.dawn.com/news/145614.
100. Ibid.
101. 'State of Privacy Pakistan' (Privacy International, January 2019), https://privacyinternational.org/state-privacy/1008/state-privacy-pakistan.
102. Government of Pakistan, Ministry of Information and Technology, 'Digital Pakistan Policy 2017', http://digitalrightsmonitor.pk/wp-content/uploads/2017/10/Digital-Pakistan-Policy-2017.pdf.
103. Jessica Fjeld, 'Clinic Supports Pakistani NGO in Shaping New Data Protection Bill', *CyberLaw Clinic | Berkman Klein Center for Internet & Society* (blog), July 13, 2018, https://clinic.cyber.harvard.edu/2018/07/13/clinic-supports-pakistani-ngo-in-shaping-new-data-protection-bill/.
104. Ibid.
105. Section 2(g) of the Personal Data Protection Bill, 2018 (Pakistan).
106. Ibid.
107. Section 2(n) of the Personal Data Protection Bill, 2018 (Pakistan).
108. Section 2(f) of the Personal Data Protection Bill, 2018 (Pakistan).
109. Section 2(d) of the Personal Data Protection Bill, 2018 (Pakistan).
110. Section 2(e) of the Personal Data Protection Bill, 2018 (Pakistan).
111. Section 3(5)(c) of the Personal Data Protection Bill, 2018 (Pakistan).
112. Ibid.
113. Ibid.
114. Section 5(1) of the Personal Data Protection Bill, 2018 (Pakistan).
115. Section 5(3) of the Personal Data Protection Bill, 2018 (Pakistan).
116. Section 5(2) of the Personal Data Protection Bill, 2018 (Pakistan).
117. Section 5(2)(d) of the Personal Data Protection Bill, 2018 (Pakistan).
118. Section 2(o) of the Personal Data Protection Bill, 2018 (Pakistan).
119. Section 7 of the Personal Data Protection Bill, 2018 (Pakistan).
120. Section 9 of the Personal Data Protection Bill, 2018 (Pakistan).
121. Section 10 of the Personal Data Protection Bill, 2018 (Pakistan).
122. Section 6 of the Personal Data Protection Bill, 2018 (Pakistan).
123. Section 22 of the Personal Data Protection Bill, 2018 (Pakistan).
124. Section 12 of the Personal Data Protection Bill, 2018 (Pakistan).
125. Section 13 of the Personal Data Protection Bill, 2018 (Pakistan).
126. Section 14 of the Personal Data Protection Bill, 2018 (Pakistan).
127. Section 17 of the Personal Data Protection Bill, 2018 (Pakistan).
128. Section 21 of the Personal Data Protection Bill, 2018 (Pakistan).
129. Section 25 of the Personal Data Protection Bill, 2018 (Pakistan).
130. Section 23 of the Personal Data Protection Bill, 2018 (Pakistan).
131. Section 20 of the Personal Data Protection Bill, 2018 (Indian).
132. Section 28(2)(a)(i) of the Personal Data Protection Bill, 2018 (Pakistan).
133. Section 28(2)(a)(ii) of the Personal Data Protection Bill, 2018 (Pakistan).
134. Section 28(e) of the Personal Data Protection Bill, 2018 (Pakistan).
135. Section 29 of the Personal Data Protection Bill, 2018 (Pakistan).
136. Section 30 of the Personal Data Protection Bill, 2018 (Pakistan); Section 31 of the Personal Data Protection Bill, 2018 (Pakistan).
137. Section 35 of the Personal Data Protection Bill, 2018 (Pakistan).
138. Section 36 of the Personal Data Protection Bill, 2018 (Pakistan).

139. Section 37 of the Personal Data Protection Bill, 2018 (Pakistan).
140. Staff Reporter, 'Lahore Police Makes Hotel Eye Software Compulsory for All the Hotels', *More*, September 10, 2016, https://www.morenews.pk/lahore-police-makes-hotel-eye-software-compulsory-hotels/.
141. 'State of Privacy Pakistan'.
142. Preamble of the Pakistan Telecommunication (Re-organization) Act, 1996.
143. Section 54 of the Pakistan Telecommunication (Re-organization) Act, 1996.
144. Section 57(2)(ah) of the Pakistan Telecommunication (Re-organization) Act, 1996.
145. Staff Reporter, 'Govt Asks Telecom Firms to Check Use of Encrypted VPN', *Dawn*, September 5, 2011, https://www.dawn.com/news/656853/govt-asks-telecom-firms-to-check-use-of-encrypted-vpn.
146. Section 22 of the Investigation for Fair Trial Act, 2013 (Pakistan); Section 23 of the Investigation for Fair Trial Act, 2013 (Pakistan).
147. Section 16 of the Investigation for Fair Trial Act, 2013 (Pakistan).
148. Ibid.
149. Section 6 of the Investigation for a Fair Trial Act, 2013 (Pakistan).
150. Section 8 of the Investigation for a Fair Trial Act, 2013 (Pakistan).
151. Staff Reporter, 'Fair Trial Act Signed into Law', *Dawn*, February 20, 2013, https://www.dawn.com/news/787426.
152. Section 31 of the Prevention of Electronic Crimes Act, 2016 (Pakistan).
153. Section 33 of the Prevention of Electronic Crimes Act, 2016 (Pakistan).
154. Section 34 of the Prevention of Electronic Crimes Act, 2016 (Pakistan).
155. Section 37 of the Prevention of Electronic Crimes Act, 2016 (Pakistan).
156. Section 39 of the Prevention of Electronic Crimes Act, 2016 (Pakistan).
157. Section 42 of the Prevention of Electronic Crimes Act, 2016 (Pakistan).
158. 'State of Privacy Pakistan'.
159. Ibid.
160. 'Tipping the Scales: Security & Surveillance in Pakistan', Special Report (Privacy International, July 2015), 6, https://privacyinternational.org/sites/default/files/201808/PAKISTAN%20REPORT%20HIGH%20RES%2020150721_0.pdf.
161. Glen Greenwald and Ewen MacAskill, 'Boundless Informant: The NSA's Secret Tool to Track Global Surveillance Data', *The Guardian*, June 11, 2013, https://www.theguardian.com/world/2013/jun/08/nsa-boundless-informant-global-datamining.
162. 'Tipping the Scales: Security & Surveillance in Pakistan', 6.
163. 'Country Report: Right to Information in Pakistan' (Article 19, November 13, 2015), https://www.article19.org/resources/country-report-the-right-to-information-in-pakistan/.
164. Section 17 of the Freedom of Information Ordinance, 2002 (Pakistan).
165. Section 8(g) of the Freedom of Information Ordinance, 2002 (Pakistan).
166. Section 8(h) of the Freedom of Information Ordinance, 2002 (Pakistan).
167. Section 3 of the Electronic Transactions Ordinance, 2002 (Pakistan).
168. Section 21 of the Electronic Transactions Ordinance, 2002 (Pakistan).
169. Article 14(1)(a) of the Constitution of the Democratic Socialist Republic of Sri Lanka (as amended up to 2015).
170. *Sinha Ratnatunga v. The State*, [2001] 2 SLR 172 (Supreme Court of Sri Lanka).
171. Ibid, 212.
172. Ibid, 213.
173. Althaf Marsoof, 'The Right to Privacy in the Information Era: A South Asian Perspective', *Scripted* 5, no. 3 (December 2008): 559, https://script-ed.org/wp-content/uploads/2016/07/5-3-Marsoof.pdf.
174. Greenleaf, 'Privacy in the Other Seven South Asian (SAARC) States', 15.
175. Government of Sri Lanka, Ministry of Digital Infrastructure and Information Technology, 'Data Protection Legislation finalized by Ministry of Digital Infrastructure and Information Technology', *Media Release*, September 24, 2019, http://www.mdiit.gov.lk/index.php/en/news-and-eventss.

176. Ibid.
177. Section 46 of the Personal Data Protection Bill 2019 (Sri Lanka).
178. Ibid.
179. See note 159 above.
180. Section 5 of the Personal Data Protection Bill 2019 (Sri Lanka).
181. Section 6 of the Personal Data Protection Bill 2019 (Sri Lanka).
182. Section 9 of the Personal Data Protection Bill 2019 (Sri Lanka).
183. Section 13 of the Personal Data Protection Bill 2019 (Sri Lanka).
184. Section 14 of the Personal Data Protection Bill 2019 (Sri Lanka).
185. Section 15 of the Personal Data Protection Bill 2019 (Sri Lanka).
186. Section 16 of the Personal Data Protection Bill 2019 (Sri Lanka).
187. Section 23 of the Personal Data Protection Bill 2019 (Sri Lanka).
188. Section 27 of the Personal Data Protection Bill 2019 (Sri Lanka).
189. Section 26(1) of the Personal Data Protection Bill 2019 (Sri Lanka).
190. Sections 26(2),(3),(4), and (5) of the Personal Data Protection Bill 2019 (Sri Lanka).
191. Section 18(1) of the Computer Crimes Act No. 24 of 2007 (Sri Lanka).
192. Ibid.
193. Section 18(2) of the Computer Crimes Act No. 24 of 2007 (Sri Lanka).
194. Section 24(2) of the Computer Crimes Act No. 24 of 2007 (Sri Lanka).
195. Section 19 of the Computer Crimes Act No. 24 of 2007 (Sri Lanka).
196. Section 52 of the Sri Lanka Telecommunications Act, 1991.
197. Section 53 of the Sri Lanka Telecommunications Act, 1996.
198. Section 54 of the Sri Lanka Telecommunications Act, 1996.
199. Section 61 of the Sri Lanka Telecommunications Act, 1996.
200. Section 3(1)(b) of the Payment Devices Frauds Act, 2006 (Sri Lanka).
201. Section 3(1)(c) of the Payment Devices Frauds Act, 2006 (Sri Lanka).
202. Section 8(4)(c) of the Payment Devices Frauds Act, 2006 (Sri Lanka).
203. Section 8(4)(d) of the Payment Devices Frauds Act, 2006 (Sri Lanka).
204. Article 14A of the Constitution of the Democratic Socialist Republic of Sri Lanka (as amended up to 2015).
205. Ibid.
206. Right to Information Act No. 12 of 2016 (Sri Lanka).
207. Section 5(1)(a) of the Right to Information Act No. 12 of 2016 (Sri Lanka).
208. Section 5(1)(e) of the Right to Information Act No. 12 of 2016 (Sri Lanka).
209. Section 5(1)(g) of the Right to Information Act No. 12 of 2016 (Sri Lanka).
210. Section 5(1)(j) of the Right to Information Act No. 12 of 2016 (Sri Lanka).
211. Section 39 of the Right to Information Act No. 12 of 2016 (Sri Lanka).
212. Section 43 of the Right to Information Act No. 12 of 2016 (Sri Lanka).
213. Section 11 of the Right to Information Act No. 12 of 2016 (Sri Lanka); Section 14 of the Right to Information Act No. 12 of 2016 (Sri Lanka).
214. Section 2 of the Information and Communication Technology Act, 2003 (Sri Lanka).
215. Section 6 of the Information and Communication Technology Act, 2003 (Sri Lanka).
216. Section 2 of the Electronic Transactions Act No. 19 of 2006 (Sri Lanka).
217. Section 21 of the Electronic Transactions Act No. 19 of 2006 (Sri Lanka); Section 22 of the Electronic Transactions Act No. 19 of 2006 (Sri Lanka).
218. Section 4 of the Cyber Security Bill 2019 (Sri Lanka).
219. Section 3 of the Cyber Security Bill 2019 (Sri Lanka).
220. Section 18 of the Cyber Security Bill 2019 (Sri Lanka); Section 19 of the Cyber Security Bill 2019 (Sri Lanka).
221. First Amendment to the Constitution of the United States, 1787.
222. *MP Sharma and Others v. Satish Chandra,* 1954 AIR 300 (Supreme Court of India).
223. Ibid.
224. *Kharak Singh v. State of Uttar Pradesh,* 1964 SCR (1) 332 (Supreme Court of India)
225. Ibid.

226. Centre for Communication Governance, 'The Indian Supreme Court on the Right to Privacy: 63 Years of Progress', *The CCG Blog* (blog), August 13, 2017, https://ccgnludelhi.wordpress.com/2017/08/13/h/.
227. *Govind v. State of Madhya Pradesh*, 1975 AIR 1378 (Supreme Court of India).
228. *R. Rajagopal v. State of Tamil Nadu*, 1995 AIR 264 (Supreme Court of India).
229. *People's Union for Civil Liberties v. Union of India*, AIR 1997 SC 568 (Supreme Court of India).
230. Ibid.
231. *Selvi v. State of Karnataka*, AIR 2010 SC 1974 (Supreme Court of India).
232. Ibid.
233. Centre for Communication Governance, 'CCG on the Privacy Judgment', *The CCG Blog* (blog), September 11, 2017, https://ccgnludelhi.wordpress.com/2017/09/11/ccg-on-the-privacy-judgment/.
234. The Supreme Court of India typically sits in benches of two or three judges to hear matters. When issues of constitutional importance are raised, a constitutional bench i.e. a bench of a minimum of five judges is set up to hear the matter. In this case, a nine judge bench decided on the question of whether the right to privacy is a fundamental right, the largest bench ever to decide on this subject. The nine judges in this case despite concurring with each other, authored several separate opinions.
235. *Justice K.S. Puttaswamy and Ors. vs. Union of India and Ors.*, (2017) 10 SCC 1 (Supreme Court of India).
236. Ibid., 291.
237. The SCOI in *Puttaswamy I* only partially overruled the *MP Sharma* and *Kharak Singh* cases to the extent they ruled that privacy was not a fundamental right under the Indian Constititution.
238. *Justice K.S. Puttaswamy and Ors. vs. Union of India and Ors.*, (2017) 10 SCC 1 (Supreme Court of India).
239. Resolution adopted by the United Nations General Assembly in the 51st session (1996–1997), UN Doc. NO. A/RES/51/162, Model Law on Electronic Commerce adopted by the United Nations Commission on International Trade Law.
240. Preamble, Information and Technology Act, 2000 (India).
241. The term 'body corporate' has been defined in Section 43A of the Information Technology Act, 2000, to mean a company and to include firms, sole proprietorships or other associations of individuals engaged in commercial or professional activities.
242. Rule 2(1)(i) of the Information Technology (Reasonable security practices and procedures and sensitive personal data or information) Rules, 2011.
243. Rule 3 of the Information Technology (Reasonable security practices and procedures and sensitive personal data or information) Rules, 2011.
244. Under the Information Technology (Reasonable security practices and procedures and sensitive personal data or information) Rules, 2011, certain provisions are applicable to personal information and some to SPDI. However, a clarification to the rules was issued by the State in 2011 itself, to iron out some of the issues raised in relation to compliance with these rules. This clarification provides that the rules will be applicable in relation to SPDI only. The validity of the clarification itself is in doubt, and therefore there is still some confusion on the correct applicability of the rules. For a discussion on this issue, see Smitha Krishna Prasad, '(Draft) Paper on Information Technology Act, 2000 and the Data Protection Rules', SSRN Scholarly Paper (Rochester, NY: Social Science Research Network, December 30, 2017), https://papers.ssrn.com/abstract=3094792.
245. Rule 5(5) of the Information Technology (Reasonable security practices and procedures and sensitive personal data or information) Rules, 2011.
246. Rule 5(4) of the Information Technology (Reasonable security practices and procedures and sensitive personal data or information) Rules, 2011.
247. Rule 5(9) of the Information Technology (Reasonable security practices and procedures and sensitive personal data or information) Rules, 2011.

248. Rule 5(8) and 8 of the Information Technology (Reasonable security practices and procedures and sensitive personal data or information) Rules, 2011.
249. See Krishna Prasad, '(Draft) Paper on Information Technology Act, 2000 and the Data Protection Rules'.
250. Government of India, Planning Commission, 'Report of the Group of Experts on Privacy', December 29, 2017 http://planningcommission.nic.in/reports/genrep/rep_privacy.pdf.
251. Government of India, Planning Commission, Report of the Group of Experts on Privacy (Chaired by Justice AP Shah, Former Chief Justice, Delhi High Court), October 16, 2012, https://www.dsci.in/sites/default/files/documents/resource_centre/Report%20of%20the%20Group%20of%20Experts%20on%20Privacy%20constituted%20by%20Planning%20Commission%20of%20India.pdf.
252. Staff Reporter, 'Justice Srikrishna Committee Submits Report on Data Protection. Here're its Top 10 Suggestions', *Economic Times*, July 28, 2018, https://economictimes.indiatimes.com/news/politics-and-nation/justice-bn-srikrishna-committee-submits-report-on-data-protection-herere-the-highlights/articleshow/65164663.cms?from=mdr.
253. Trisha Jalan, 'BJP's Meenakshi Lekhi appointed chair of Joint Committee for Personal Data Protection Bill', *MediaNama*, December 13, 2019, https://www.medianama.com/2019/12/223-personal-data-protection-bill-joint-committee-members-rs-prasad/.
254. Clause 2 of the Personal Data Protection Bill, 2019 (Indian).
255. Clause 3(36) of the Personal Data Protection Bill, 2019 (Indian).
256. Clause 33(2) of the Personal Data Protection Bill, 2019 (Indian).
257. Chapters II, III, IV, V and VI of the Personal Data Protection Bill, 2019 (Indian).
258. Section 27 of the Personal Data Protection Bill, 2019 (Indian); Section 29 of the Personal Data Protection Bill, 2019 (Indian).
259. Clause 41 of the Personal Data Protection Bill, 2019 (Indian); Clause 49 of the Personal Data Protection Bill, 2019 (Indian).
260. Clause 35 of the Personal Data Protection Bill, 2019 (Indian); Clause 36 of the Personal Data Protection Bill, 2019 (Indian).
261. Clause 50 of the Personal Data Protection Bill, 2018 (Indian).
262. The Competition Act, 2002, s 9; The Lokpal and Lokayuktas Act, 2013, s. 4.
263. *National Securities Depository Limited v. Securities and Exchange Board of India*, (2017) 5 SCC 517.
264. *Rojer Mathew v. South Bank India Ltd. & Ors*, 2019 (15) SCALE 615.
265. Section 5(2) of the Indian Telegraph Act, 1885 (Indian).
266. *PUCL v. Union of India* (1997) 1 SCC 301 (Supreme Court of India); Chinmayi Arun, 'Paper-thin Safeguards and Mass Surveillance in India', *National Law School of India Review* 26 (2014): 105.
267. Section 69 of the Information Technology Act, 2000 (Indian).
268. Chaitanya Ramachandran, 'PUCL v. Union of India Revisited: Why India's Surveillance Law Must be Revised for the Digital Age', *NUJS Law Review* 7, no. 2 (2014): 105.
269. See Arun, 'Paper-thin Safeguards and Mass Surveillance in India'.
270. See Ibid.
271. Rishab Bailey et al., 'Use of Personal Data by Intelligence and Law Enforcement Agencies', *Data Governance Network*, August 1, 2018, http://datagovernance.org/files/research/BBPR2018-Use-of-personal-data.pdf.
272. *Justice K.S. Puttaswamy and Ors. vs. Union of India and Ors.*, (2017) 10 SCC 1 (Supreme Court of India).
273. For a detailed examination of these tests, see Amber Sinha, Nehaa Chaudhari, and Smitha Krishna Prasad, 'Reading "Necessity" in India's New Data Protection Bill', *Digital Debates CyFy Journal*, GP-ORF Series 5 (2018): 112, https://www.orfonline.org/wp-content/uploads/2018/10/Digital-Debates-Journal_v13.pdf.
274. Chinmayi Arun, 'Three Problems with India's Draft Data Protection Bill', *Council on Foreign Relations* (blog), October 3, 2018, https://www.cfr.org/blog/three-problems-indias-draft-data-protection-bill; Aditi Agrawal, 'Government's Approach to Data is Dangerous, says

Justice Srikrishna', *MediaNama*, August 27, 2019, https://www.medianama.com/2019/08/223-srikrishna-on-privacy-data-collection-aadhaar/.
275. Clause 42 of the Personal Data Protection Bill 2018 (Indian).
276. Clause 43 of the Personal Data Protection Bill 2018 (Indian).
277. Clause 40 of the Personal Data Protection Bill, 2018 (Indian). See also Yuthika Bharagav, 'Experts Pick Holes in Data Protection Bill', *The Hindu*, July 28, 2018, https://www.thehindu.com/news/national/experts-pick-holes-in-data-protection-bill/article24542431.ece.
278. Clause 35 of the Personal Data Protection Bill 2019 (Indian).
279. Clause 42 of the Personal Data Protection Bill 2019 (Indian).
280. *Internet Freedom Foundation v. Union of India,* Writ Petition (C) No. 46/2019; also see https://internetfreedom.in/supreme-court-issues-notice-on-iffs-petition-for-survelliance-reform-saveourprivacy/.
281. Asmita Nandy, 'Govt Knew NSO, Other Spyware Firms Operated in India: Ex-home Secy', *The Quint*, November 1, 2019, https://www.thequint.com/news/india/whatsapp-pegasus-nso-spyware-former-home-secretary-gk-pillai.
282. *Central Public Information Officer, Supreme Court of India v. Subhash Chandra Agarwal*, 2019 Indlaw SC 1114.
283. Ibid.
284. *Navtej Singh Johar v. Union of India* 2018 (10) SCALE 386 (Supreme Court of India).
285. M.B. Subba, 'BICMA Act 2006 to be Scrapped', *KUENSEL*, November 19, 2016, https://kuenselonline.com/bicma-act-2006-to-be-scrapped/.
286. Graham Greenleaf, 'Privacy in South Asian (SAARC) States: Reasons for Optimism', *Privacy Laws & Business International Report* (2017): 3.
287. Section 464(76) of the Information, Communications and Media Act of Bhutan 2018. Section 464(89) of the of the Information, Communications and Media Act of Bhutan 2018 also defines sensitive personal data or information.
288. Section 179 of the Information, Communications and Media Act of Bhutan 2018.
289. Section 271 of the Information, Communications and Media Act of Bhutan 2018.
290. Section 376 of the Information, Communications and Media Act of Bhutan 2018.
291. Section 379 of the Information, Communications and Media Act of Bhutan 2018.
292. Article 24, Constitution of Maldives.
293. Greenleaf, p. 18 of 33.
294. Article 16(d) of the Constitution of Maldives.
295. Article 16(a) of the Constitution of Maldives.
296. See Greenleaf, 266 and Greenleaf, 70.
297. Article 37, Constitution of the Islamic Republic of Afghanistan (2004).
298. Ibid.
299. Ibid.
300. 'Electronic Frontier Foundation', Mandatory National IDs and Biometric Databases, n.d., https://www.eff.org/issues/national-ids.
301. 'World Stumbling Zombie-like into a Digital Welfare Dystopia, Warns UN Human Rights Expert', United Nations Human Rights Office of the High Commissioner, October 17, 2019, https://www.ohchr.org/EN/NewsEvents/Pages/DisplayNews.aspx?NewsID=25156.
302. 16.9, Global indicator framework for the Sustainable Development Goals and targets of the 2030 Agenda for Sustainable Development, https://unstats.un.org/sdgs/indicators/Global%20Indicator%20Framework%20after%202019%20refinement_Eng.pdf.
303. Government of India, Planning Commission, Gazette Notification No. A-4301/02/2009-Admn.I, January 28, 2009, https://uidai.gov.in/images/notification_28_jan_2009.pdf.
304. The Aadhaar (Targeted Delivery Of Financial And Other Subsidies, Benefits And Services) Act, 2016.
305. Ibid.
306. PUCL Vs Union of India.
307. Ibid,
308. Section 14 of the Aadhaar and Other Laws (Amendment) Act, 2019 (Indian).

309. See note 252 above; also see Gopal Sathe, 'What is the Aadhaar Judgment of the Supreme Court About?' *HuffPost*, September 25, 2018, https://www.huffingtonpost.in/2018/09/25/what-is-the-aadhaar-judgement-of-the-supreme-court-about_a_23538865/.
310. 'The Right to Privacy in the Islamic Republic of Pakistan', Stakeholder Report (Privacy International, March 2017), 9, https://privacyinternational.org/sites/default/files/2017-11/UPR28_Pakistan.pdf.
311. Section 10 the National Database and Registration Authority Ordinance, 2000 (Pakistan).
312. Section 9 of the National Database and Registration Authority Ordinance, 2000 (Pakistan).
313. Section 19 of the National Database and Registration Authority Ordinance, 2000 (Pakistan); Responses to Information Requests, Immigration and Refugee Board of Canada, https://www.justice.gov/eoir/page/file/1130671/download.
314. Section 7(1)(a) of the National Database and Registration Authority Ordinance, 2000 (Pakistan).
315. Section 7(1)(b) of the National Database and Registration Authority Ordinance, 2000 (Pakistan).
316. Section 7(1)(c) of the National Database and Registration Authority Ordinance, 2000 (Pakistan).
317. Section 7(1)(i) of the National Database and Registration Authority Ordinance, 2000 (Pakistan).
318. Section 22 of the National Database and Registration Authority Ordinance, 2000 (Pakistan).
319. Staff Reporter, 'NADRA's innovative services', *The News*, April 8, 2019, https://www.thenews.com.pk/print/455030-nadra-s-innovative-services.
320. Section 7(1)(j) of the National Database and Registration Authority Ordinance, 2000 (Pakistan).
321. Zainab Durrani, 'DRF Condemns yet Another Breach of NADRA Database and Demands Strong Data Protection Legislation', *Digital Rights Foundation* (blog), May 28, 2018, https://digitalrightsfoundation.pk/drf-condemns-yet-another-breach-of-nadra-database-and-demands-strong-data-protection-legislation/.
322. Ibid.
323. Staff Reporter, 'Nadra Wins Sri Lanka ID Card Project', *The Nation*, November 9, 2013, https://nation.com.pk.
324. Ibid.
325. Government of Sri Lanka, Department for Registration of Persons, https://www.drp.gov.lk/Templates/eNIC.english.Department-for-Registration-of-Persons.html.
326. Section 39A of the Registration of Persons Act, 1968 (Sri Lanka).
327. M. Ratnasabapathy, 'Central Database for Citizen Information', *Daily News*, November 1, 2018, https://www.dailynews.lk/2018/11/01/features/167152/central-database-citizen-information.
328. Staff Reporter, 'Bangladesh Introduces "Smart" National Identity Cards', *GlobalVoicesAdvox*, October 7, 2016, https://advox.globalvoices.org/2016/10/07/bangladesh-introduces-smart-national-identity-cards/.
329. 'Review of National Identity Programs', Focus Group Technical Report (International Telecommunication union, May 2016), https://www.itu.int/en/ITU-T/focusgroups/dfs/Documents/09_2016/Review%20of%20National%20Identity%20Programs.pdf.
330. Staff Reporter, 'Bill Related to National ID Endorsed', *The Himalayan Times*, August 28, 2019, https://thehimalayantimes.com/kathmandu/bill-related-to-national-id-card-endorsed/.
331. Ibid.
332. Indu Nepal, 'ID-ing Nepal', *Nepali Times*, April 2010, http://archive.nepalitimes.com/news.php?id=17017#.Xh7hWi2B0dU.
333. See note 18 above.
334. See note 18 above.
335. Alex Perala, 'Maldives' New Biometric ID Combines Passport, Driver License, Payment Card, and More', *FindBiometrics*, October 12, 2017, https://findbiometrics.com/maldives-biometric-id-410121/.

336. Thad Rueter, 'The Maldives Digital ID Drives Multi-application to the Next Level', *SecureID News*, November 13, 2017, https://www.secureidnews.com/news-item/maldives-digital-id-drives-multi-application-next-level/.
337. Alex Perala, 'Maldives' New Biometric ID Combines Passport, Driver License, Payment Card, and More', *FindBiometrics*, October 12, 2017, https://findbiometrics.com/maldives-biometric-id-410121/.
338. See note 18 above; Frud Bezhan, 'Controversial ID Cards Expose Ethnic Divisions In Afghanistan', *Radio Free Europe Radio Liberty*, December 18, 2013, https://www.rferl.org/a/afghanistan-id-cards-ethnic-divisions/25205181.html.
339. Sayed Salahuddin and Pamela Constable, 'Afghanistan's New National ID Card has Finally Debuted, and it's Already Plagued by Problems', *The Washington Post*, May 4, 2018, https://www.washingtonpost.com/world/asia_pacific/afghanistans-new-national-id-card-has-finally-debuted-and-its-already-plagued-by-problems/2018/05/03/b9449ba4-4ee8-11e8-85c1-9326c4511033_story.html.
340. 'Literacy Rates Rise ffffrom One Generation to Next, But Challenges Remain in Region', UNESCO, September 8, 2017, https://bangkok.unesco.org/content/literacy-rates-rise-one-generation-next-challenges-remain-region.
341. Government of Sri Lanka, Ministry of Digital Infrastructure and Information Technology (MDIIT), 'Draft National Digital Policy for Sri Lanka 2020–2025', http://www.mdiit.gov.lk/index.php/en/component/jdownloads/send/6-legislation/76-national-digital-policy.
342. Government of Pakistan, Ministry of Information and Technology, 'Digital Pakistan Policy 2017', http://digitalrightsmonitor.pk/wp-content/uploads/2017/10/Digital-Pakistan-Policy-2017.pdf.
343. Neha Alawadhi and Karan Choudhury, 'Economic Survey Suggests Govt Can Monetise Citizen's Data as A Public Good', *Business Standard*, July 4, 2019, https://www.business-standard.com/article/economy-policy/economic-survey-suggests-govt-can-monetise-citizen-s-data-as-a-public-good-119070401558_1.html.
344. Government of India, Ministry of Electronics and Information Technology, 'A Free and Fair Digital Economy, Protecting Privacy, Empowering Indians (Committee of Experts under the Chairmanship of Justice B.N. Srikrishna)', https://meity.gov.in/writereaddata/files/Data_Protection_Committee_Report.pdf.

Disclosure statement

No potential conflict of interest was reported by the author(s).

The long arm of GDR in Africa: re flection on data privacy law reform and practice in Mauritius

Alex B. Makulilo

ABSTRACT

The recently adopted General Data Protection Regulation (GDPR) in the European Union has certainly set the highest standards of all data privacy policies across the world. In theory such standards have provided more control to individuals over their personal data. Due to the strengthened third-party obligations in the GDPR for data export to non-European Union countries and fear of loss of foreign investment if such countries fail to provide adequate protection of personal data, the GDPR exerts profound influence on data privacy law reform and practice outside Europe. This article analyses the impact of the GDPR in Africa by using Mauritius as an intrinsic case study. Mauritius is selected in this analysis due to its leading role in the privacy policy reforms in Africa and the internationalisation of its data protection systems. Accordingly, the development of the data protection system in Mauritius from the repealed Data Protection Act 2004 to the current Data Protection Act 2017 is analysed in detail, drawing on the largest body of reported complaints, appeals and judicial decisions so far decided by courts.

1. Introduction

Regulation (EU) 2016/679 on the protection of natural persons with regard to the processing of personal data and on the free movement of such data which is commonly referred to as the General Data Protection Regulation (GDPR) represents a decisive step in the policy reform of data privacy framework in the European Union. The GDPR entered into force on 24 May 2016 and became operational since 25 May 2018. The GDPR replaces the European Union Data Protection Directive 95/46/EC. One of the fundamental aspects of the EU data privacy policy reform is that, as a 'regulation', the GDPR is a binding legislative act which has direct effect on all EU member states. This is in contrast to a 'directive' which had to be transposed to national laws of the EU member countries to take effect. In the field of data protection, Data Protection Directive 95/46/EC had resulted into problem of fragmentation of data protection regulations in Europe and the different legislation and application of the Directive between EU member countries. Concomitantly, change in the regulatory approach from 'directive' to 'regulation' is perhaps one of the main aspects of the reform of the EU data privacy regime with the view of achieving harmonisation of law and practice across the European Union.

It is important to note that harmonisation of the EU law and practices in the field of data protection were not the only reason for the reform of the data protection regime in Europe. Given the significant technological changes since the Directive was passed in 1995, the GDPR seeks to preserve EU harmonisation while modernising data privacy laws.[1] There are quite many dimensions of modernisation. Suffice to point here that mobile Internet devices, web-user generated content and the rise of social networking sites based on Web 2.0 have changed the ways and manner through which personal data may be processed. Above all, modern technologies have increased many possibilities of personal data processing that could have not been imagined before. Individuals who were mainly data subjects have now become data controllers just like organisations. Empowered by modern technologies millions of people use social networking sites every day to keep in touch with friends, upload an unlimited number of photos, share links and videos, and learn more about the people they meet.[2] All of this is based on personal data processing.[3] Similarly, security of personal data in the digital age has become a critical issue. This is partly due to the fact that data stored in the 'cloud' is beyond the control of an individual to whom it relates. Loss of control over one's personal data in the 'cloud' has far reaching privacy implications.

Perhaps one of the aspects of the GDPR that has ramifications on law reform in the field of data privacy to non-European Union states including Africa is its global reach. The Proposal for General Data Protection Regulation issued in 2012 by the European Commission, partly states that

> Individuals' rights must continue to be ensured when personal data is transferred from the EU to third countries, and whenever individuals in Member States are targeted and their data is used or analysed by third country service providers. This means that EU data protection standards have to apply regardless of the geographical location of a company or its processing facility.[4]

This part of the proposal was finally enshrined in the GDPR through the extraterritorial jurisdictional claims as well as through the requirement of adequacy standard for privacy protection in third-countries. This latter criterion has exerted indirect pressure on third-countries resulting into the exportation of privacy norms.

This article analyses the impact of the GDPR in Africa by using Mauritius as an intrinsic case study. Mauritius is selected in this analysis due to its leading role in the privacy policy reforms in Africa and the internationalisation of its data protection systems. Accordingly, the development of the data protection system in Mauritius from the repealed Data Protection Act 2004 to the current Data Protection Act 2017 is analysed in detail, drawing on the largest body of reported complaints, appeals and judicial decisions so far decided by courts.

2. The context of Mauritian data protection law reform

2.1. Overview

The Republic of Mauritius is among the earliest countries in Africa to enact comprehensive data protection legislation. Inspired by the European Data Protection Directive

95/46/EC on the protection of individuals with regard to the processing of personal data and on the free movement of such data, Mauritius passed its first data protection legislation in 2004, the Data Protection Act 2004 (i.e. DPA 2004). However, it was not until 2009 when the substantive provisions of the Data Protection Act 2004 came into operation.

Mauritius adopted the DPA 2004 due to two main reasons. The first is that the Act was adopted in order to give effect to the constitutional right to privacy as a result of potential risks posed by use of computers.[5] The Constitution of Mauritius 1968 explicitly recognises privacy as a basic fundamental human right in Articles 3 and 9. Besides the Constitution, the other general law from which the DPA 2004 obtains its legal foundation is the Civil Code. Article 22 of the Civil Code states that everyone has the right to respect for his private life. Accordingly, this provision empowers courts to make orders to prevent or stop an invasion to the right of privacy. The second reason and perhaps the one which carries more weight is economic one. Mauritius adopted a data privacy law in order to attract foreign investment in the island from the European Union. This reason appears to be recited over and again during the parliamentary discussion (Hansard) of 1 June 2004.[6] Indeed Article 25 of the EU Data Protection Directive 95/46/EC restricted EU countries to export personal data of data subjects in EU to non-EU countries, if the latter do not provide adequate protection of personal data. Through this provision EU indirectly exercised pressure on third countries to adopt data protection legislation for fear of loss of trading relations.

Since it was enacted, the DPA 2004 was amended twice in 2009 before it was eventually repealed on 8 December 2017. The first amendment of the DPA 2004 was passed on 15 April 2009 through section 2 of the Additional Stimulus Package (Miscellaneous Provisions) Act 2009. This provision, among others, amended section 17 of the Data Protection Act 2004 on Commissioner's powers of entry and search. Such powers which were confined to the Commissioner were now extended to his subordinates called authorised officers. However, in case of entry and search by authorised officers, a warrant issued by a Magistrate was to be obtained. Similarly, section 2 of the Additional Stimulus Package (Miscellaneous Provisions) Act 2009 repealed the contentious section 21 of the DPA 2004 that compromised the independence of the Commissioner. Such provision empowered the Prime Minister to give direction to the Commissioner. The second set of amendments was introduced by the Finance (Miscellaneous Provisions) Act 2009. Such amendments introduced new powers of the Data Protection Commissioner to obtain information in the course of investigation.

Overall, the amendments of the DPA 2004 were meant to bring Mauritian data protection system and practices in line with the European and international data protection standards and best practices. This reflects the spirit of the National ICT Policy which clearly states that it was adopted to meet the need for Mauritius to be potentially recognised by the European Union as a third country with an adequate level of protection.[7] The Mauritian Data Protection Commissioner has explained the reasons behind DPA 2004 amendments in order to enhance prospective registration of data processors and also to give more independence to the Commissioner in the exercise of his function under the Act.[8] However, in the First Annual Report (February 2009–February 2010), the Commissioner assigns a slight different reason:

> the Commissioner was required to amend and update the Data Protection Act to secure better chances of accreditation with the European Union for Mauritius to be recognised as an adequate country in data protection to facilitate the transfers of personal data from the European Union to Mauritius and thus attract more investment in mainly the ITES/BPO sectors of the Mauritian economy.[9]

Admittedly, both reasons advanced by the Commissioner are broadly in line with the policy statement of the Mauritian National ICT Policy.[10] This is because the need for independent data protection authority as previously stated by the Data Protection Commissioner is central to the functioning of data privacy legislation under the European Directive 95/46/EC.

2.2. The influence of international and regional human rights and privacy policies

Mauritius is a party to the United Nations (UN), African Union (AU) and Southern African Development Community (SADC). Accordingly, human right treaties as well as data privacy policies at the UN, AU and SADC levels are relevant to the Mauritian data protection system. The most important human rights instrument at the United Nations addressing privacy is the International Covenant on Civil and Political Rights 1966 (ICCPR). In Africa there are two main instruments at the AU relevant for privacy protection namely, the African Charter on Human and Peoples' Rights (ACHPR or the African Charter) 1981 and the African Union Convention on Cyber Security and Personal Data Protection 2014 (the Malabo Convention). While the ACHPR was not adopted specifically to address data privacy issues the Malabo Convention was adopted to address the challenges of modern technologies including the right to privacy. In the SADC region, the Southern African Development Community (SADC) Model Law on data protection adopted in 2012 is relevant. Outside of Africa, the data protection system in Mauritius has been inspired by the EU data protection regime as well as the Council of Europe Convention 108 and its Additional Protocol.

(a) ICCPR

The ICCPR is the United Nations based treaty on human rights. Article 17 of the ICCPR protects the rights to privacy. It states that

> No one shall be subjected to arbitrary or unlawful interference with his privacy, family, home or correspondence, nor to unlawful attacks on his honour and reputation. Everyone has the right to the protection of the law against such interference or attacks.

Bygrave argues that case law developed around Article 17 of the ICCPR provides the clearest indication that the right to privacy in international law harbours core data protection principles. However, this case law currently falls short of data protection laws in terms of both ambit and prescriptory guidance.[11] Although Mauritius is a party to the ICCPR, the *travaux préparatoires* to DPA 2017 makes no reference to ICCPR. Similarly, the Mauritian Supreme Court did not make any reference to Article 17 of the ICCPR in the landmark case of *Madhewoo v The State of Mauritius & Another*[12] implying there is little influence of the ICCPR in the data privacy discourse in Mauritius. Further discussion of this case law is provided in subsequent parts of this article.

(b) The ACHPR

The African Charter on Human and Peoples' Rights is the continental human right treaty that addresses fundamental human rights and obligation of peoples. The Charter came into force on 21 October 1986. As far as the right to privacy is concerned, and in contrast to core international and regional human treaties,[13] the African Charter does not explicitly protect the right to privacy. Commentators in the field of data privacy have argued that the right to privacy may be implied from other provisions of the Charter especially those that guarantee respect for dignity of human beings and freedom from all forms of exploitation and degradation, including torture.[14] However, up until now, there is no case law of the African Court on Human and Peoples' Rights on the right to privacy that has read in the right to privacy in other provisions of the African Charter. Neither is there any complaint filled to the Human Rights Commission on this subject. Nonetheless, the African Court on Human and Peoples' Rights has broad jurisdiction to adjudicate a right that is not covered in the African Charter. The power of the Court in this regard arises when a right is not provided in the African Charter but it is covered by another international human rights treaty. Commentators have argued that privacy is an example of such right which, although, is not provided in the ACHPR may be adjudicated through Article 17 of the International Covenant on Civil and Political Rights 1966 (ICCPR).[15]

Mauritius signed and ratified the ACHPR in 1992. Up to now Mauritius has submitted three combined periodic reports on the implementation of the African Charter.[16] Nonetheless, it is only in the third report (2016–2019) where Mauritius reports the implementation of the right to privacy by making reference to its DPA 2017. Much as there is no explicit provision on the protection of the right to privacy in the African Charter and also no case law has been developed by the African Court on Human and Peoples' Rights, there appears to be quite limited influence of the ACHPR on the data privacy reform in Mauritius. None of the *travaux préparatoires* make reference to the ACHPR either.

(c) The Malabo Convention

The African Union Convention on Cyber Security and Personal Data Protection 2014 is the only binding data protection treaty outside Europe. The Convention was adopted in Malabo, Equatorial Guinea on 27 June 2014. Up to now fourteen out of fifty-five African countries have signed the Convention and only five countries have ratified it.[17] The Convention has not yet come into force for want of fifteen ratifications.

In contrast to other regional data privacy treaties, the Malabo Convention covers three diverse subjects in one document: electronic transactions, data protection and cybersecurity. Data protection is covered in Chapter 2 of the Convention.

With respect to data privacy, the objectives of the Malabo Convention are to commit the AU member states to establish a legal framework aimed at strengthening fundamental rights and public freedoms, particularly the protection of physical data and to punish any violation of privacy without prejudice to the principle of free flow of data. The other objective of the Convention is to ensure that member states respect fundamental freedoms and human rights in the course of undertaking any form of data processing while recognising the right of the state, local communities and the purposes for which businesses were established.

The Convention has a broad scope. It is applicable to any processing carried out in the territory of a state party to the AU. Also, it applies to any operation which is performed upon personal data whether or not by automatic means.

The Convention contains six principles of data processing namely, the principle of consent and legitimacy of personal data processing, the principle of lawfulness and fairness of personal data processing, the principle of purpose, relevance and storage of processed personal data, the principle of accuracy of personal data, the principle of transparency of personal data processing and the principle of confidentiality and security of personal data processing.[18] Besides the data protection principles, the Malabo Convention establishes rights and obligations of the data subjects as well as the data controllers, respectively.

As regards enforcement, the Convention requires AU member states to establish an authority in charge of protecting personal data known as National Protection Authorities (NPAs). The NPAs must be independent administrative authorities whose overall duty is to ensure that the data processing is carried out in accordance with the Convention.

It is noteworthy that Mauritius ratified the African Union Convention on Cyber Security and Personal Data Protection on 6 March 2018 well after it had passed its new Data Protection Act 2017 on 8 December 2017. There is therefore little or no reference at all to the Malabo Convention in the *travaux préparatoires* and/or discussion of the Mauritian data protection reform.

(d) SADC Model Law

The Southern African Development Community (SADC) adopted the model law on data protection adopted in 2012.[19] The primary objectives of the Model Law are to provide protection of an individual's right to privacy as well as harmonisation of data privacy policies and laws across the sub-region. The Model Law applies to both automatic and non-automatic processing of personal data.[20]

The heart of the Model Law lies in parts IV, V, VI and VII which contain basic principles and condition for processing personal data. These principles include in a nutshell: fair and lawful processing; explicit purpose; legitimacy; sensitivity; data quality; security; openness and accountability. Besides the basic principles of data processing, part VI of the Model Law contains the obligations imposed on data controllers while part VII provides for the rights of the data subjects. Part III of the Model Law provides for the establishment of protection authority in member states. This part provides for the composition, functions and powers, sanctions and remedies for breaches of the provisions of the Model Law.

The Model Law as its name suggests is not binding on SADC member states. It is soft law. As such, it is meant to guide SADC member states when adopting their national legislation to take into account of the provisions of the Model Law. Due to its nature the Model Law has had little influence in the data privacy law reform in Mauritius. It is interesting to note that none of the *travaux préparatoires* refers to the SADC Model Law.

(e) EU Data Protection Regime

The EU data protection regime is currently comprised in the GDPR. The philosophical basis of the GDPR is human rights. The latter is reflected in the objectives of the instrument which are to protect fundamental rights and freedoms of natural persons particularly their rights to protection of personal data and to ensure free flow of information within the European Union.[21]

The GDPR applies to the processing of personal data wholly or partly by automated means. Geographically, the GDPR has an extra territorial jurisdiction broader than its predecessor in the EU Directive. Article 3(2) (a) and (b) of the GDPR partly states:

> This Regulation applies to the processing of personal data of data subjects who are in the Union by a controller or processor not established in the Union, where the processing activities are related to: (a) the offering of goods or services to such data subjects in the Union; or (b) the monitoring of their behaviour.

The above clause is fundamentally different from Article 4(1)(c) of the EU Directive. Instead of focusing on the use of equipment situated in the EU as it was the case with Article 4 (1) (c) of the Directive, Article 3(2) describes two circumstances under which the GDPR applies to a data controller or data processor not established in the Union but whose activities seek to 'target' [Article 3(2)(a)] and 'monitor' [Article 3(2)(b)] individuals within it. Professor Dan Jerker Svantesson argues that Article 3 of the GDPR and again, in particular Article 3(2), and potentially Article 3(3) of the GDPR goes too far, thereby giving the GDPR a scope of application that is difficult to justify on the international stage, as the GDPR may end up applying in situations in relation to which the EU may be argued to lack legitimate interest to apply its laws and to which it has only a very weak connection.[22] Accordingly the GDPR has a worldwide effect. It does not only apply to all EU nations but also on every company holding data on EU citizens regardless of its geographical location.

There are a number of new definitions in the GDPR. For example, the definition of 'personal data' has been expanded to include a wider range of consumer data. Previously the Directive confined the definition of 'personal data' to information used to identify an individual while the GDPR goes far to include online identification markers, location data, genetic information and more, in the definition of 'personal data'.

The GDPR sets out seven principles for the lawful processing of personal data.[23] Processing of personal data is defined in Article 4(2) of the GDPR as any operation or set of operations which is performed on personal data or on sets of personal data whether or not by automated means. Broadly, the seven principles in the GDPR are: lawfulness, fairness and transparency, purpose limitation, data minimisation, accuracy, storage limitation, integrity and confidentiality and accountability. These principles are similar to the ones in the Directive 95/46/EC. However, to make the GDPR stronger, additional elements have been introduced notably the transparency principle, clarification of the data minimisation principle and establishment of a comprehensive responsibility and liability of the data controller.[24] Also, the criteria of lawful processing have remained the same as in the Directive, only that the balance of interest criterion has to be applied. Similarly, the GDPR clarifies conditions regarding re-purposing of the processing as well as conditions of consent with regard to processing of personal data.

The rights of the data subjects in the GDPR have been somehow redefined. However, one of the new right introduced in the GDPR is 'the right to be forgotten' which simply mandates a data subject to direct the controller or processor, as the case may be, to erase and destroy completely any information relating to him or her, especially when its purpose or period required has expired or consent has been withdrawn.[25] The other right introduced by the GDPR is data portability which allows individuals to obtain and reuse their personal data for their own purposes across different services. It allows them to move, copy or transfer personal data easily from one IT environment to another in a safe and secure way, without hindrance to usability.[26]

The GDPR retains most of the obligations placed on data controllers and processors in the EU Directive 95/46/EC. It also clarifies obligations of joint data controllers. However, the GDPR introduces in clear terms the 'principle of accountability' as an obligation on the part of data controllers and processors. Controllers and processors are also obliged to carry out a data protection impact assessment prior to risky processing operation.[27] Also important to note is that the GDPR puts obligation on data controllers and processors to employ Data Protection Officers with knowledge on issues of data protection law and regulations.[28] The officer is required to discharge his or her duties with some levels of independence. There is also a requirement of data breach notification. The GDPR introduces a security breach communication framework for all data controllers regardless of the sector in which they operate. Notification obligations (to supervisory authorities and to data subjects) are triggered by accidental or unlawful destruction, loss, alteration, unauthorised disclosure of, or access to, personal data.[29]

The GDPR has also introduced another obligation not covered in the Directive 95/46/EC. This is privacy by design and by default. Article 25 of the GDPR requires a data controller to implement appropriate technical and organisational measures for ensuring that, by default, only personal data which is necessary for each specific purpose of the processing is processed. This obligation somehow relates to the amount of personal data collected, the extent of their processing, the period of their storage and their accessibility.

The EU Directive was the first international instrument to control exports of personal data to countries not bound by the same data privacy rules (in this case, non-EU/EEA countries).[30] Article 25 permitted such exports from EU member states 'only if … the third country in question ensures an adequate level of protection'. The GDPR retained the 'adequacy clause' in Article 45. It is also interesting to note that in assessing the level of adequacy of protection of a third country, the EU takes into account the third country's accession to the Council of Europe Convention of 28 January 1981 for the Automatic Processing of Personal Data and its Additional Protocol.[31] It is arguable that the adequacy clause puts indirect pressure on third countries to enact data privacy laws to allow free flow of personal data. Since the majority of third countries have trade relations with Europe, the lack of legal framework for protection of personal data would mean restriction of trade with third countries. The adequacy mechanism has great influence of the EU data protection regime to law reforms in the third countries.

As regards enforcement, the GDPR clarifies a number of enforcement measures available for data subjects to enforce their rights. Data protection authorities remain the central institution of administrative enforcement. Sanctions and compensations have been enhanced. Previously the Directive did not clarify most of these issues as they were only left to the member states to provide them in their national data protection legislation.

In contrast to the ACHPR, Malabo Convention and SADC Model Law on data protection, the EU data protection regime has significantly inspired privacy law reform in Mauritius. This is clearly evidenced in the *travaux préparatoires* of the Mauritian data protection reform as outlined above. Therefore, in view of attracting investment from Europe and bringing the Mauritian data protection system in line with the international standards and best practices, Mauritius made a request for accreditation of its data protection system to the European Union in 2010. This request sought to make Mauritius in the EU white list for exchange of personal data of data subjects in the two jurisdictions. This would enable Mauritius to step up trading relations with member states of the Europe Union in an off-shore investment services and business process outsourcing. A preliminary assessment by EU consultant found that the Mauritian data protection system did not meet the adequacy standard.[32] Some of the reasons for this finding include the following:

- the concept of personal data in the EU refers to 'individuals' rather generally while in the Mauritian system is it limited to 'living individuals' excluding deceased persons;
- contrary to the EU Directive, the DPA 2004 does not foresee that processing might be legitimate when necessary for the purposes of legitimate interests pursued by the controller or by the third party or parties to whom the data are disclosed;
- the Mauritian system exempts several sectoral activities from the obligations defined by the DPA 2004;
- in the Mauritian system consent has a normative priority over other legal grounds of lawful processing of personal data;
- the Mauritian system with respect to onward transfers of personal data appears more restrictive than the European one since the Commissioner's approval is always requested, whether the transfer occurs towards an adequate destination or in the framework of adequate safeguards;
- the Commissioner's interpretation as to automated decisions lacks legal basis in the DPA 2004;
- the DPA 2004 contains several exemptions thereby compromising such principles as purpose limitation, data quality and proportionality principles;
- the independence of the Data Protection Office and its Commissioner is not directly addressed in the DPA 2004; and
- the Data Protection Office has no direct sanction powers. These have to be dealt with by the Intermediate Court.

The unfavourable finding called for more reforms in the Mauritian data protection system and practices. In order to offer assistance to Mauritius so that it would align its data protection system to the EU, a project titled 'Ensuring the compliance of the data protection legislation and principles of Mauritius with EU standards'[33] was designed. The overreaching objective of the project states as follows:

> The Government of Mauritius needs to achieve compliance of the Mauritian Data Protection Act and related legislations with EU data protection laws. The global objective of this assignment is to amend the Data Protection Act in the perspective of achieving compliance with the EU data protection laws, and to improve the existing institutional set-up of the Data Protection Office to meet international standards.

It is interesting to note that since the final report of the above project was completed in 2011, it has taken about eight years for Mauritius to adopt a new legislation in 2017. As alluded to, the *travaux préparatoires* of the Mauritian DPA 2017 extensively relies upon the EU data privacy regime as the source of inspiration and primary reference.

(f) Council of Europe Convention 108

Founded in 1949, the Council of Europe is an international entity of 47 members states, 28 of which are member states of the European Union. The overall aim of Council of Europe is to uphold human rights, democracy and the rule of law in Europe. It is noteworthy that in the field of data privacy, the Council of Europe adopted the Convention for the Protection of Individuals with regard to Automatic Processing of Personal Data (CoE Convention 108) in 1981. So far, the Convention 108 has two protocols. The first protocol was adopted in 2001, the Additional Protocol to the Convention for the Protection of Individuals with regard to Automatic Processing of Personal Data, regarding supervisory authorities and transborder data flows. The second one, the Protocol amending the Convention for the Protection of Individuals with regard to Automatic Processing of Personal Data was adopted in 2018. The aim of the Protocol of amendment is to modernise and improve the Convention 108, taking into account the new challenges to the protection of individuals with regard to the processing of personal data which have emerged since the Convention was adopted in 1980.

The Convention 108 has similar data protection principles as the GDPR especially following the modernisation process. However, currently, the Convention has the following principles fair and lawful processing, purpose specification, limitation, data quality, data retention, data security and sensitivity. The Convention also provides for the rights of the data subject similar to the GDPR. There is a requirement for establishment of an independent supervisory authority. The Convention provides for a requirement of transborder data flow to countries which provide adequate protection of personal data. It noteworthy that the Protocol amending the Convention for the Protection of Individuals with regard to Automatic Processing of Personal Data was adopted in 2018 has strengthened the Convention 108.[34] However, it has not yet come into force.

Up until recently, the Convention 108 is the only existing legally binding international treaty with global relevance in the field of data privacy. Article 23(1) of the Convention 108 offers possibilities for non-European countries to accede to it. Through this provision, Mauritius acceded to the Convention 108 and its Additional Protocol on 17 June 2016. The Convention came into force with respect to Mauritius on 1 October 2016. Since the assessment of the EU adequacy of protection of a third country takes into account, among other factors, a third country's accession to the Council of Europe Convention 108 and its Additional Protocol, it is arguable that, this will increase the chances of Mauritius to fulfil its long term desire to be accredited by the EU through the GDPR.[35]

3. Mauritian Data Protection Act 2017

The starting point of the new data protection legislation in Mauritius is the Budget Speech of 2017–2018. Through this speech, the Prime Minister made it clear that the Data Protection Act 2004 would be amended to comply with the new EU data protection regulation which came in force on 25 May 2018. According to the Prime Minister, the motive behind the amendment is to encourage companies in the ICT sector to use Mauritius as a platform for their services.[36] In the July 2017 deliberations, the Mauritian Cabinet took note that the Data Protection Act 2004 would be overhauled with a view to aligning it with the current technological and other advancements, and relevant international standards, namely the New European Union General Data Protection Regulation 2016/679 and the European Convention for Protection of Individuals with regard to Automatic Processing of Personal Data. The Cabinet agreed to introduce the Bill on data protection legislation in December 2017. Accordingly, the Data Protection Act 2017 was passed by the National Assembly on 8 December 2017. It was assented to by the President on 23 December 2017 and officially came into force on 15 January 2018. The new Act repeals the Data Protection Act 2004. However, it retains all the Code of Practice and Guidelines made under the repealed law.[37]

While the original reasons for the adoption of a data protection law in Mauritius primarily remain the same, there are four main reasons why the Data Protection Act 2004 has been repealed. The first, is to strengthen the control and personal autonomy of data subjects over their personal data following the recent developments of technologies which have seen the rise of big data, the internet of things and cloud computing, to mention but a few examples. Such technologies have the tendencies of diminishing an individual's ability to control his personal data. Second, is to ensure Mauritian data protection system is in line with current relevant international standards, in particular the European Union's General Data Protection Regulation (GDPR) 2016/679 on the protection of natural persons with regard to the processing of personal data and on the free movement of such data. The Explanatory Memorandum to the Data Protection Bill 2017 and the parliamentary discussion (*Hansard*) of 8 December 2017 clearly state that the idea of strengthening the control and personal autonomy of data subjects is to ensure respect for their human rights and fundamental freedoms, in particular their right to privacy, in line with current relevant international standards, in particular the European Union's General Data Protection Regulation 2016/679 on the protection of natural persons with regard to the processing of personal data and on the free movement of such data.[38] Thirdly, the Act seeks to simplify the regulatory environment for business in the country's digital economy; and finally, to promote the safe transfer of personal data to and from foreign jurisdictions, given the diversification, intensification and globalisation of data processing and personal data flows.

3.1. Scope of the Act

The Data Protection Act applies to all kinds of automated processing as well as manual files and other forms of manual processing where the personal data form part of a filing system or are intended to form part of a filing system.[39] Processing by both public and private sectors are covered under the Act.[40] This scope is similar to Article 2 (1) of the GDPR.

However, the Data Protection Act excludes from its scope certain types of processing, particularly those related to exchange of information between ministries, government departments and public sector agencies where such exchange is required on a need-to-know basis.[41] Also, the Act does not apply to processing of personal data by an individual in the course of a purely personal or household activity.[42] The exemptions under the Data

Protection Act appear to be narrower than the GDPR which excludes under Article 2 processing of personal data by competent authorities for the purposes of the prevention, investigation, detection or prosecution of criminal offences or the execution of criminal penalties, including the safeguarding against and the prevention of threats to public security. It is also interesting to note that unlike the Data Protection Act 2004 which excluded the activities of the media from the purview of the Act, the 2017 Data Protection Act fails to exempt media from the application of the legislation. It is submitted that the Act has the potential of limiting freedom of expression.

The Data Protection Act 2017 has the same scope as the repealed Data Protection Act 2004 [section 3(3)].[43] The Act applies to a data controller who is established in Mauritius. To put it differently, the Act applies when the activities of the establishment are located in Mauritius. If a controller is not established in Mauritius but uses equipment in Mauritius for processing data, such a controller is subject to the application of the Data Protection Act. In that case he has an obligation to nominate a representative who resides in Mauritius to carry out his data processing activities through an office in Mauritius. Section 3(7) of the Data Protection Act 2017 provides that the notion of 'establishment' is confined to a person who is ordinarily a resident in Mauritius or a person who carries out data processing operations through an office, branch or agency in Mauritius. In contrast, the GDPR applies even to a controller who is not established in the EU and who is not using equipment in the EU. The GDPR does not focus on the 'use of equipment located in the EU' as it was the case with the EU Directive 96/46/EC. That is why the GDPR is considered to have an extra-territorial applicability.[44] It is also important to note that the DPA 2017 just as it was the case with its predecessor the DPA 2004, does not apply by virtue of public international law. This is another scenario where the GDPR applies to the processing of personal data by a controller not established in the EU but only by virtue of public international law.

As regards exemptions, both the GDPR and the Data Protection Act have similar scope. Both laws do not apply to the processing of personal data by a natural person in the course of a purely personal or household activity. Similarly, the two instruments exempt processing of personal data in the domain of enforcement of criminal law and national security. There are dissimilarities as regards exemptions. While the Mauritian DPA 2017 exempts the processing of personal data for the purpose of historical, statistical or scientific research,[45] the GDPR appears not to provide such exemptions as such. Instead it gives special safeguards to the processing of such data subject to few derogations.[46] It is also interesting to note that the Data Protection Act does not provide exemption and /or any regulation to personal data processing pursuant to the freedom of expression and information, including processing for journalistic purposes and the purposes of academic, artistic or literary expression. In contrast, Article 85 of the GDPR provides extensive and detailed provision of these aspects. One wonders why the policy makers and legislators in Mauritius decided not to retain section 49 of the Data Protection Act 2004 which covered exemptions for processing personal data for journalistic, literary and artistic purposes.

3.2. Key definitions

The Data Protection Act 2017 introduces in section 2 new definitions in line with the GDPR. Such definitions include biometric data, encryption, genetic data, physical or mental health, personal data breach, profiling and pseudonymisation. Most of these definitions and concepts are a result of the advancement of modern technologies and their application.

3.3. Principles of processing personal data

The Data Protection Act sets out six basic principles of processing personal data in section 21 (a) – (f). These principles apply to all kinds of personal data. The six principles of data processing are as follows:

(a) '21. that personal data must be processed lawfully, fairly and in a transparent manner in relation to any data subject;
(b) that personal data must be collected for explicit, specified and legitimate purposes and not further processed in a manner incompatible with those purposes;
(c) that personal data must be adequate, relevant and limited to what is necessary in relation to the purposes for which they are processed;
(d) that personal data must be accurate and, where necessary, kept up to date, with every reasonable step being taken to ensure that any inaccurate personal data are erased or rectified without delay;
(e) that personal data should be kept in a form which permits identification of data subjects for no longer than is necessary for the purposes for which the personal data are processed; and
(f) that personal data must be processed in accordance with the rights of data subjects.'

The principles of processing personal data in the Data Protection Act are copycat of Article 5 (a) – (f) of the GDPR. The wordings of these provisions are exactly the same. However, there is one difference. Section 21(f) of the Data Protection Act adds a 'new principle' previously not provided in any international or regional data protection policy, that is, personal data must be processed in accordance with the rights of data subjects. Part VIII of the Data Protection Act covers 'data protection rights'. In contrast, Article 5(f) of the GDPR covers the principle of integrity and confidentiality which states that personal data shall be processed in a manner that ensures appropriate security of the personal data, including protection against unauthorised or unlawful processing and against accidental loss, destruction or damage, using appropriate technical or organisational measures. The Data Protection Act covers the security of processing in section 31. However, this section is slightly different in wordings from a corresponding provision on security of processing in Article 32 of the GDPR but with similar scope.

3.4. Legal grounds for lawful processing

The specific conditions of processing personal data must be interpreted within the context of the principles of processing personal data. The conditions depend upon the kinds of personal data that is subject of processing, i.e. whether personal data are ordinary or special categories of personal data.

Section 28 of the Data Protection Acts sets out eight legal grounds for the lawful processing of personal data. Out of the eight legal grounds in the Act, six are copycat of

Article 6 of the GDPR.[47] The six grounds in Article 6 of the GDPR are exhaustive and there is no ranking between Article 6 (1)(a) – (f) in the sense that one ground has normative priority over the others.[48] It is interesting to note that, section 24 of the repealed Data Protection Act 2004 had a normative priority of consent over the other grounds. As alluded to, this was among the issues raised by the EU consultant's report in Mauritius.[49] However, this is no longer the case with section 28 of the Data Protection Act 2017.

The two additional legal grounds for lawful processing in the Data Protection Act which are not covered by Article 6 of the GDPR are:

- Section 28(1)(b)(v) of DPA 2017, no person shall process personal data unless the processing is necessary for the performance of any task carried out by a public authority.
- Section 28(1)(b)(v) of DPA 2017, no person shall process personal data unless the processing is necessary for the purpose of historical, statistical or scientific research.

It is important to note that 28(1)(b)(v) of the DPA 2017 is somehow a repetition of section 28(1)(b)(iv). The latter section provides that no person shall process personal data unless the processing is necessary for the performance of a task carried out in the public interest or in the exercise of official authority vested in the controller. Section 28 (1)(b)(iv) of the Data Protection Act is equivalent to Article 6 (1) (e) of the GDPR. This provision is the general basis for lawful processing of personal data for public sector purposes.[50] The other legal ground which is not covered by the GDPR is that no person shall process personal data unless the processing is necessary for the purpose of historical, statistical or scientific research.[51] It is awkward for this clause to be considered as a condition for processing personal data. This is because, it is an exemption of data processing in section 44 (2) of the Data Protection Act. In any case, it may not stand as a condition as such.

The other condition, warranting discussion, upon which data processing may take place under the Data Protection Act is consent for specified purposes.[52] The Data Protection Act defines consent in section 2 as any freely given specific, informed and unambiguous indication of the wishes of a data subject, either by a statement or a clear affirmative action, by which he signifies his agreement to personal data relating to him being processed. This definition is identical to the definition of the term consent in Article 4(11) of the GDPR. In this definition consent may be made by express statement or clear affirmative action. The latter takes care of the notion of passive consent or what is known as acquiescence or implicit consent in which case, for example, an individual fails to tick the ubiquitous box to declare lack of consent. The notion of passive consent by the Data Protection Commissioner has been criticised by Makulilo under the Data Protection Act 2004 due to the fact that it failed to be compatible with the definition of consent. It could also be used by data controller against many data subjects who were still ignorant of the data processing of their personal data in Mauritius.[53]

The essential conditions for a valid consent are provided in section 24 of the Data Protection Act. Section 24(1) of the Act places on the data controller the burden of proof for establishing a data subject's consent to the processing of his personal data for a specified purpose. This provision is identical to Article 7(1) of the GDPR. The second condition for a valid consent is provided for in section 24(2) of the Data Protection Act. It accords the data subject the right to withdraw his consent at any time. This right is an essential part of the most important 'right to be forgotten' under Article 7(3) of the GDPR. The third condition is provided in section 28(3) of the Data Protection Act. It states that that in determining whether consent was freely given, account shall be taken of whether, inter alia, the performance of a contract, including the provision of a service, is conditional on consent to the processing of personal data that is not necessary for the performance of that contract. This condition is identical to Article 7(4) of the GDPR. The GDPR contains an additional legal ground for the lawful processing of personal data which is not present in the Data Protection Act. Article 7(2) of the GDPR requires that consent needs to be distinguishable from other matters when it is given in the context of a written declaration which also contains other matters. This clause states further that any part of the written declaration of the data subject concerning other matters which infringe the GDPR shall not be binding. The requirement in Article 7(2) is aimed at stopping the common practice whereby businesses include the text for consenting to processing of personal data in the fine print of agreements.[54]

The other legal ground for lawful processing that needs the attention of this article is section 28(1)(b)(vii) of the Data Protection Act 2017. Section 28(1)(b)(vii) of the Data Protection Act is a copycat of Article 7(f) of the GDPR. This provision governs processing of personal data on grounds of legitimate interests pursued by the controller or by a third party. It is worth noting that this provision did not exist in the repealed Data Protection Act 2004. As a result, the Mauritian data protection system was partly criticised on account of this lacuna.[55]

There are also great similarities between the Data Protection Act and the GDPR as far as the processing of special categories of personal data is concerned. The Data Protection Act defines in section 2 'special categories of personal data' as personal data pertaining to: –

- i racial or ethnic origin
- ii political opinion or adherence
- iii religious or philosophical beliefs
- iv membership of a trade union
- v physical or mental health or condition
- vi sexual orientation, practices or preferences
- vii genetic data or biometric data uniquely identifying a person
- viii commission or alleged commission of an offence by a person
- ix proceedings for an offence committed or alleged to have been committed by him, the disposal of such proceedings or the sentence of any court in the proceedings
- x such other personal data as the Commissioner may determine to be sensitive personal data.

The GDPR does not define the term special categories of personal data. Nonetheless, Article 9(1) of the GDPR provides a list of such data to include those contained in section 2 of the Data Protection Act. The GDPR does not cover processing of personal data in numbers (viii), (ix) and (x) above. It is arguable that the list of special categories of personal data under the Mauritian data protection system is broader than what is in the GDPR. This is because the Commissioner may determine additional list of sensitive data. In contrast, the list of sensitive data in Article 9(1) of the GDPR is exhaustive, so that additional types of sensitive data may not be added to it.[56]

Processing of personal data of special categories attracts more stringent conditions. First and foremost, processing of such data must comply with the legal grounds of lawful processing in section 28 of the Data Protection Act.[57] In addition, such processing must fulfil the conditions set out in section 29(1)(b) – (d) of the Act. It is important to note that the requirements of the Data Protection Act in processing special categories of personal data are similar to Article 9 of the GDPR. However, the GDPR is broader in scope than the Data Protection Act in these aspects. For example, while the GDPR covers situations of processing necessary for reasons of public health like in the case of the COVID 19 pandemic, the Data Protection Acts does not provide for such situation.

3.5. Rights of the data subject

The rights of the data subjects have been somehow strengthened under the Data Protection Act 2017. The Act provides the right of access as it was the case in the Data Protection Act. However, the provision on the right to access has been significantly improved to allow transparent processing and accountability of the data controller. Section 37 of the Data Protection Act provides for the right to information relating to processing of personal data such as the identity of the controller, the purpose of the collection of personal data as well as all the operations relating to such data. Furthermore, the right of access is made free of charge and information has to be provided timely upon request and in a written form. This is an improvement from the Data Protection Act 2004 where fees were charged in connection with the exercise of this right. The idea behind section 37 of the Data Protection Act 2017 is to enhance transparency and enable the possibility of self-determination with respect to personal data. Section 37 of the Data Protection Act corresponds to Article 15 of the GDPR. In terms of substance, both provisions are identical save for few aspects which are insignificant.

The other data subject right concerns about automated individual decision making. According to section 38 of the Data Protection Act, which is a copycat of Article 22 of the GDPR, a data subject shall have the right not to be subject to a decision based solely on automated processing, including profiling, which produces legal effects concerning him or significantly affects him. There are exceptions to this general prohibition. Such exceptions are identical in both the Data Protection Act and the GDPR.

Section 39 of the Data Protection Act covers three types of data subject rights: the right to rectification, the right to erasure (also known as the 'right to be forgotten') and the right to restriction of processing. The corresponding rights in the GDPR are covered in Articles 16, 17 and 18 respectively. To say the least, the scope and substance of section 39 of the Data Protection Act are identical to Articles 16, 17 and 18 of the GDPR. The Data Protection Act appears to reproduce the provisions of the GDPR verbatim.

The other data subject right in the Data Protection Act is the right to object. Section 40 of the Act provides that the data subject has the right to object the processing of personal data concerning him. There is one exception to this general right where the data controller demonstrates compelling legitimate grounds for the processing which override the data subject's interests, rights and freedoms or for the establishment, exercise or defence of a legal claim. The right to object extends to the processing of personal data for the purpose of direct marketing. According to section 40, the data subject may object to processing of personal data concerning him for such marketing, which includes profiling to the extent that it is related to such direct marketing. The latter is defined as the communication of any advertising or marketing material which is directed to any particular individual. The GDPR covers the right to object in Article 21. Section 40 of the Data Protection Act appears to copy and paste the provision of the GDPR.

Despite the great similarities in the provisions providing for the rights of data subjects in the Data Protection Act and the GDPR, the former does not address the right to data portability similar to Article 20 of the GDPR. Data portability is an emerging essential right in the discourse of data protection law which allows a data subject to receive the personal data concerning him from one data controller and be able to transmit it to any another controller without any hindrance as to technology. In other words, the law requires data to be provided in a machine-readable format that is supported by different technologies.

3.6. Privacy enforcement

3.6.1. The data protection office

The Data Protection Office (DPO) is the administrative institution of privacy enforcement under the Data Protection Act 2017. The Commissioner is the head of the DPO. He is assisted by other public officers. In order to qualify as Commissioner, one must be a barrister with at least five years standing at the Bar. This is in sharp contrast with the GDPR which requires specific qualifications, experience and skills in the area of protection of personal data.[58] The Data Protection Act is silent as to who appoints the Commissioner and under which terms of reference. However, *hansard* shows that the Commissioner is appointed by the Public Service Commission.[59]

Most of the functions and powers of the Commissioner in the DPA 2017 are the same as in the repealed DPA 2004. However, an addition of the new function of the Commissioner is to foster international cooperation with supervisory authorities of other countries, especially to exchange relevant information that would be necessary for the performance of his duties.[60] The functions as well as powers of the Commissioner in the DPA 2017 are typical of any supervisory authority and hence similar to the ones in Articles 57–60 of the GDPR on tasks, powers, activity report and cooperation, respectively.

The other improvement of the DPA 2017 is that it incorporates an explicit provision that the DPO shall act with complete independence and impartiality and shall not be subject to the control or direction of any other person or authority in the discharge of its functions.[61] In the Data Protection Act 2004, the Data Protection Office was closely tied to the Prime Minister's Office and accordingly the Commissioner was under general direction of Prime Minister.[62] In addition, the Commissioner and public officers in the DPO are given immunity against civil and criminal prosecutions arising from actions connected with their office.

One shortcoming of the Data Protection Act is that, it does not clearly state to whom the Data Protection Commissioner is accountable to. He is only required to lay an annual report of the activities of the DPO before the National Assembly. Arguably, this leaves a lot to be desired in terms of the security of tenure of the Commissioner and may compromise the principle of independence. The same is true with regard to the financial independence of the DPO. The Act does not state where the budget of the Office comes from and how its availability is guaranteed without putting the independence of this Office under the mercy of administrative authorities.

The question of independence of a supervisory authority is specifically dealt in Article 51(1) - (6) of the GDPR. While this provision is similar to the one in the Data Protection Act, its scope is broader than the Mauritian legislation on this aspect. For example, the GDPR has an incompatibility clause which prohibits members of the supervisory authority to engage in any incompatible occupation, whether gainful or not.[63] Similarly, the GDPR requires the supervisory authority to be provided with human, technical and financial resources, premises and infrastructure necessary for the effective performance of its tasks.[64] Since the DPO was established, the Data Protection Commissioner in Mauritius has complained about the serious shortage of staff in his office and financial resources for the efficient discharge of the functions of the DPO. In the 2018–2019 Annual Report, the Commissioner posits:

> Unfortunately, over the past years, one long outstanding problem faced by this office is the severe insufficiency of human resources, which inevitably hampers on the efficiency of service delivery. The effect of limited staff was felt even worse in 2018 because with the coming into force of the Data Protection Act 2017, the volume and complexity of work increased substantially with the introduction of new functions in line with international practices regarding personal data breaches, data protection impact assessments, certification, seals, sensitisation, auditing, security checks, hearing of complaints and preparing and swearing of information in Court for offences under the DPA.[65]

The above passage clearly shows one of the aspects likely to erode the independence of the Commissioner in Mauritius.

3.6.1.1. Enforcement powers. Section 5 of the Data Protection Act vests the Commissioner with a wide range of functions typical of any data protection authority. However, in order to carry out such functions, the Act gives the Commissioner different powers:

(a) Receiving and investigating complaints

In section 6 of the Act, the Commissioner is given powers to investigate any complaint made to his Office or cause it to be investigated by an authorised officer, unless he is of the opinion that the complaint is frivolous or vexatious. The Act further gives the Commissioner powers to undertake the amicable resolution by the parties concerned of the complaint, notify, in writing, the individual who made the complaint of his decision in relation to it so that the individual may, where he considers that he is aggrieved by the decision, appeal against it. The DPA 2017 does not change the Commissioner's power to receive and investigate complaints only that it clearly states that the Commissioner will only mediate the parties with the view of achieving an amicable resolution. Since it was established in 2004–2018, the Mauritius Data Protection Commission had decided 46 complaints.[66] The practice under the DPA 2004 shows that the Commissioner's primary focus was to mediate such complaints although the law did not clearly provide for such powers.

(b) Power to require information

The Commissioner is given powers under section 7 of the Act, to request from any person such information as is necessary or expedient for the discharge of his functions and the exercise of his powers under the Data Protection Act. These powers are only limited where there is an express written law.

(c) Preservation orders

In case of emergence, the DPA 2017 empowers the Commissioner under section 8 to apply to a Judge in Chambers for a Preservation Order for the expeditious preservation of data, including traffic data, where he has reasonable ground to believe that the data are vulnerable to loss or modification. The maximum duration of the order to remain in force is 90 days. The Commissioner may apply for extension.

(d) Enforcement notice

An enforcement notice can be issued under section 9 of the DPA 2017. The Commissioner may exercise this power where he is of the opinion that a controller or a processor has contravened, is contravening or is about to contravene the provisions of the Act. The enforcement notice normally specifies the provision contravened and measures which have to be taken within such period as specified in the notice. None compliance to the terms of the enforcement notice constitute an offence.

(e) Power to seek assistance

The Commissioner may also seek assistance in the course of discharging his duties. Particularly under section 10 of the Act, for the purpose of gathering information or for the proper conduct of any investigation, the Commissioner may seek the assistance of such person or authority as he thinks fit and that person or authority may do such things as are reasonably necessary to assist the Commissioner in the discharge of his functions.

(f) Power of entry and search

The power of entry and search are exercised by authorised officers in the Data Protection Office. According to section 11 of the Act, an authorised officer may enter and search any premises for the purpose of discharging any function or exercising any power granted under the Act. However, an authorised officer must obtain a warrant from court before he enters or searches any premises. The authorised officer must show to the owner or occupier a warrant issued by a Magistrate for the purpose entry and search. The Act allows the authorised officer to be accompanied by such person as the Commissioner may determine.

(g) Delegation of powers

The Commissioner may delegate any investigating or enforcement power conferred on him by the Act to an officer of the Office or to a police officer designated for that purpose by the Commissioner of Police.

(h) Other powers

Other categories of powers vested in the Commissioner under the DPA 2017 include power to carry out prior security checks (section 32) and power to carry out periodic audits of the systems of data controllers or processors to ensure compliance to the data protection principles (section 46). Finally, the Commissioner has powers to refer the matter to the police following a revelation of commission of offence from his investigation (section 13).

One of the shortcomings of the enforcement powers of the Commissioner is the inability to impose administrative fines for breaches of the Data Protection Act. As pointed out earlier, the Data Protection Commissioner plays mediation role when he receives complaints from data subjects. In case he fails to amicably resolve the dispute, the aggrieved person has the right of appeal. It is submitted that, the enforcement powers in the DPA 2017 is almost the same as it was in the DPA 2004. Makulilo has criticised the privacy enforcement regime in Mauritius as it undermines the main objective of the Act.[67] A similar comment has recently been made by Ammar Oozeer who posits:

> It is doubtful that a criminal law regime would greatly assist in ensuring compliance with data protection law. To date, there has been no reported prosecution and/or conviction under the Act, even though a few data controllers have been found to have contravened it. A financial penalty regime, as provided under the GDPR, would have ensured stricter compliance with data protection law.[68]

It is important to note that while the Commissioner has no power to impose administrative fines as this can only be done by a court of law, the GDPR empowers supervisory authorities to impose fines of administrative nature on controllers upon breach of the law.[69]

3.6.2. Special jurisdiction of ICT appeal tribunal

The ICT Appeal Tribunal (the Tribunal) is established under section 35 of the Information and Communication Technologies Act 2001. According to section 51 of the Data Protection Act, the Tribunal hears and determine appeals from the decisions of the Commissioner. However, an aggrieved personal who reached a settlement with the consent of parties or their representatives is barred from making appeal to the Tribunal. It is therefore important that the Commissioner fully explains the implication of any amicable resolution reached by the parties with regard to possibility of appeal prior to the commencement of the settlement process. If this is not explained, complainants who would otherwise wish to appeal would be blocked to appeal. It is important to note that, the Tribunal does not report appeals decided by it on its website nor does the DPO report such appeals on its webpage. There is therefore little knowledge to the public about the existence of appeals and available decisions. This article may not further discuss appeals from the DPO to the Tribunal due to this limitation.

3.6.3. Role played by courts

Mauritian courts have different roles in implementing the Data Protection Act. First, any entry and search under the Act has to be sanctioned by the warrant issued by the Intermediate Courts. This means that courts play an important part in the criminal investigation of any violation of the Act. Secondly, all offences committed under the Data Protection Act are heard and determined by the Intermediate Court. However, before any prosecution takes place the Director of Public Prosecutions must provide his consent. Thirdly, the Mauritian Supreme Court hears and determines appeals from the ICT Appeal Tribunal. It is interesting to note that any further appeal from the Supreme Court lie to the United Kingdom (UK) Privy Council. This is the court of last resort. Up to now, only one appeal relating to privacy has reached the UK Privy Council. This is an appeal in *Madhewoo v The State of Mauritius and another.*[70] In this appeal, *Madhewoo* challenged the constitutionality of four matters: the obligation to provide fingerprints and other biometric information under section 4 of the National Identity Card Act 1985 as amended by the National Identity Card (Miscellaneous Provisions) Act 2013, the storage of that material on the identity card under section 5, the compulsory production of an identity card to a policeman under section 7(1A) in response to a request under section 7(1)(b), and the gravity of the potential penalties under section 9(3) for non-compliance. He claims, first, that the implementation of the new biometric identity card is in breach of various sections of the Constitution coupled with section 22 of the Civil Code (which provides that everyone has the right to respect for his private life and empowers courts with competent jurisdiction to prevent or end a violation of privacy) and, secondly, that the collection and permanent storage of personal biometric data, including fingerprints, on the identity card are in breach of those sections of the Constitution and that article of the Civil Code. The Privy Council upheld the decision of the Supreme Court of Mauritius and dismissed the appeal on the ground that the action by the government to collect and store the fingerprints was saved by the derogations under the Constitution.

The role of the court with regard to civil claims is not clearly provided in the Data Protection Act which appears to have relied upon the criminal law regime as the main scheme for the enforcement of the Act. There is nowhere the Act provides for civil remedies arising from breach of the provisions of the Act. It is therefore doubtful if a complainant may institute a civil claim in court. Perhaps this may be so under section 22 of the Civil Code.

3.7. Specific issues

3.7.1. Trans-border data flow

Transfer of personal data outside Mauritius is no longer based on the adequacy decision as provided in the DPA 2004. Currently the Mauritian Data Protection Act 2017 provides under section 36 for two main situations in which personal data can be transferred outside Mauritius. First, is where there are appropriate safeguards with respect to protection of personal data as provided under section 36(1) (a) of the Act. However, the Act fails to specify what are those safeguards. Perhaps these would include binding corporate rules, standard data protection clauses or contractual clauses authorised by the Commissioner as it is the case under Article 46 of the EU GDPR. Secondly, personal data may be transferred outside of Mauritius under specific situations as provide in section 36(1) (b)–(d) of the Act.

It is worth noting that while the general rule under the GDPR restricts transfer of personal data to third countries unless they provide adequate level of protection[71] and only in the absence of adequate level of protection, transfer on the basis of appropriate safeguards and specific situations is permitted,[72] in Mauritius there is no such general restriction. Transfer is generally permitted subject to appropriate safeguards and in specific situations. How in actual practice this is going to affect transfer of personal data outside Mauritius remains unknown at the moment. Time has to pass to allow assessment of the effectiveness of the Mauritian law on this aspect.

3.7.2. Processing operations likely to present risk

This is what is sometimes referred to as *Data Protection Impact Assessment.* According to section 34 of the Act which is a copycat of Article 35 of the GDPR, where there is processing of personal data by using new technologies which is likely to result in a high risk to the rights and freedoms of natural persons, a data controller or processor will be required to carry out an impact assessment prior to the processing. The controller or processor will be required to provide the DPO with the data protection impact assessment report so as to allow the Office to make an assessment of the compliance of the processing and in particular of the risks for the protection of personal data of the data subject and of the related safeguards.

3.7.3. Data protection by design and by default

The Data Protection Act imposes a duty on controllers and processors in section 22(2)(a) and section 31(1) to implement appropriate data security and organisational measures at the time of determining the means for processing and at the time of the processing. Such measures are required to ensure that personal data are protected against unauthorised access, alteration, disclosure, accidental loss and destruction. The appropriate level of security of data must be effective. Privacy by design and by default was not part of the repealed DPA 2004. It is a new requirement based on Article 25 of the GDPR. The two provisions are identical.

3.7.4. Other important issues

The Data Protection Act 2017 imposes in sections 25 and 26, the requirement of notification of personal data breach on data controllers and processors to the DPO as well as to the data subject. These provisions reproduce Article 33 and 34 of the GDPR. Such notification has to be made within 72 h. There is also a requirement that a data controller must employ a data protection officer who would ensure in-house compliance to the Act.

4. Decisions on complaints by the data protection office

The DPO has so far (2011–2019) decided sixty-one complaints (Figure 1). Forty-five of these decisions were decided in the past eight years based on the repealed Data Protection Act 2004 while sixteen of them have been decided on the new Data Protection Act 2017 just in the first two years of the coming into operation of the Act. All of the decisions of complains of the Data Protection Commissioner are published on the official website of

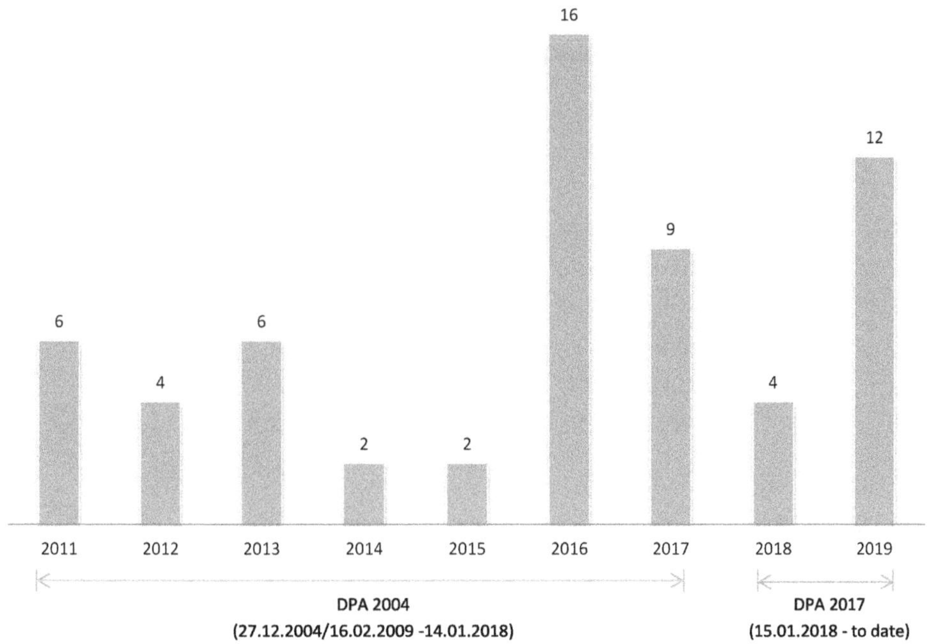

Figure 1. Decisions on complaints (2011–2019).

the DPO.[73] In relative terms, the number of complaints has increased since the Data Protection Act 2017 came into force on 15 January 2018 suggesting that the Act has provided conducive environment for individuals to exercise their fundamental right to privacy.

A breakdown of complaints types over the period from 2011 to 2018 indicates that disclosure of personal information (27%) was the prominent complaint followed by unauthorised use of CCTV footage (20%) and biometrics (20%) especially for monitoring employees' attendance at work places (Table 1, Figure 2 and 3). However, since 15 January 2018 when the Data Protection Act 2017 became operational, unauthorised use of CCTV (44%) is the prominent type of complaint followed by disclosure (33%). Overall, there is a promising future that with time the Data Protection Act 2017 will enable individuals to lay complaints to the DPO as they become aware of their rights.

Table 1. Breakdown by complaint type (2011–2019).

	DPA 2004		DPA 2017	
Type of complaints	Percentage	Totals	Percentage	Totals
Disclosure	27%	12	31%	5
Use of CCTV footage	20%	9	44%	7
Unauthorized access	4.4%	2	13%	2
Biometrics	20%	9	0%	0
Direct Marketing	11%	5	0%	0
Use of personal data	11%	5	0%	0
Retention	2.2%	1	0%	0
Request of sensitive personal data	2.2%	1	0%	0
Excessive data	2.2%	1	0%	0
E-mail monitoring	0%	0	6%	1
False and Malicious information	0%	0	6%	1
Total	100	45	100	16

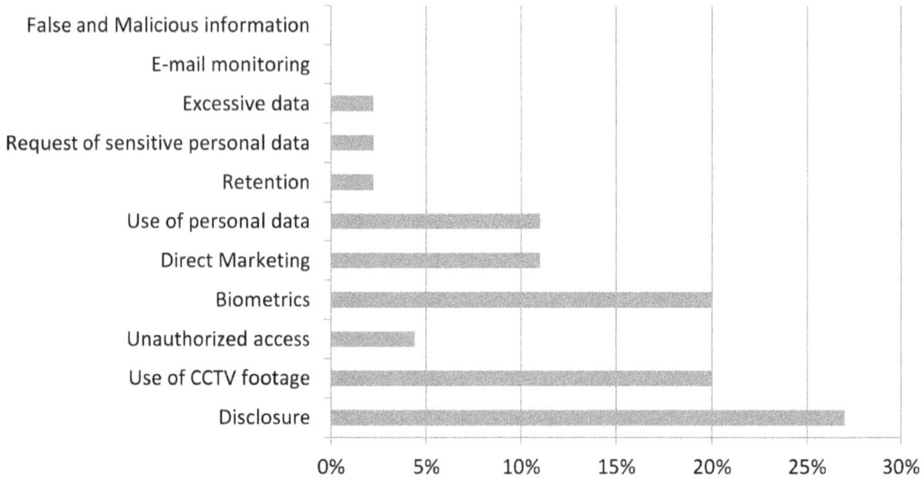

Figure 2. DPA 2004 (2011–2018) - Breakdown by complaint type.

Of all decisions given by the Commissioner over complaints reported to his Office, only nine have so far been referred to the police for prosecution. The rest of the decisions ended up by the Commissioner closing inquiries or setting them aside. It is interesting to note from the nine decisions of the Commissioner that ended up with referral to police for prosecution, the Commissioner may have reached one of the following conclusions: that the respondent was in a serious breach of the provision of the Data Protection Act or he failed to comply with enforcement notice and sometimes the respondent had failed to cooperate. However, one of the following conclusions by the Commissioner was the reason for closing or setting aside a complaint: if the Commissioner finds that there was lack of proof of the complaint; lack of cooperation from the complainant in the sense that he does not give his view or opinion in a specified time to the response from the respondent;

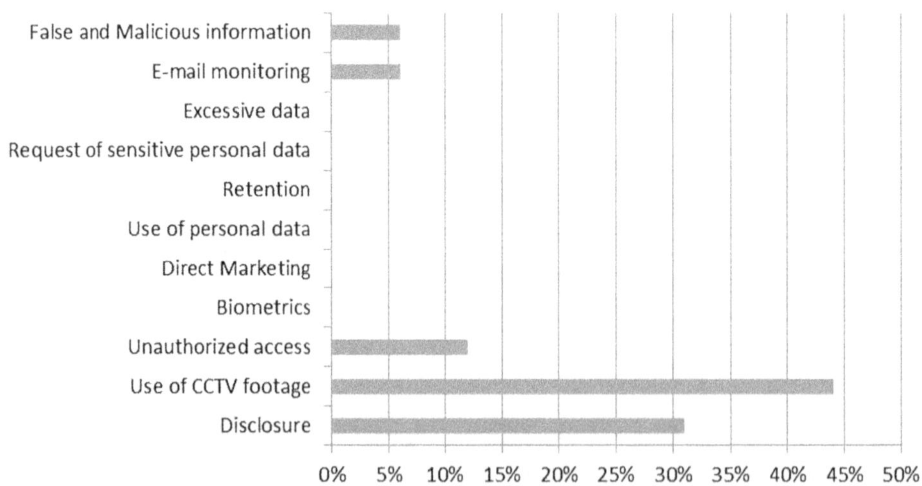

Figure 3. DPA 2017 (2018–2019) - Breakdown by complaint type.

a complainant decides to withdraw a complaint; although the Commissioner finds the respondent in breach of the provisions of the Data Protection Act she gives the respondent corrective measures through enforcement notice and the respondent complies or both parties agree to settle the matter under the guidance of the Commissioner. It is interesting to note that since the Data Protection Act 2017 came into force on 15 January 2018, there is no decision which was made by the Commissioner to refer the matter to the police for prosecution (Figure 4). This is partly due to the effective use of section 6(1)(b) of the Data Protection Act, which is a new provision empowering the Commissioner to attempt an amicable resolution by the parties concerned of the complaint.

It is important to note that the decisions of the Commissioner are relatively short. In the beginning the Commissioner gave detailed opinion on complaints reported to his Office with cited provisions of the law. However, with time he reduced the details of his opinion to one or half a page. All the decisions are published publicly on the DPO's website and annual reports of the Commissioner. The publication of the decisions of the Commissioner is subject to removing names of the parties. In addition, such decisions are numbered serially. In the past, the decisions were given reference numbers in addition to the serial numbers upon being published on DPO's website.

The time the DPO takes to complete one complaint varies from case to case depending upon the complexity of the matter involved. In his last annual report, the Commissioner has pointed out that inquiries take long because of limited human and financial resources.[74] For example, while the DPO received twenty complaints in 2018, only five of them were completed.

An analysis of early decisions (Nos. 1–10) of the complaints by the Commissioner broadly reflects the basic data protection principles laid down in the Data Protection

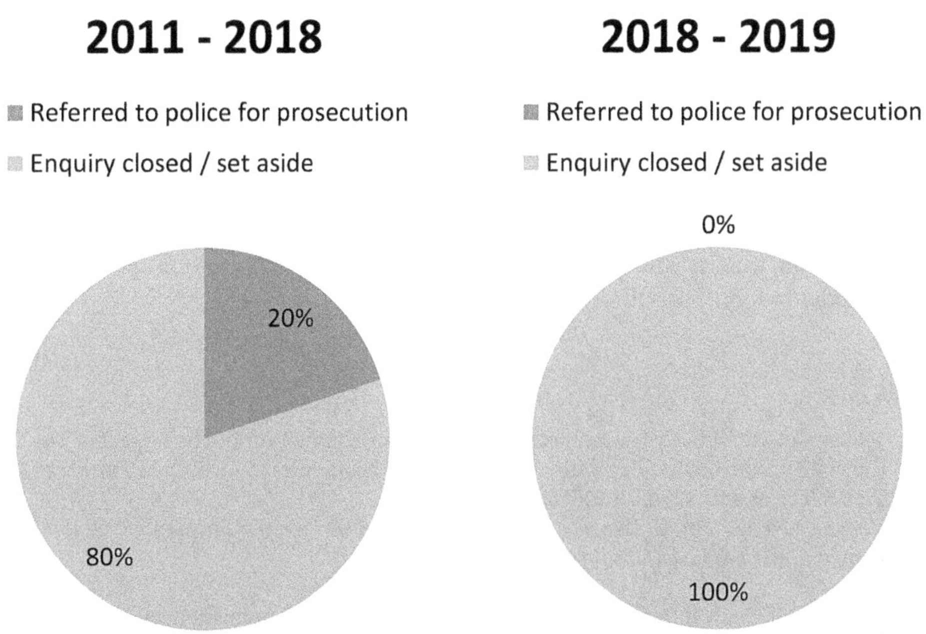

Figure 4. Complaint outcomes.

Act 2004. However, they are not consistent. Similarly, such decisions have at times taken into account factors beyond the provisions of the law.[75] In subsequent decisions the Commissioner has strived to maintain consistency. For example, she has referred to her previous decisions on unauthorised use of CCTV footage (Nos. 2,4,11,13,14,21,22,25,31,52,53,54,55,56,59,61) as well as on biometrics particularly those related to unauthorised processing of fingerprint data for attendance at workplace (No. 17,19,33,34,36,39,40,46) in deciding future complaints. Also, the Commissioner has in certain decisions cited with approval case law of the European Court of Human Rights, the Court of Justice of the European Union as well as opinion of the Article 29 of the Working Party of the European Union on a number of complex subjects such as use of biometrics in the context of employment mandatory attendance. The practice of citing foreign case law and expert opinion particularly from Europe has been largely a result of accession to the Council of Europe Convention 108 by Mauritius and attempt to obtain EU accreditation of the Mauritian data protection system. All in all, such reference has increased the quality of opinion of the Commissioner and achievement of consistency.

5. Final remarks

The comparative analysis in this article reveals that the impact of the GDPR on law reform in Mauritius is profound. The *travaux préparatoires* to both the DPA 2004 and DPA 2017 make it clear that it has been a long-term agenda by Mauritius to create a friendly environment that supports Business Process Offshoring (BPO) mostly by European companies that relocated their business operations from their countries to Mauritius. This is due to the fact that BPO is based upon exchange of personal data between the parent company and its subsidiary, which is far away from Europe. In the context of the restrictions of transfer of personal data from the EU to third countries if the latter fail to provide adequate protection of personal data, the compliance to the EU data protection standards becomes inevitable. It is arguable that the influence of the GDPR on Mauritius data protection system is not only seen in the rationale as provided in the *travaux préparatoires* but also in the textual similarities between the DPA 2017 and the GDPR. The former is mostly a copycat of the latter. It is also important to note that there has been little and/or no influence from the human rights instruments applicable to Mauritius (ICCPR, ACHPR), on the data protection law reform in the country. This is also the case with data protection treaties and policies such as the Malabo Convention as well as the SADC Model Law on Data Protection.

Notes

1. Tiffany Curtiss, 'Privacy Harmonization and The Developing World: The Impact of The EU's General Data Protection Regulation on Developing Economies', *Washington Journal of Law, Technology & Arts* 12, no. 1 (2016): 97.
2. Viviane Reding, 'The Upcoming Data Protection Reform for the European Union Viviane Reding', *International Data Privacy Law* 1, no. 1 (2011): 4.
3. Ibid.
4. Proposal for General Data Protection Regulation (European Commission, 2012), https://eur-lex.europa.eu/LexUriServ/LexUriServ.do?uri=COM:2012:0011:FIN:EN:PDF (accessed May 20, 2020).

5. See the Explanatory Memorandum to the Data Protection Bill (No. XV of 2004) which expressly states that the object of this Bill is to provide for the protection of the privacy rights of individuals in view of the developments in the techniques used to capture, transmit, manipulate, record or store data relating to individuals.
6. See The parliamentary discussion (Hansard) of 1 June 2004, Mauritius National Assembly, Debate No. 12 of 01.06.04, Public Bills: Data Protection Bill (No. XV of 2004), pp. 77–78.
7. See, e.g. Mauritius National ICT Policy 2007–2011, pp. 1–18, at pp. 7–8.
8. Drudeisha Madhub, 'Data Protection Implications for Our DNA Bill', Awareness Workshop on Legal Aspects of the Use of Human DNA, 9.06.2009, http://dataprotection.govmu.org/English/Publications/Pages/Presentation.aspx (accessed May 20, 2020).
9. Mauritius Data Protection Office, First Annual Report of the Data Protection Commissioner February 2009-February 2010, p. 4, http://dataprotection.govmu.org/English/Documents/Publications/annrep150611.pdf (accessed May 20, 2020).
10. Mauritius National ICT Policy 2007–2011, pp. 1–18, at pp. 7–8.
11. Lee A Bygrave, 'Data Protection Pursuant to the Right to Privacy in Human Rights Treaties', *International Journal of Law and Information Technology* 6 (1998): 247–84.
12. *Madhewoo v. The State of Mauritius & Another* 2015 SCJ 177, https://ionnews.mu/wp-content/uploads/2015/05/Biometric-ID-Card_Madhewoo-vs-State.pdf (accessed May 20, 2020).
13. See, e.g. Universal Declaration of Human Rights 1948 (Article 12); International Covenant on Civil and Political Rights (ICCPR) 1966 (Article 17); Convention on the Rights of the Child 1989 (Article 16); Convention for the Protection of Human Rights and Fundamental Freedoms 1950 (Article 8); and Arab Charter on Human Rights 2004 (Article 21).
14. Kinfe Micheal Yilma and Alebachew Birhanu, 'Safeguards of Right to Privacy in Ethiopia: A Critique of Laws and Practices', *Journal of Ethiopian Law* 26, no. 1 (2013): 106; See also., Kinfe Micheal Yilma, 'Data Privacy Law and Practice in Ethiopia,' *International Data Privacy Law* 5, no. 3 (2015): 180.
15. Nani Jansen Reventlow and Rosa Curling, 'The Unique Jurisdiction of the African Court on Human and People's Rights: Protection of Human Rights Beyond the African Charter', *Emory International Law Review* 2 (2019): 208.
16. Mauritius, State Report, https://www.achpr.org/states/detail?id=33 (accessed May 20, 2020).
17. African Union, List of countries which have signed, ratified/acceded to the African Union Convention on Cyber Security and Personal Data Protection 2014, https://au.int/sites/default/files/treaties/29560-sl-AFRICAN%20UNION%20CONVENTION%20ON%20CYBER%20SECURITY%20AND%20PERSONAL%20DATA%20PROTECTION.pdf (accessed May 20, 2020).
18. For a critical appraisal of the data protection principles of the Malabo Convention, see Lukman Adebisi Abdulrauf and Charles Manga Fombad, 'The African Union's Data Protection Convention 2014: A Possible Cause for Celebration of human rights in Africa?' *Journal of Media Law* 8, no. 1 (2016): 67–97.
19. SADC Model Law on Data Protection 2012.
20. SADC Data Protection Model Law, Art 2(1).
21. GDPR, Art 1.
22. Dan Jerker B. Svantesson, 'Article 3. Territorial Scope', in The EU General Data Protection Regulation (GDPR): A Commentary, eds. Christopher Kuner, Lee A. Bygrave, Christopher Docksey (Oxford: Oxford University Press, 2020), 95; Dan Jerker B. Svantesson, 'Extraterritoriality in the Context of Data Privacy Regulation', *Masaryk University Journal of Law and Technology* 7, no. 1 (2013): 87–96.
23. See, the GDPR, Part II.
24. Explanatory Memorandum to the First Draft Proposal of the GDPR, p. 8.
25. GDPR, Art. 17.
26. GDPR, Art. 20.
27. GDPR, Art. 35.
28. GDPR, Art. 37.
29. GDPR, Arts. 33 & 34.

30. Graham Greenleaf, *Asian Data Privacy Laws, Trade and Human Rights Perspectives* (Oxford: Oxford University Press, 2014), 31.
31. GDPR, Recital 105.
32. See, e.g. CRID, University of Namur (Belgium)., 'Analysis of the adequacy of protection of personal data provided in Mauritius: draft final report, 2010; Alex B. Makulilo, 'Data Protection Regimes in Africa: Too Far from European 'Adequacy' Standard?' *International Data Privacy Law* 3, no. 1 (2013): 42–50.
33. Tira Green, 'Ensuring the Compliance of the Data Protection Legislation and Principles of Mauritius with EU Standards', Framework Contract Beneficiaries – Lot 07, Letter of Contract No. 2009/ 272357, Final Report, 9 December 2011.
34. Some of the innovations contained in the Protocol are the following: stronger requirements regarding the proportionality and data minimisation principles, and lawfulness of the processing; extension of the types of sensitive data, which will now include genetic and biometric data, trade union membership and ethnic origin; obligation to declare data breaches; greater transparency of data processing; new rights for the persons in an algorithmic decision making context, which are particularly relevant in connection with the development of artificial intelligence; stronger accountability of data controllers; requirement that the "privacy by design" principle is applied; application of the data protection principles to all processing activities, including for national security reasons, with possible exceptions and restrictions subject to the conditions set by the Convention, and in any case with independent and effective review and supervision; clear regime of transborder data flows; reinforced powers and independence of the data protection authorities and enhancing legal basis for international cooperation.
35. See, e.g. Alex B. Makulilo, 'African Accession to Council of Europe Privacy Convention 108: Moving Towards Stronger Privacy Protection', *Datenschutz und Datensicherheit-DuD* 41, no. 6 (2017): 364–7.
36. Republic of Mauritius, Budget Speech 2017-2018, Paragraph 133, http://budget.mof.govmu.org/budget2017-18/2017_18budgetspeech.pdf (accessed May 20, 2020).
37. Art. 57(7) GDPR.
38. Mauritius National Assembly, Debate No. 19 of 08.12.2017, Public Bills: Data Protection Bill (No. XIX of 2017), pp. 58–60.
39. Data Protection Act, s. 3(3).
40. Data Protection Act, s. 3(1) & (2).
41. Data Protection Act, s. 3(4) (a).
42. Data Protection Act, s. 3(4) (b).
43. Data Protection Act, s. 3(5).
44. See Part 2.2(e) of this article for a detailed discussion about the overreaching effect of Article 3(2) of the GDPR.
45. Data Protection Act, s. 44(2).
46. GDPR, Art. 89.
47. GDPR, Article 6 (1) (a) Consent: the individual has given clear consent for you to process their personal data for a specific purpose; (b) Contract: the processing is necessary for a contract you have with the individual, or because they have asked you to take specific steps before entering into a contract; (c) Legal obligation: the processing is necessary for you to comply with the law (not including contractual obligations); (d) Vital interests: the processing is necessary to protect someone's life; (e) Public task: the processing is necessary for you to perform a task in the public interest or for your official functions, and the task or function has a clear basis in law; (f) Legitimate interests: the processing is necessary for your legitimate interests or the legitimate interests of a third party, unless there is a good reason to protect the individual's personal data which overrides those legitimate interests. This cannot apply if you are a public authority processing data to perform your official tasks.

48. Waltraut Kotschy, 'Article 6. Lawfulness of Processing', in *The EU General Data Protection Regulation (GDPR): A Commentary*, eds. Christopher Kuner, Lee A. Bygrave, Christopher Docksey (Oxford: Oxford University Press, 2020), 329.
49. CRID, University of Namur (Belgium)., 'Analysis of the adequacy of protection of personal data provided in Mauritius: draft final report, 2010, pp. 26–7.
50. Kotschy, 'Article 6', 335.
51. Data Protection Act, s. 28(1)(b)(viii).
52. Data Protection Act, s. 28(1) (a).
53. Alex B. Makulilo, "Peel off the Mask': Enforcement of the Data Protection Act in Mauritius', *Datenschutz und Datensicherheit-DuD* 38, no. 12 (2014): 845–9.
54. Eleni Kosta, 'Article7. Conditions for Consent', in *The EU General Data Protection Regulation (GDPR): A Commentary*, eds. Christopher Kuner, Lee A. Bygrave, Christopher Docksey (Oxford: Oxford University Press, 2020), 350.
55. See, e.g. CRID, University of Namur (Belgium)., 'Analysis of the adequacy of protection of personal data provided in Mauritius: draft final report, 2010.
56. Ludmila Georgieva and Christopher Kuner, 'Article9. Processing of Special Categories of Personal Data', in *The EU General Data Protection (GDPR): A Commentary*, eds. Christopher Kuner, Lee A. Bygrave, Christopher Docksey (Oxford: Oxford University Press, 2020), 373.
57. Data Protection Act, s. 29(1)(a).
58. GDPR, Art. 53(2).
59. Mauritius National Assembly, Debate No. 19 of 08.12.2017, Public Bills: Data Protection Bill (No. XIX of 2017), pp. 58–60.
60. Data Protection Act 2017, sec 5(j).
61. Data Protection Act 2017, s. 4(2).
62. Data Protection Act 2004, s. 21.
63. GDPR, Art. 51(3).
64. GDPR, Art. 51(4).
65. Mauritius Data Protection Office, Annual Report of the Data Protection Commissioner January – December 2018, p. 9.
66. Mauritius Data Protection Office., Decisions on Complaints', http://dataprotection.govmu.org/English/Pages/Decisions-on-Complaints.aspx (accessed May 20, 2020). For a critical analysis of complaints decided by the Commissioner see, Alex B. Makulilo, 'Mauritius Data Protection Commission: An Analysis of its Early Decisions', *International Data Privacy Law* 3, no. 2 (2013): 131–9.
67. Makulilo, supra note 21, p. 848.
68. Ellen O'Brien, 'Mauritius: Data Protection Bill Should "in principle" Lead to EU Adequacy', *DataGuidance*, December 7, 2017, https://www.dataguidance.com/mauritius-data-protection-bill-principle-provide-eu-adequacy/ (accessed May 20, 2020).
69. GDPR, Art. 83.
70. *Madhewoo (Appellant) v The State of Mauritius and another (Respondents) (Mauritius)*, Privy Council Appeal No 0006 of 2016 [2016] UKPC 30, https://www.jcpc.uk/cases/docs/jcpc-2016-0006-judgment.pdf (accessed May 20, 2020). For a critical review of *Madhewoo (Appellant) v The State of Mauritius and another (Respondents) (Mauritius)*, read Roopanand Mahadew, 'Does the Mauritian Constitution Protect the Right to Privacy? An Insight from *Madhewoo v The State of Mauritius*', *African Human Rights Law Journal* 18, no. 1 (2018): 189–204.
71. GDPR, Art. 45.
72. GDPR, Arts. 46–9.
73. Mauritius Data Protection Office., Decisions on Complaints', http://dataprotection.govmu.org/English/Pages/Decisions-on-Complaints.aspx (accessed May 20, 2020). The author has presented such decisions of complaints in charts and tables to ease their analysis and discussion.
74. Mauritius Data Protection Office, Annual Report January to December 2018, 10th Edition, p. 9.

75. Alex B. Makulilo, 'Mauritius Data Protection Commission: An Analysis of its Early Decisions', *International Data Privacy Law* 3, no. 2 (2013): 131–9.

Disclosure statement

No potential conflict of interest was reported by the author(s).

From privacy to data protection: the road ahead for the Inter-American System of human rights

Carlos Affonso Souza, Caio César de Oliveira, Christian Perrone and Giovana Carneiro

ABSTRACT

The right to privacy and data protection are key elements to understand how data has become the centerpiece of many changes in human interaction, new business models and technological development in an increasingly hyperconnected world. In a so-called data driven economy, the task of asserting principles, concepts and legal bases for data processing is fundamental to devise how such rights can be indeed protected. The Inter-American System of Human Rights recognises this right. In contrast to the European system that since 2000 recognises the right to data protection as an autonomous right – differentiating it from the right to privacy – the Inter-American System is on track to improve the standards of protection of both rights. Considering all thirty-five States of the Americas, eighteen have a specific data protection regulation; seven are discussing the Bill and eleven do not have a specific data protection regulation. The purpose of this article is to present the stage of development of the inter-American System of Human Rights in relation to the protection of the right to privacy and data protection and also demonstrate the challenges that such system will have to face as it move towards the effective guarantee of such rights.

1. Introduction

The Inter-American Human Rights System (IAHRS) is a regional human rights system responsible for monitoring, promoting, and protecting human rights in the 35 independent countries of the Americas that are members of the Organization of American States (OAS).[1]

The IAHRS is composed by two organs: the Inter-American Commission on Human Rights (IACHR) and the Inter-American Court of Human Rights ('the Court' or 'IACtHR'). The IACHR is an autonomous quasi-judicial organ established by the Charter of the OAS in 1959. Its mandate is to promote and protect human rights in the American hemisphere, overseeing all thirty-five member States of the OAS. The Court is a judicial organ established under the American Convention on Human Rights, whose purpose is to interpret and apply the convention in a adjudicatory and advisory fashion.[2]

The IACHR's work is on three main pillars: an individual petition system, where individuals and groups of individuals may denounce violations of human rights committed by the States under the jurisdiction they are in; a overall monitoring mechanism, which provides both general overview of the trends and meta-trends of human rights' advancements and challenges; and a advisory and technical cooperation apparatus that can guide States towards fulfilling their human rights obligations.[3] Under such framework the Commission collaborates with the States enhancing laws, practices, policies, and institutions in order to improve the conditions of all person under the jurisdictions of the Americas.

Thus, the IACHR has both quasi-jurisdictional mechanisms and non-jurisdictional mechanisms in order to advance human rights standards and contributing to State action in the field. This means the commission is organised internally broadly in two different areas, one dealing with petitions and cases and another with both monitoring and technical assistance and cooperation.[4] The work is supported by eight thematic rapporteurships, two special rapporteurships – one for Freedom of Expression (which has taken a leadership role in the topic of this article) and another on Economic, Social, Cultural, and Environmental Rights – and three institutional thematic units.[5] The idea is to provide a broad view on the rights of a particular vulnerable group or on relevant overarching theme.

The Court serves as the interpretative institution for the American Convention and for the net of human rights instruments that countries in the Americas are a part of.[6] It not only interprets the convention within a particular case presented to it, but also has a guidance function whenever an advisory opinions is requested.[7]

The IAHRS, thus, deal with a broad range of thematic issues regarding both concrete individual violations and general guidance. The Commission can set its own agenda and has done so in the past taking into consideration the major human rights issues of the Continent and prioritising them under its own thematic and rights-based concerns. The Court, on the other hand, cannot act *motu proprio*, yet has some relative latitude towards its analysis of rights taking into consideration a wide range of factors, including national and international legislative and judicial developments.

The right to privacy has always been a topic of heated debate in the IAHRS. It has appeared under different headings, as a right to be left alone, as a guarantee of personal development, of family life and a as part and parcel of the formation of individual opinion and thought within a democratic society. New technologies have changed the context in with this right is exercised.

The Internet, for instance, has changed the way humans relate to each-other, produce and consume information. Individuals stopped being just receivers and started to be producers of content and with this an intense volume of information has been formed. Other types of technologies such as smartphones and the digitalisation and 'sensorization' of many aspects of society have allowed for a lot more records on many more elements including many aspects of each individual's life. This means a gargantuan increase in the volume of personal data in circulation, thus, reframing the traditional meaning of privacy; waking us up for a desire of control and transparency in the treatment of such personal data.[8]

The IAHRS has not been inert to such a phenomenon as the development in the understanding of the right to privacy has evolved. A few reports, particularly of the Special

Rapporteurship for Freedom of Expression, have pointed out to the dimension of data protection for the right to privacy. Yet, the agenda of the IAHRS has not caught up with the other human rights systems not even with the countries in the Americas.

Taking into considering that out of the thirty-five States of the Americas, eighteen already have a specific data protection regulation; seven are discussing a bill and only ten do not have a specific general data protection regulation, it can be inferred the relative importance of the topic for the Region. This includes the fact that some of the countries do have already added as a constitutional stand-alone guarantee the dimension of data protection to the right of privacy.

The purpose of this article is to present the stage of development of the IAHRS in relation to the protection of the right to privacy and data protection. It will seek to map out the development from a right of privacy in a traditional sense to its data privacy dimension within the IAHRS. Later, it will propose that a majority of the countries in the region – both of parties and not of the American Convention on Human Rights – have advanced, particularly in the last few years, towards a data privacy regulation. From that it can be inferred the relative importance of personal data protection for the understanding of the right of privacy in the Americas. Finally, after an overview of the certain technologies and their potential impact for the right of data privacy, the article aims at demonstrating the challenges that the IAHRS will have to face as it moves towards the effective guarantee of such right.

The proposal here is that in view of the relevance of data privacy for personal development and for the future of the exercise of many other human rights and inline with the complexity of the matter and its many different technological aspects, the Commission should move the topic beyond a marginal aspect viewed mostly by the Special Rapporteur for Freedom of Expression and streamline it. This will provide the stuffing for more harmonised regional human rights standards and eventually settled decisions of the IACtHR.

2. The development of the right to privacy in the Inter-American System of human rights

2.1. The development of the right to data privacy in other human rights systems

Privacy is a constantly changing concept. The definition of Brandeis and Warren, in 1890, in the famous article 'The Right to Privacy',[9] in which privacy is seen as *a right to be left alone*, is remarkable. Back then, the challenges that new technologies could pose for personality rights were discussed.

It is possible to note that the concept of privacy has come to be related to a guard against third party interference and, currently, in an economy driven by the processing of personal data, privacy is related to the control of personal data.

The different human rights systems have recognised data protection as either a stand-alone right or as a dimension of the right to privacy. The European Human Rights System, for instance was crucial for the development of privacy and for data protection to be included as a protected cluster right.[10] This is particularly true taking into consideration Convention 108 (Council of Europe's Convention for the protection of individuals with regard to automatic processing of personal data, 1981), the only multilateral international treaty open to universal ratification.[11] It provides a framework for dealing with protection of personal data within the context of automatic processing.[12] This was a watershed moment where the Council of Europe proved to be at the vanguard of the safeguard of the interests of privacy through the international protection of personal data.

The European Convention on Human Rights (ECHR), however, had its focus for long on the context of 'private life'.[13] For the most part, it still is, as the European Court of Human Rights (ECtHR) understands that the 'essential object of article 8 of the ECHR [right to privacy] is to protect the individual against arbitrary action by the public authorities'.[14]

Early on, however, the European Human Rights System understood that privacy and private life under the Convention was an elastic, broad term that encompassed both negative and positive obligations.[15] The notion that such right covers not only the interest to be left alone, but also to build one's own personality and relationship with other individuals and to the world was very soon acknowledged.[16] Personal autonomy was brought to the forefront and became one of the main pillars underpinning a whole dimension of the article 8 of the ECHR.

Such autonomy was seen as embracing the protection of 'multiple aspects of a person's physical and social identity'.[17] Control over its own information was seen as paramount.[18] A series of cases regarding health data underscored the necessary need for a protection of personal information, later understood by the ECHR as personal data.[19] The ECtHR itself moved to connect privacy with data protection and used the definition of personal data from Convention 108 as a stepping stone to interpret the rights of personal and family life.[20]

It is not hard to perceive the direction the European System has taken. The guarantee to a private and family life has led to the need to safeguard the development of human personality, which branched out to the defense of personal autonomy and human agency through the protection of personal information[21] and personal data.[22]

This was not a matter covered solely by human rights instruments. In 1980, the Organization for Economic Co-operation and Development (OECD) has published guidelines and principles for the processing of personal data: (i) Collection Limitation Principle; (ii) Data Quality Principle; (iii) Purpose Specification Principle; (iv) Use Limitation Principle; (v) Security Safeguards Principle; (vi) Openness Principle; (vi) Individual Participation Principle and; (vii) Accountability Principle.[23] To this day such principles are understood as the backbone of data privacy and are an integral inspiration of most data protection laws.

It should be noted that the developments within the European Union with the approval of Directive 46/95 and later the General Data Protection Regulation (GDPR – Reg. 679/2016)[24] have influenced and, in many ways, strengthened the cluster of rights involved in privacy and data protection. Not to mention, the approval of the Charter of Fundamental Rights of the EU has crystalised the relevance of privacy and data protection within that Region.

The European Human Rights System, based on the Council of Europe, does not directly follows the path taken by the EU. The ECHR, as a much older instrument, has not been updated to reflect the advances of time and grant data protection an autonomous standing as much as the aforementioned Charter of the EU.[25] Yet, the regulations issued from the EU have served as a beacon and a much needed source of inspiration. The European System strives to maintain a unity that represents the continents cultural heritage, which encompass as well the dimension of data protection and the emerging consensus that comes from the majority of the member states that data protection is a protected dimension of the right to private life and privacy.

It is clear that the right to privacy has evolved in Europe and that it has added a dimension of data protection, even if, originally the ECHR had not and could not have foreseen such developments. The Court in Strasbourg understood that it was harmonious with the spirit of the convention and its objectives coupled with growing national consensus that data protection was part of the cluster of rights protected under article 8 of the ECHR.

The same way it happened in the European Union, action by the IAHRS would be valuable to the harmonic emergence, within the States of the Americas, of a data protection fundamental right. In this sense, it is possible to say that the European model is a source of inspiration for the IAHRS as explored below.

2.2. Data privacy in the Inter-American System of human rights

The right to privacy at the IAHRS developed following an emphasis on private life, family life, protection of home and communications.[26] This is probably so due to the very language of article 11 of the American Convention,[27] where the aforementioned expressions are directly present and data protection *per se* is not.[28]

The content and scope of the right, however, has had an asymmetrical development comparing to other systems, particularly from Europe.[29] On the European side, there was an explicit recognition that 'data protection' felt within the protections afforded by the Regional Human Rights System. Within the Americas, as much as in the Universal Human Rights System,[30] the lack of specific autonomous rights may have afforded a protected development of a deeper understanding of the personal data dimensions of privacy as a human right.[31]

As will be explored bellow, the countries in the Hemisphere have not shied away from having their own set of rules proving a body of regulation to data protection. It is true that not all States have enshrined data protection in their Constitutions,[32] nor it is an unanimity to have an *omnibus* data protection legislation. Yet, as it will be argued, data protection had become a wide concern for at least wide majority of the Continent.

The European Human Rights System has set its own trail from a focus on a negative obligation of non-interference on a personal life and family – privacy in a traditional, brandeisian way, to be left alone – to the upholding of data protection. The IAHRS has given signs to follow in much the similar way.

The concept of privacy, as understood in the Americas, goes beyond solely the right to be left alone or no interference in someone's residence or correspondence. For instance, monitoring, recording and publishing of conversations and communications are encompassed within the right to privacy (private life).[33] The IACtHR has already recognised that '[t]oday, the fluidity of information places the individual's right to privacy at greater risk owing to the new technological tools and their increased use'.[34]

This notion is perceived, then, as 'a wide-ranging term, which cannot be defined exhaustively'[35], '[it] includes the way in which the individual views himself and to what extent and how he decides to project this view to others'.[36] The Court goes on and expands:

The protection of private life encompasses a series of factors associated with the dignity of the individual, including, for example, the ability to develop his or her own personality and aspirations, to determine his or her own identity and to define his or her own personal relationships. The concept of private life encompasses aspects of physical and social identity, including the right to personal autonomy, personal development and the right to establish and develop relationships with other human beings and with the outside world. The effective exercise of the right to private life is decisive for the possibility of exercising personal autonomy on the future course of relevant events for a person's quality of life. Private life includes the way in which individual views himself and how he decides to project this view towards others and is an essential condition for the free development of the personality.[37]

Thus, the IACtHR has set the basic tenets to understand privacy in an expansive fashion, plastic enough to encompass a personal data protection dimension. The IACtHR has noted the connection of privacy with personal autonomy and the possibility of developing one's own self-image, personality and identity. The terrain is prepared for the recognition of autonomy over one's own information akin to a right of data protection.

In fact, the IACHR has recognised since 2013 that the right to privacy protects at least four legal rights: (a) the right to have an individual sphere impervious to arbitrary interference from the State or third parties; (b) the right to govern oneself by one's own rules defined autonomously according to one's individual life plan; (c) the right to the confidentiality of all the data produced in that private space, with a corresponding prohibition on disclosure or circulation of information captured without the consent of its owner, in that space of private protection reserved for the individual; and (d) the right to one's own image.[38]

In addition, the Commission 'highlighted that it is crucial to *develop rules for data protection* that regulate the storage, processing, and use of personal data, as well as its transfer, whether among State entities or third parties'.[39]

The Special Rapporteur for Freedom of Expression has also manifested that the protection of personal data works *pari-passu* with the right to privacy. Actually, there is a concern that 'the growing processing power of computers exacerbates the challenge as information can be harvested from multiple sources, processed and re-processed and then sold on. In fact the entire business model of the most successful companies directly impinges upon the right to privacy'.[40] Thus, the Rappourteur stated that '[t]o protect privacy on the Internet, the confidentiality of personal online data must be guaranteed'.[41] Even more so, it includes the protection of personal data as one of 'five [...] challenges that arise or are magnified by the phenomenon of the Internet'.[42]

More recently, the Special Rapporteur, considering the situation of freedom of expression in Cuba, took notice and manifested its concerns regarding data protection online, particularly, the recollection of personal data by the government in the island.[43] This shows that data protection has entered the agenda of the IACHR, even if, it has not been articulated in a case or given a specific standing in an independent document.

Within the Organization of American States (OAS) in general, as will be developed below (topic 3.1), the Inter-American Juridical Committee has published a Guide of Principles on Privacy and Personal Data Protection, which recognises the interrelation of privacy and data protection.[44] This highlights the relevance given by the States in the region to the subject and the importance of the IAHRS to be prepared to face the issue head on.

3. Data protection as a right – where does it stand in the Americas?

As it can be noted, the right to privacy is ripe for development in the Intern-American system. Yet, data protection has not yet blossomed as a stand-alone dimension of such right. Most of the references to data privacy tend to relate to general reports particularly issued from the Special Rapporteur for Freedom of Expression. This does not seem to reflect the importance of the matter given by the majority of the States in the Region and for the OAS as such where the Human Rights System is one of its four pillars.[45]

Specifically on data protection, both the OAS and the States of the Americas have taken steps towards an approach regarding privacy that fully considers the digital age, therefore treating data privacy as a significant dimension of a fundamental right to be protected. This approach on data protection should have echo in the IAHRS, in order to provide an extra layer of protection and to properly consider it a human right part of the scope of the right to privacy. Therefore, at this point the article aims to paint a full picture of the OAS's initiatives and of the local developments on data protection.

3.1. Data protection and the Organization of American States

The OAS has recognised the relevance of data protection from an early stage. It has taken into consideration the important points of convergence between access to information and data protection. Between 2003 and 2010, the OAS' General Assembly have published Resolutions on Access to Public Information and also a Model Inter-American Law on Access to Public Information, adopted in 2010.[46] The Model Inter-American Law on Access to Public Information already mentioned 'data protection', stating in a commentary to the Model Law that 'data protection regimes should live harmoniously with the access to information legislation'.[47]

On data protection itself, considering both public and private sectors, the Department of International Law presented the Draft Preliminary Principles and Recommendations on the Protection of Personal Data[48] (revised in 2011). Afterwards, via General Assembly Resolution AG/RES.2661, the Organization has paved the way for further action on data protection, considering 'the growing importance of privacy and the protection of personal data, and the need to encourage and protect cross-border flows of information in the Americas'.[49]

In 2012, instructed by this Resolution, the OAS' Department of International Law released a comparative study on data protection in the Americas, presenting national legal frameworks of eleven countries in details and international instruments on privacy and data protection.[50] The document was an important contribution to the international community, especially the thirty-five States of America, as it was the first document elaborated by a public international organisation focused in the Region. A further and update analyses on the local legal framework will be provided later in this article, but that comparative study was just the initial step to the actions the OAS would take in the coming years.

In 2015, the Inter-American Juridical Committee released a proposed legislative guide on data protection for the States of the Americas, based on a set of 12 reviewed Principles from the initial 2010s draft. The report itself states that 'In the Rapporteur's view, the field of personal privacy and data protection continues to be characterised by rapid technological developments as well as constantly evolving threats to personal privacy'[51], clearly showing the connection between privacy and data protection.

3.1.1. OAS Principles on privacy and personal data protection

As stated above, the Principles were elaborated with the intention to provide a guide to local legal implementation in the States of the Americas. As stated in the document:

> Each Member State must decide how best to implement these Principles in its domestic legal system. Whether by means of legislation, regulations or other mechanisms, Member States should establish effective rules for personal data protection that give effect to the individual's right to privacy and demonstrate respect for their personal data, while at the same time safeguarding the individual's right to benefit from the free flow of information and access to the digital economy.[52]

The twelve principles (and official definitions)[53] are:

(1) Lawful and fair purposes (Personal data should be collected only for lawful purposes and by fair and lawful means);
(2) Clarity and consent (The purposes for which personal data is collected should be specified at the time the data is collected. As a general rule, personal data should only be collected with the consent of the individual concerned);
(3) Relevant and necessary (The data should be accurate, relevant and necessary to the stated purposes for which it is collected);
(4) Limited use and retention (Personal data should be kept and used only in a lawful manner not incompatible with the purpose(s) for which it was collected. It should not be kept for longer than necessary for that purpose or purposes and in accordance with relevant domestic law);
(5) Duty of confidentiality (Personal data should not be disclosed, made available or used for purposes other than those for which it was collected except with the knowledge or consent of the concerned individual or under the authority of law);
(6) Protection and security (Personal data should be protected by reasonable and appropriate security safeguards against unauthorised access, loss, destruction, use, modification or disclosure);
(7) Accuracy of Data (Personal data should be kept accurate and up-to-date to the extent necessary for the purposes of use);
(8) Access and correction (Reasonable methods should be available to permit individuals whose personal data has been collected to seek access to that data and to request that the data controller amend, correct or delete that data. If such access or correction needs to be restricted, the specific grounds for any such restrictions should be specified in accordance with domestic law);
(9) Sensitive personal data (Some types of personal data, given its sensitivity in particular contexts, are especially likely to cause material harm to individuals if misused. Data controllers should adopt privacy and security measures that are commensurate with the sensitivity of the data and its capacity to harm individual data subjects);
(10) Accountability (Data controllers should adopt and implement appropriate procedures to demonstrate their accountability for compliance with these Principles);

(11) Trans-border flow of data and accountability (Member States should cooperate with one another in developing mechanisms and procedures to ensure that data controllers operating in more than one jurisdiction can be effectively held accountable for their adherence to these Principles);
(12) Disclosing Exceptions (When national authorities make exceptions to these Principles for reasons relating to national sovereignty, internal or external security, the fight against criminality, regulatory compliance or other public order policies, they should make those exceptions known to the public).

There is no study so far on whether these principles were or not adopted in the local legal frameworks, but, as it will be seen in the next topic, many developments have occurred in the Region between 2015 and today. Many new bills on data protection have been proposed and some such as the Brazilian General Data Protection Legislation and the Argentinian data protection reform of 2018 have gain shape an incorporate many aspect present in the legislative guide.

Although data protection's approaches vary within the States of the Americas, regarding its scope and content, its regulation as in the right to privacy's umbrella is notorious. In any case, the proposal of a set of Principles by the OAS on data protection demonstrates the concern and development of the right of data privacy, which should resonate in the IAHRS.

3.2. Data protection and the 35 States of the Americas

If the IAHRS has yet to directly spell out data protection as a part of the cluster of rights pertaining to the protection of personal and family life and privacy; the States of the Americas have already started establishing their own domestic data protection framework. They are joining an international trend that in many ways is being fostered by Europe and in which legislations such as the articles 7 and 8 of the EU Charter of Fundamental Rights and the EU General Data Protection Regulation (GDPR) are particularly crucial examples. Such regulatory frameworks tend to provide a basis for a domestic protection of the right to data protection as a cluster right for privacy.[54]

This international trend, according to the United Nations Conference on Trade and Development (UNCTAD) database on Data Protection and Privacy Legislation Worldwide[55], accounts for at least 107 countries around the globe that have a legislation to secure the protection of data and privacy. This part aims to call attention to the fact that many of the thirty-five members of the OAS' member states are included in that number. The countries have realised the need to regulate data protection for social, economic and political reasons. Firstly, business development and the protection of rights of individuals needed to be equalized.[56] Secondly, the frameworks needed to be adapted to a digitalised economy, result of the rapid technological advancement.[57] Finally, data protection started to be a trade concern, as the individuals' right to data protection needed to be foreseen also in trade agreements and international cooperation instruments.[58]

As it will be seen, data protection is already a concern in the Region and the States have, in its majority, started dealing with it and inserting it in its local legal frameworks. This is an important evidence of the commitment of such States to data protection and that the IAHRS should follow suit.

After all, if all or the majority of the member states are willing to take action towards a safer and more protected data environment, this should be at least an important indicative for the IAHRS guide its agenda as well.

The concept of privacy has evolved to cover data protection. Therefore, it is neither far-fetched nor innovative to say that this right should also be encompassed by the IAHRS. On the contrary, consensus on the domestic understanding of a right should be seen as a guiding factor for the System to interpret it as encompassing such understanding as part and parcel of the common standards of protection.[59]

In order to better analyse this issue, there will be four major questions to be examined: (i) whether a country has a specific data protection regulation and when it was enacted; (ii) whether it has a provision about international data transfer; (iii) whether it has an institutional framework that supports the data protection system (a 'Data Protection Authority' – DPA); and (iv) whether data protection is per se a constitutional right (See Table 1).

Concerning the first pillar (whether a country has a specific data protection regulation), it was found that:

- Eighteen countries have a specific data protection regulation: Antigua and Barbuda; Argentina; The Bahamas; Brazil; Canada; Chile; Colombia; Costa Rica; Dominican Republic; Mexico; Nicaragua; Panama; Peru; Saint Kitts and Nevis; Saint Lucia; Trinidad and Tobago; United States of America; Uruguay.
- Seven countries are discussing the Bill: Barbados; Ecuador; El Salvador; Guatemala; Honduras; Jamaica; Paraguay.
- Ten countries do not have a specific data protection regulation: Belize; Bolivia; Cuba; Dominica; Grenada; Guyana; Haiti; Saint Vincent and the Grenadines; Suriname; Venezuela.

By 2012, according to the previously mentioned comparative study conducted by the OAS' Department of International Law, twenty-four countries had no Data Protection Law.[60] This number, as it can be assessed from Table 1, has diminished to ten, meaning a rise on the Region's concern on data protection. Even in that scenario, from the ten countries, which still do not have a specific data protection regulation, the majority are part of other international initiatives or organisations that are acting towards a stronger data protection framework.

From the ten countries that do not have a specific data protection regulation, Dominica, Grenada and Saint Vincent and the Grenadines are member states of the Organization of Eastern Caribbean States (OECS), which drafted a Data Protection Bill in 2016.[61] The Bill is part of the E-Government for Regional Integration Project and provides safeguards to the collection, use and disclosure of personal data, both to private and public sectors.

Another international agreement worth mentioning is the EU-CARIFORUM Agreement signed in 2008.[62] It set objectives, definitions, principles and rules on cooperation between the signing states in different areas. On data protection, Chapter 6 ('protection of personal data') combines a principiological and a functional approach[63] in order to create a comprehensive and enforceable data protection framework. Article 197 states that the Parties recognise 'their common interest in protecting fundamental rights and freedoms of natural persons, and in particular their right to privacy, with respect to the

Table 1. OAS member states – data protection in local legal frameworks.[105]

	Does the country have a specific data protection regulation? If yes, when was it enacted?	Does the data protection regulation have any provision about international data transfer?	Does the country have an established Data Protection Authority ('DPA')?	Is data protection *per se* right under the Constitution?
1. Antigua and Barbuda	Yes. 2013.[106]	No.	Yes.[107]	No.[108]
2. Argentina	Yes. 2000.[109]	Yes.[110]	Yes.[111]	Yes.[112]
3. The Bahamas	Yes. 2003.[113]	Yes.[114]	Yes.[115]	No.[116]
4. Barbados	Under discussion.[117]	–	No.[118]	No.[119]
5. Belize	No.	–	No.	No.[120]
6. Bolivia	No.[121]	–	No.	No.[122]
7. Brazil	Yes. 2018.[123]	Yes.[124]	No.	Under discussion.[125]
8. Canada	Yes. 2000.[126]	Yes.[127]	Yes.[128]	No.[129]
9. Chile	Yes. 1999.[130]	No.	No.	Yes.[131]
10. Colombia	Yes. 2012.[132]	Yes.[133]	Yes.[134]	Yes.[135]
11. Costa Rica	Yes. 2011.[136]	Yes.[137]	Yes.[138]	No.[139]
12. Cuba	No.[140]	–	No.	No.[141]
13. Dominica	No.	–	No.	No.
14. Dominican Republic	Yes. 2013.[142]	Yes.[143]	No.[144]	Yes.[145]
15. Ecuador	Under discussion.[146]	–	No.	Yes.[147]
16. El Salvador	Under discussion.[148]	–	No.	No.[149]
17. Grenada	No.	–	No.	No.[150]
18. Guatemala	Under discussion.[151]	–	No.	No.[152]
19. Guyana	No.	–	No.	No.[153]
20. Haiti	No.	–	No.	No.[154]
21. Honduras	Under discussion.[155]	–	Yes.[156]	No.[157]
22. Jamaica	Under discussion.[158]	–	No.	No.[159]
23. Mexico	Yes. 2010.[160]	Yes.[161]	Yes.[162]	Yes.[163]
24. Nicaragua	Yes. 2012.[164]	Yes.[165]	No.[166]	No.[167]
25. Panama	Yes. 2019.[168]	Yes.[169]	No.	Yes.[170]
26. Paraguay	Under discussion.[171]	–	No.	No.[172]
27. Peru	Yes. 2011.[173]	Yes.[174]	Yes.[175]	Yes.[176]
28. Saint Kitts and Nevis	Yes. 2018.[177]	No.	Yes.[178]	No.[179]
29. Saint Lucia	Yes. 2011.[180]	Yes.[181]	Yes.[182]	No.[183]
30. Saint Vincent and the Grenadines	No.[184]	–	No.	No.[185]
31. Suriname	No.	–	No.	No.[186]
32. Trinidad and Tobago	Yes. 2011.[187]	Yes.[188]	Yes.[189]	No.[190]
33. United States of America	Yes. 1974.[191]	No.	Yes.[192]	No.[193]
34. Uruguay	Yes. 2008.[194]	Yes.[195]	Yes.[196]	Yes.[197]
35. Venezuela	No.	–	No.	No.[198]

processing of personal data' and Article 107 that the signatories 'shall adopt adequate safeguards to the protection of privacy and fundamental rights, and freedom of individuals, in particular with regard to the transfer of personal data', confirming the point that personal data is a fundamental right parallel to the right to privacy. Belize, Guyana, Haiti and Suriname are part of the CARICOM (together with other Caribbean countries).[64]

Therefore, out of the ten countries listed above which has no national provision on the matter, the majority is not only included in the initiatives already taken by the IAHRS, but also in other international agreements. In different levels, all of the thirty-five States of the

Americas are taking important steps towards data protection, mainly under the assumption that it is a fundamental right.

3.2.1. Remarkable local scenarios

In order to better explain the local developments on data protection legislation, there are a few remarkable countries worth of further explanation.

Of major importance are the cases of Argentina and Uruguay. They are the only States of Americas besides the United States (limited to the Privacy Shield framework) and Canada (commercial organisations) considered by the European Commission to have an adequate level of data protection.[65]

Brazil signals the high level of commitment and a willingness to interact with other like-minded countries forming a stronger environment of data protection. Since July 2019, the National Congress is discussing the inclusion of data protection as a fundamental right in the Constitution.[66] Whilst local authors argue that this inclusion would be unnecessary as scholars and caselaw extract the right to data protection from the right to privacy,[67] there are strong arguments for its inclusion. One of them is precisely the harmonisation with international practice.

The Dominican Republic, by its turn, already has a data protection legislation and citizen's rights to access personal data and to have information about its use are recognised in the Constitution. However, it is currently working on a new legislation more in line with international standards (specifically the European).[68] Barbados' data protection legislation, although yet not passed into law, has already passed by the Senate and by the House of Assembly and has been heavily influenced by the European General Data Protection Regulation.[69]

Finally, Chile has started a major overhaul of its domestic legislation aiming at aligning itself with the most sophisticated data protection regulations in the world. It has started a legislative process to modernise Law n° 19.628 and the on-going discussion is expected to be concluded by the first semester of 2020.[70] It includes, for instance, the imposition of fines for non-compliance and the framework of an equivalent Data Protection Authority.[71] Moreover, Chile has joined the 108 Convention as an observer.[72]

3.2.2. Data protection as a constitutional provision

Finally, in what concerns data protection as a fundamental right in the States of the Americas' Constitutions, Table 1 indicates that eight (Chile, Colombia, Dominican Republic, Ecuador, Mexico, Panama, Peru and Uruguay) of the thirty five States of the Americas treat data protection as a fundamental and autonomous right in their Constitutions and one (Brazil) is discussing its inclusion. This formal recognition of data protection as a new constitutional right is one more evidence of the growing importance of data protection in the Region and one more reason for the IAHRS to start treating it as a fundamental right.

4. The next steps for privacy and data protection within the Inter-American System of human rights

As demonstrated by this survey, the vast majority of countries in the Americas have given a high regard to the dimension of data protection on the right to privacy. They have acknowledged the relevant technological change that has occurred and still occurring and its impact on privacy. This relevance and its impact are yet to be reflected in the IAHRS.

There is a lot to be done. For one, the concern regarding data privacy should move up in the agenda of the IAHRS. The Commission has the authority to set its own priorities. In the past, it has created either specific units,[73] or even rapporteurships or special rapporteurships[74] in order to streamline specific topics and rights it believed to be deserving of particular attention. The commissioners even decided to prioritise individual petitions from particular topics so that a jurisprudence would emerge and with it spell out concrete standards. Data privacy should be one such priority themes.

This is particularly pressing in view of the challenges new technologies bring for human rights chiefly for privacy and in view of the significance of personal data will have in the coming future. This part of the part aims at charting such future challenges and point out the forthcoming issues and debates that should be part of the agenda of the IAHRS.

4.1. Future challenges regarding data protection in the Americas

The countries in the Americas and the IAHRS seem to be converging in a similar path of Europe's. Data protection is becoming a significant dimension of the right of privacy and having instances of being recognised as an autonomous right. Yet, the Hemisphere will face future challenges under a different context from its European counterparts.

To the one hand, it is a very diverse Continent. Both some of the most advanced markets and some of the least advanced are a part of it. This sheds a different perspective on the intensity and mode of production and use of technology from the consumer, business and government sides. Some of the States can be better characterised as consumers of technology rather than producers and some are amongst the heaviest of users of technologies.[75] All this touch upon the challenge of protecting personal data and regulating its uses.

The background becomes even more intricate taking into consideration the history of many of nations in the Region. There is still a looming shadow of dictatorships and undemocratic governments, not to mention fragile democracies. The risk of mass surveillance, abuse of facial recognition (and other techniques of recognition), and content, speech and action monitoring are very high.

The IAHRS has developed an extensive expertise dealing with analogue and offline forms of repression, from massacres to forced disappearances, from censorship of journalists to shutting down newspapers. Much of the 'repression 2.0' can and sadly is not only moving online, it is integrating both environments (on and off) and, what may make it all harder, it is being done not only by States but by technology companies.[76]

4.1.1. Challenges arriving from the implementation of new technologies

The IAHRS will have to provide a strong framework in order to protect people's privacy and personal data in face of the challenges that many new technologies bring. It is not only the Americas that will to face such challenges, but on top of the aforementioned background, they will be particularly steep in the Region.

Three aspects of the new technologies can be highlighted. One the one hand we are seeing an extensive deployment of technologies on the cyberspace that are designed to be data intensive. They tend to collect information in order to optimise functions of their algorithms. Some are designed to create profiles of our inclinations and desires based on clicks we make, the information we share, and the time we expend. We are in an age of using algorithms that find our online footprint and retrace our steps in order to try to figure out our what we want, what we like, who we are.[77]

This is, yet, just the tip of the iceberg, because this is within the environment we call cyber or 'online'.[78] Combined with the 'Internet of Things' (IoT),[79] the distance between what we do in the internet and outside it will most likely either disappear or be very much lowered in relevance.[80]

The importance of the aforementioned changes relates precisely to the digitalisation of our lives.[81] Not only the user's information is being digitised, but also the environment around them. Houses and domestic appliances are imbued not only with the connection to the internet but also the capacity to make many services online and, in many places in not so distant future, will be able to do various domestic tasks that humans would have to do, such as ordering food and house cleaning.[82]

To see the glass half full or half empty depends on some of the focus on the advantages or on the risks. Possible advantages are an increase in daily productivity or in leisure time, as people will not have to focus on many of the mindless tasks that bother our daily existence such as cleaning. On the reverse of the coin, there are the risks, the great amassing of data about our lives: what we do and do not do; when we wake up and sleep (for how long); who is with us; how we dress; what we think; what we read; what we say. So much information in any hand can mean the possibility of influencing our choices, changing our minds, even shaping the development of our personalities.

Another point remains with the digitalisation of the public space.[83] Different technologies are changing the way our public spaces are understood. In the beginning of the 2000s, cameras started to be deployed in many cities, creating what we called the 'CCTV' systems of many cities. This was just a small step. Now there are many cities in the world and many in our Hemisphere that debating the advantages and disadvantages of having not only cameras, but facial and vehicular recognition software.[84] It is brewing a debate on expanding the uses of new technologies in to change the landscape of our cities. Our municipalities want to become 'smart cities' providing technological solutions and digital services. This start with traffic monitoring and possible the use of autonomous vehicles, but goes way beyond, providing many public services in a digital format.

These too have both positive and negative aspects that have to be understood and dealt with. The security implications of such new technologies are playing a central role. Many of the major cities in the region are not safe both from the standpoint of criminality and from deficient or insufficient services. Deaths due to vehicular accidents can be examples of the latter. This tips in favour of using such technologies. Yet, many aspects have to be taken into consideration such as the implications of their deployment,[85] for instance, what about the liberty we feel walking down the streets, developing our own personalities with the interaction in the public market of ideas. There are many possible effects depending on how they are deployed, one not less important is the chilling effect it may have on people's' lives, how more controlled they will behave if they know that someone is watching? Imagine if our whole lives would be a complete panopticon?

As a final point, the use of Artificial Intelligence (AI) creates another layer of challenges, as the study from the Berkman Klein Center from Harvard points out '[p]rivacy is not only implicated in prominent implementations of AI, but also behind the scenes, in the development and training of these systems'.[86] Thus, a framework for the right of privacy and data protection is important not only for the services powered by AI, but also for the development of the technique itself.'[87]

It is clear that our relationship with such new technologies has to be approached in a careful and even minded way.[88] In times of crises and especially under the COVID-19 pandemic, the dark face of technology is even more evident. Around the globe, different governments have taken steps to tackle the pandemic using technological tools that raised concerns regarding the citizens' privacy.[89] In that context, the IACHR has adopted the Resolution no. 1/2020,[90] motivated by what the IACHR itself described as the use of surveillance technology 'to track the propagation of the coronavirus, and to store data on a massive scale'.[91] By this Resolution, the Commission has explicitly made recommendations on the right to data protection, namely that:

> Governments, health providers, businesses and other economic actors involved in the efforts to contain and treat the pandemic must obtain the consent of such persons when gathering or sharing their sensitive data. Personal data gathered during the emergency must only be stored for the limited purpose of combatting the pandemic, and the data must not be shared for commercial or other purposes. People affected and patients shall retain their right to delete their sensitive data.[92]

People in general and in the Americas in particular can only reap the benefits of the new technologies if the core values of our society (our human rights) are preserved. None are more on the basis of such changes than privacy and data protection. The IAHRS, thus, will have to deal with such issues and will have to face the fact that many of the countries will deploy such technologies and that without a strong human rights framework, there will be abuses and there will be a string of other human rights violations. At the very core is data protection.

4.1.2. Forthcoming issues and debates

As we have already mentioned, the challenges relate – and the way to face them – to the protection of privacy and personal data. There is a series of specific aspects regarding personal data and privacy that will have to be addressed through strong human rights standards as well as a framework for the implementation of the positive obligation States have to provide protective regulation.

One of the first aspects that will have to be dealt with concerns the definition of the nature and extent data can be processed. Looking through the security lenses and surveilled cities, there is the question of which categories of data should be treated differently. There is a growing consensus that biometric data, for instance, should have be part of a special category and granted a different level of protection.[93]

For instance, the map of one's face or the way someone talks or even walks. These are very personal data which cannot be changed.[94] Historically as well, some classes of information have a propensity to be used in a discriminatory way. A person's political affiliation, ethnicity, gender, sexual orientation, economical situation, religion, and many others fit into categories that should be treated differently.[95]

The IAHRS will have to define whether failing to provide such differentiation is a violation of the positive obligations under the American Convention. The OAS in its guide already recognises this differentiation as presupposition, part of the 'definitions' necessary to apply principles of data protection.[96]

Not only such differentiation is necessary, but also an emphasis on how the technologies are structured. Algorithms deployed to make them work may not directly collect and use personal data that is within such categories, but might use 'proxies', information that leads to a similar conclusion on a personal characteristic that is sensitive. One example is not using specific data on economic status or race, but the algorithm may exclude a person from a specific zip code, an area where there is a higher concentration from people that do carry one or the other characteristic.[97]

Such situations happen without the use of new technologies or, even less, of artificial intelligence software. Yet, they are exacerbated by their uses in at least three ways. First, ingrained in many algorithms there may be a bias towards one group or the other. The engineers that developed them might not even be aware of such consequences. One very quoted example is a hiring algorithm trained with a database that was majorly of male applicants. The artificial intelligence algorithm, even if not instructed, ended up favouring male applicants even if there were eligible – even better qualified – female ones.[98] This phenomenon has been named 'algorithmic bias'. A discriminatory *praxis* that are either wilfully embedded in the systems (algorithm) or is an unintended result of either erroneous selection in the database or of a mistake in structuring the algorithm.[99]

The risks of singling out persons and groups are further strengthened by the fact that the data collected goes beyond what a person has imparted. It is collected the information provided, the behaviour within the environment (on and offline) and what can be inferred from the previous two. One popular example is in a study from Cambridge University that could infer with a high level of accuracy a person's intellectual prowess from a 'like' in a photograph of a Curly Fry and could predict individuals political inclinations from their 'likes' in a photograph of a Kit-Kat.[100] Out of very unsuspecting, innocent information, other, sometimes much more personal info can be predicted.[101]

Big data and artificial intelligence challenge the idea of control over the shared data. Out of ordinary information, much more sensitive can be predicted. The question is how to deal with the possible abuses of such data. Coming from the private sector, there has to be a way to limit and restrict their abuses. From the public sector, there reminds us of another possible layer of social surveillance. The misuses can be for the singling out of political dissidents or the monitoring of opposition or even of journalists and dissonant voices.[102] It can even prevent access to public services in a not so distant future.

The challenge is intensified by the fact that many services are being automatised.[103] The decision-making processes that are being employed does not require or take into account the ability of having a human being either revising or explaining the decisions after its deployment. For instance, if someone wants access to microcredit, the analysis of one person's financial history takes a long time for an analyst, for an algorithm, it may take nano-seconds. Yet, who makes the decision? The algorithm. The questions here are whether that person can complain if s/he was not accepted; whether s/he will have access to the criteria being used; whether s/he has a right to a human intervention or review.[104]

5. Conclusion

The IAHRS stands in the middle of a road that begins with the very concept of privacy as related to the protection of family life and that, along the turns of the last decades, have steered the System towards an increasingly complex scenario. As everything turns into data in a so-called data-driven economy, the challenge of the IAHRS will be to develop a coherent protection that singles out which are the situations that could trigger the mandate of the System. The IAHRS has to face such challenge and the only way is to a priority in its agenda. It has to give the centrality that it deserves and has been given by the countries in the Region.

Additionally, the development of new technologies will likely challenge the scope and limits of the protection of data privacy upheld by the IAHRS. Profiling, algorithmic biases, and the 'black box' aspect of automated decision-making processes are just a small sample of what is at stake on the road ahead.

In order to comply with its mandate, the System will have to determine the level of transparency and access to information individuals will have. The minimum basis for information security and what is the guarantees related to biometric and sensitive data are also important topics that will likely come along.

As privacy and data protection grow in importance to understand the world, the IAHRS will face the challenge of protecting them under the umbrella of many different cultural, economic and legal landscapes. The perils of the road will be many, but the System has proven reliable in the past to adapt and to carve out, in a creative way, standards for protection of rights that are in tune with trying times. Technology might be just one piece of a much larger puzzle but addressing this one right could be the most important challenge ahead in the road that leads to a better safeguarding of privacy and data protection in the Americas.

Notes

1. 'Inter-American Human Rights System', *International Justice Resource Center (IJRC)*, https://ijrcenter.org/regional/inter-american-system/ (accessed May 03, 2020).
2. OAS, 'What is the IACHR?', *About the IACHR*, https://www.oas.org/en/iachr/mandate/what.asp (accessed May 03, 2020). The Court is, in principle, the interpretative authority under the Inter-American Convention on Human Rights, yet its jurisdiction, under principles of public international law, is constrained by both the States that adhere to the Convention and those that accepted it jurisdiction either a compulsory matter or in a *ad hoc* fashion. This means that whereas the Commission can act in regard to the whole 35 members of the OAS, the Court only to the members bound by the American Convention and that accepts its jurisdiction.
3. IACHR, *Strategic Plan 2017–2021*, https://www.oas.org/en/iachr/mandate/StrategicPlan2017/docs/StrategicPlan2017-2021.pdf.
4. For an overall understanding of the IACHR, the organisational charter is available at: https://www.oas.org/en/iachr/mandate/docs/Organization-chart-IACHR.pdf.
5. A general view on the IACHR rapporteurships is available at: https://www.oas.org/en/iachr/mandate/rapporteurships.asp.
6. A list of the Inter-American human rights instruments is available at: https://www.corteidh.or.cr/instrumentos-en.cfm.
7. It is widely understood that the Court has four types of jurisdiction: adjudicative, advisory, provisional
8. United Nations, Frank La Rue, *Report of the Special Rapporteur on the promotion and protection of the right to freedom of opinion and expression*, May 16, 2011, https://www2.ohchr.org/english/bodies/hrcouncil/docs/17session/A.HRC.17.27_en.pdf.

9. Samuel D. Warren and Louis D. Brandeis, 'The Right to Privacy', *Harvard Law Review* 4, no. 5 (1890): 193–220.
10. Viktor Mayer-Schönberger, 'General development of data protection in Europe', in *Technology and privacy: The new landscape* (Cambridge: MIT Press, 1997).
11. In 2018, it was approved a modernised version of the Convention known as Convention 108+.
12. Christopher Kuner, Fred H Cate, Orla Lynskey, Christopher Millard, Nora Ni Loideain, and Dan Jerker B. Svantesson, 'Introducing the global data privacy prize', *International Data Privacy Law* 9, no. 1 (February 2019): 1, https://doi.org/10.1093/idpl/ipz002.
13. In a handbook relatively recently published in conjunction by the EU and the Council of Europe they showcase the intertwined nature of both rights: 'The right to respect for private life and the right to the protection of personal data are closely related. Both strive to protect similar values, i.e. the autonomy and human dignity of individuals, by granting them a personal sphere in which they can freely develop their personalities, think and shape their opinions'. European Union Agency for Fundamental Rights and Council of Europe, Handbook on European data protection law (2018), https://www.echr.coe.int/Documents/Handbook_data_protection_ENG.pdf.
14. ECtHR, Case *Arvelo Apont v the Netherlands* App no 28770/05, judgement of 3 November, 2011, para. 53.
15. ECtHR, Case *Certain aspects of the Laws on the Use of Languages in Education in Belgium v Belgium* App nos 1474/62, 1677/62, 1691/62, 1769/63, 1994/63 and 2126/64, judgement of 23 July, 1968; ECtHR, Case *Marckx v Belgium* App no 6833/74, judgement of 13 June, 1979. An interesting overview of this aspect can be found at: A.R. Mowbray, *The Development of Positive Obligations under the European Convention on Human Rights by the European Court of Human Rights* (Oxford: OUP, 2004).
16. At the X v. Iceland Case, for instance the Court understood that '[the right of privacy] comprises also, to a certain degree, the right to establish and to develop relationships with other human beings, especially in the emotional field for the development and fulfilment of one's own personality'. (ECtHR, Case *X v Iceland* App no 6825/74, judgement of 18 May, 1976).
17. ECtHR, Case *Mikulić v. Croatia*, no. 53176/99, judgement of 7 February, 2002, para. 53.
18. Both in the imparting and receiving side. For the latter, the leading case is *Odièvre v. France*, dealing with a French procedure that allowed the identity of the mother be a secret preventing the child to know her origins. To one side a personal information protects, to the other, a personal information (family origin) kept from the data subject (ECtHR, Case *Odièvre v. France*, judgement of 13 February, 2003).
19. ECtHR, Case *Z. v. Finland* App no. 22009/93 judgement of 25 February, 1997; ECtHR, Case *M. S. v. Sweden*, judgement of 2 August, 1997. In the former the Court stated that it would take into account that the protection of personal data, not least medical data, is of fundamen-' tal importance to a person's enjoyment of his or her right to respect for private and family life as guaranteed by Article 8 of the Convention (art. 8). Respecting the confidentiality of health data is a vital principle in the legal systems of all the Contracting Parties to the Convention' (para. 95).
20. In COE's and EU's Handbook, it is stated that '[o]ver the years, the Court has ruled that personal data protection is an important part of the right to respect for private life (Article 8), and has been guided by the principles of Convention 108 in determining whether or not there has been an interference with this fundamental right'. European Union Agency for Fundamental Rights and Council of Europe, *Handbook on European Data Protection Law* (2018).
21. The connection between privacy to personal identification can be seen for instance at the Case Burghartz v. Switzerland dealing with the correction of stored personal data, at this time, family surname. (ECtHR, Case *Burghartz v. Switzerland*, 22 February 1994, § 24, Series A no. 280-B).
22. ECtHR, Case *Amann v. Switzerland* [GC], No. 27798/95, judgement of 16 February 2000, para. 65; ECtHR, Case *S. and Marper v. the United Kingdom*, judgment (Grand Chamber) of 4 December 2008, para. 66.

23. OECD, *Guidelines on the Protection of Privacy and Transborder Flows of Personal Data* (1980), https://www.oecd.org/sti/ieconomy/oecdguidelinesontheprotectionofprivacyandtransborder flowsofpersonaldata.htm (accessed May 03, 2020).
24. One should bear in mind that those two norms are not the only EU Laws that deal with data protection.
25. The Charter of Fundamental Rights of the EU grants two specific articles to deal with the matter, art. 7 and 8, rights to private life and data protection, respectively.
26. The cases from the IACtHR, as seen above, highlight the matter. Home: IACtHR, Case of the Ituango Massacres v. Colombia. Judgment of July 1, 2006. Merits, Reparations and Costs. Series C No. 148; IACtHR, Case Escué-Zapata v. Colombia. Judgment of July 4, 2007. Merits, Reparations and Costs. Series C No. 165; IACtHR, Case Fernández-Ortega et al. v. Mexico. Judgment of August 30, 2010. Merits, Reparations and Costs. Series C No. 215. Communications: IACtHR, Case Tristán Donoso v. Panama. Preliminary Objection, Merits, Reparations and Costs. Judgment of January 27, 2009. Series C No. 193; ase of Escher v. Brazil. Judgment of July 6, 2009. Merits, Reparations and Costs. Series C No. 200. Family life: IACtHR, Case Escué-Zapata v. Colombia. Judgment of July 4, 2007. Merits, Reparations and Costs. Series CNo. 165; IACtHR, Case Atala Riffo and children vs. Chile, Sentencia de Merits, Reparations and Costs, of February 24, Series C No.; IACtHR, Case Artavia Murillo and Others ('*In vitro* fecundation') vs. Costa Rica, Preliminary Objection, Merits, Reparations and Costs, judgement of November 28, 2012, Series C No.
27. Office of the Special Rapporteur for Freedom of Expression of the IACHR. *Standards for a Free, Open and Inclusive Internet* (2016), para. 186, https://www.oas.org/en/iachr/expression/docs/publications/INTERNET_2016_ENG.pdf.
28. 'Art. 11(2): No one may be the object of arbitrary or abusive interference with his private life, his family, his home, or his correspondence, or of unlawful attacks on his honor or reputation'. (Art. 11(2) American Convention on Human Rights, 1989).
29. There are Latin American scholars who understand that the development of the right to privacy has been mostly focused on personal development than personal data. María Solange Maqueo Ramírez, Jimena Moreno González, and Miguel Recio Gayo, 'Protección de datos personales, privacidad y vida privada: la inquietante búsqueda de un equilibrio global necesario', *Revista de Derecho (Valdivia)* XXX, no. 1 (2017): 77–96, https://scielo.conicyt.cl/pdf/revider/v30n1/art04.pdf.
30. Ramírez, González, and Gayo, 'Protección de datos personales, privacidad y vida privada'.
31. At the Universal System, there has been lately a higher emphasis on data protection as a human right. See for instance: UNGA Res. 68/167, The Right to Privacy in the Digital Age (Jan. 21, 2014); UNGA Res. 69/166, The Right to Privacy in the Digital Age (Dec. 18, 2014); UNGA Res. 71/199, The Right to Privacy in the Digital Age (Dec. 19, 2016); Human Rights Council Res. 28/16 (Mar. 24, 2015). In the past, the UN Human Rights Committee has addressed the issue under the heading of '[t]he gathering and holding of personal information on computers, data banks and other devices, whether by public authorities or private individuals or bodies, must be regulated by law' (UN Human Rights Committee, General Comment no. 16, Article 17 (The right to respect of privacy, family, home and correspondence, and protection of honour and reputation), HRI/GEN/1/Rev.9 (Vol. I), 8 April 1988.) As a part of the UN general response on the matter, it had as well the non-binding Guidelines for the Regulation of Computerized Personal Data Files, UNGA Res. 45/95 (Dec. 14, 1990).
32. Brazil has approved in a committee of its Lower Chamber an Amendment to its Constitution that would include autonomously data protection as a fundamental right. Brazil, *PEC 17/2019,* https://www.camara.leg.br/proposicoesWeb/fichadetramitacao?idProposicao=2210757 (accessed 03 May, 2020).
33. IACtHR, Case Tristán Donoso vs. Panama, Judgement of 27 January, 2009, Merits, Reparations and Costs, paras. 55 and 76; and IACtHR, Case Escher et al. vs. Brazil, Judgment of July 6, 2009. Merits, Reparations and Costs. Series C No. 200. para. 114.

34. IACtHR, Case Escher et al. vs. Brazil, Judgment of July 6, 2009. Merits, Reparations and Costs. Series C No. 200. para. 115.
35. IACtHR, Case Fernández Ortega et al. vs. México, Judgement of 30 August, 2010, Merits, Reparations and Costs, para. 129; and Caso Rosendo Cantú et al. vs. México, Judgement of 31 August, 2010, Merits, Reparations and Costs, para. 119.
36. IACtHR, Case Atala Riffo and Daughters vs. Chile, Judgement of 24 February, 2012, para. 162.
37. IACtHR, Case Artavia Murillo et al. ('*In vitro fertilization*') vs. Costa Rica, Judgement of 28 November, 2012, Merits, Reparations and Costs, para. 143. (Original footnotes omitted).
38. IACHR, *Report of the Special Rapporteur for Freedom of Expression* (2013), Chapter IV (Freedom of Expression and the Internet). OEA/Ser.L/V/II.149. Doc. 50. December 31, 2013. para. 131.
39. IACHR, *Report of the Special Rapporteur for Freedom of Expression* (2013), Chapter IV (Freedom of Expression and the Internet). OEA/Ser.L/V/II.149. Doc. 50. December 31, 2013. para. 138. (grifo provided).
40. Office of the Special Rapporteur for Freedom of Expression of the IACHR, *Standards for a Free, Open and Inclusive Internet* (2016), para. 199, https://www.oas.org/en/iachr/expression/docs/publications/INTERNET_2016_ENG.pdf.
41. Office of the Special Rapporteur for Freedom of Expression of the IACHR, *Standards for a Free, Open and Inclusive Internet* (2016), para. 204, https://www.oas.org/en/iachr/expression/docs/publications/INTERNET_2016_ENG.pdf.
42. Office of the Special Rapporteur for Freedom of Expression of the IACHR, *Standards for a Free, Open and Inclusive Internet* (2016), para. 202, https://www.oas.org/en/iachr/expression/docs/publications/INTERNET_2016_ENG.pdf.
43. IACHR, *Annual Report of the Office of the Special Rapporteur for Freedom of Expression 2018* (2019), para. 404, https://www.oas.org/en/iachr/expression/docs/reports/annual/IA2018RELE-en.pdf.
44. Inter-American Juridical Committee of the Organization of American States, *OAS Principles on Privacy and Personal Data Protection with Annotations* (2015), https://www.oas.org/en/sla/dil/docs/CJI-doc_474-15_rev2.pdf.
45. More information on the standing of the Inter-American Human Rights System within the Organization of American States, see: https://www.oas.org/en/about/what_we_do.asp.
46. See for instance: OAS, *Access to Public Information: Strengthening Democracy* (2009), AG/RES. 2514 (XXXIX-O/09), https://www.oas.org/en/sla/dil/docs/AG-RES_2514-2009_eng.pdf, *Access to Public Information: Strengthening Democracy* (2008), AG/RES. 2418 (XXXVIII-O/08), https://www.oas.org/en/sla/dil/docs/AG-RES_2418_XXXVIII-O-08_en.pdf, *Access to Public Information: Strengthening Democracy* (2007), AG/RES. 2288 (XXXVII-O/07), https://www.oas.org/DIL/AG-RES_2288_XXXVII-O-07_eng.pdf and *Model Inter-American Law on Access to Public Information* (2010), AG/RES. 2607 (XL-O/10), https://www.oas.org/dil/AG-RES_2607-2010_eng.pdf.
47. OAS, *Commentary And Guide For Implementation For The Model Inter- American Law On Access To Information* (2010), item D (4), 5, https://www.oas.org/dil/AG-RES_2607-2010_eng.pdf.
48. OAS, Department of International Law, of the Secretariat for Legal Affairs, *Preliminary Principles and Recommendations on Data Protection (The Protection of Personal Data)* (2010/2011), https://www.oas.org/dil/CP-CAJP-2921-10_rev1_corr1_eng.pdf.
49. OAS, *Access To Public Information And Protection Of Personal Data* (2011), AG/RES. 2661 (XLI-O/11), https://www.oas.org/DIL/AG-RES_2661-XLI-O-11_eng.pdf.
50. OAS, Department of International Law, of the Secretariat for Legal affairs, *Comparative Study: Data Protection In The Americas, Different existing legal regimes, polices and enforcement mechanisms for the protection of personal data, including domestic legislation, regulation, and self-regulation* (2012), https://www.oas.org/es/sla/ddi/docs/CP-CAJP-3063-12_en.pdf.

51. Inter-American Juridical Committee of the Organization of American States, *Privacy and Data Protection* (2015), CJI/doc. 474/15 rev.2, p.1, https://www.oas.org/en/sla/dil/docs/CJI-doc_474-15_rev2.pdf.
52. Inter-American Juridical Committee of the Organization of American States, *Privacy and Data Protection* (2015), CJI/doc. 474/15 rev.2, p.3, https://www.oas.org/en/sla/dil/docs/CJI-doc_474-15_rev2.pdf.
53. Inter-American Juridical Committee of the Organization of American States, *Privacy and Data Protection* (2015), CJI/doc. 474/15 rev.2, pp. 6–19, https://www.oas.org/en/sla/dil/docs/CJI-doc_474-15_rev2.pdf.
54. The European Human Rights System does not outright adopt standards of data protection from the GDPR or of the former European normative the Directive 46/95. Yet, the EU standards serve as guidance and further evidence that data protection is a right and safeguarded under the domestic law of each country member.
55. UNCTAD, *Data Protection and Privacy Legislation Worldwide* database, https://unctad.org/en/Pages/DTL/STI_and_ICTs/ICT4D-Legislation/eCom-Data-Protection-Laws.aspx (accessed January 27, 2020). There is dispute on these numbers, Although the classification as a general data protection regulation varies, it is clear that more than 100 jurisdictions in the world do have a privacy and data protection legislation.
56. Economic Commission for Latin America and the Caribbean (ECLAC), *Corporate governance and data protection in Latin America and the Caribbean, Production Development series*, no. 223 (LC/TS.2019/38), Santiago, 2019, p.32, https://repositorio.cepal.org/bitstream/handle/11362/44629/S1900395_en.pdf?sequence=1&isAllowed=y.
57. Ibid.
58. Economic Commission for Latin America and the Caribbean (ECLAC), *Corporate governance and data protection in Latin America and the Caribbean, Production Development series*, no. 223 (LC/TS.2019/38), Santiago, 2019, p. 33, https://repositorio.cepal.org/bitstream/handle/11362/44629/S1900395_en.pdf?sequence=1&isAllowed=y.
59. Article 29 of the American Convention supports such interpretation. It states that rights established domestically should be treated and guaranteed as well, *in verbis*:
    Art. 29 No provision of this Convention shall be *interpreted* as: [...]
    b. restricting the enjoyment or exercise of any right or freedom recognised by virtue of the laws of any State Party[; or]
    c. precluding other rights or guarantees that are inherent in the human personality or derived from representative democracy as a form of government.
60. OAS, Department of International Law, of the Secretariat for Legal affairs, *Comparative Study: Data Protection in the Americas, Different existing legal regimes, polices and enforcement mechanisms for the protection of personal data, including domestic legislation, regulation, and self-regulation* (2012), 8, https://www.oas.org/es/sla/ddi/docs/CP-CAJP-3063-12_en.pdf.
61. Organization of Eastern Caribbean States (OECS), 'Data Protection Act' (2016), https://www.oecs.org/en/procurement/e-gov/data-protection-act.
62. 'Economic Partnership Agreement between the CARIFORUM States and the European Community', 2008, https://www.sice.oas.org/Trade/CAR_EU_EPA_e/careu_in_e.ASP.
63. José Augusto Fontoura Costa, 'Data Protection in International Trade Law', *Data Protection in the Internet*, eds. Dário Moura Vicente and Sofia de Vasconcelos Casimiro (Switzerland: Springer, 2020): 487.
64. CARICOM's Member States are 15: Antigua and Barbuda, Bahamas, Barbados, Belize, Dominica, Grenada, Guyana, Haiti, Jamaica, Montserrat, Saint Lucia, St Kitts and Nevis, St Vincent and the Grenadines, Suriname and Trinidad and Tobago. There are also 5 associate members, namely Anguilla, Bermuda, British Virgin Islands, Cayman Island and Turks and Caicos Islands. CARICOM, https://caricom.org/about-caricom/who-we-are/our-governance/members-and-associate-members/ (accessed May 03, 2020).
65. EU, European Commission, 'Adequacy decisions', https://ec.europa.eu/info/law/law-topic/data-protection/international-dimension-data-protection/adequacy-decisions_en (accessed May 03, 2020).

66. The Proposal was not yet voted by the National Congress in its entirety. Brazil, National Congress, https://www.camara.leg.br/proposicoesWeb/fichadetramitacao?idProposicao=2210757 (accessed May 03, 2020).
67. See for instance Anderson Schreiber. Anderson Schreiber, 'PEC 17/19: Uma Análise Crítica', *Gen Jurídico* (2019), https://genjuridico.com.br/2019/07/19/analise-critica-pec-17-2019/.
68. 'The Dominican Republic Works on New Data Protection Law', *Council of Europe* (December 18, 2019), https://www.coe.int/en/web/cybercrime/-/glacy-the-dominican-republic-works-on-new-data-protection-law
69. Bartlett D. Morgan, 'Barbados, A Modern Data Protection Regime', *Data Guidance* (September 2019), https://platform.dataguidance.com/opinion/barbados-modern-data-protection-regime.
70. Jaime Urzúa. *Avances en el Proyecto de ley sobre protección de datos personales: Consejo para la Transparencia será la nueva Agencia de protección de datos* (September 2019), https://www.alessandri.legal/avances-en-el-proyecto-de-ley-sobre-proteccion-de-datos-personales/.
71. Local scholars consider two existing alternatives: a new body of regulation or deliverying the attribution to an existing body, the Transparency Counsel – *Consejo para la Transparencia* – CPLT (María Paz Canales and Pablo Viollier, 'Chile necesita una regulación de protección de datos con dientes', *Derechos Digitales* (July 12, 2019), https://www.derechosdigitales.org/13443/proteccion-de-datos-con-dientes/). Most recent news has indicated that the Congress would end up choosing the second one, but there are still concerns as to its independence and autonomy (Jaime Urzúa. *Avances en el Proyecto de ley sobre protección de datos personales: Consejo para la Transparencia será la nueva Agencia de protección de datos* (September 2019), https://www.alessandri.legal/avances-en-el-proyecto-de-ley-sobre-proteccion-de-datos-personales/).
72. 'European Commission Joint press statement by Commissioner Věra Jourová and Felipe Larraín Bascuñán, Minister of Finance, and Hernán Larraín Fernández, Minister of Justice and Human Rights of Chile on cooperation on data protection', *European Commission Statements*, 2019, https://ec.europa.eu/commission/presscorner/detail/en/STATEMENT_19_4029 (accessed May 03, 2020).
73. One example is the creation of the unit for dealing with LGBTI right in 2011 and this further development in a Rapporteurship. IACHR, *IACHR Creates Unit on the Rights of Lesbian, Gay, Bisexual, Trans, and Intersex Persons* (November 3, 2011), https://www.oas.org/en/iachr/media_center/PReleases/2011/115.asp (accessed May 03, 2020). The Commission also amended its rules on prioritising cases, the registry of individual petitions tends to take from 2 to 4 years and then starts the petition's processing. Petitions concerned LGBTI rights took priority and were reviewed in advance.
74. Another example comes from the institution of an Office of the Special Rapporteur on Economic, Social, Cultural, and Environmental Rights: https://www.oas.org/en/iachr/media_center/PReleases/2014/034.asp.
75. Mexico and Brazil, for instance, are amongst the top ten heaviest users of digital services, particularly, social media platforms. (UN ECLAC, *Regional digital market Strategic aspects* (2018), p. 7ff., https://www.cepal.org/en/publications/43633-regional-digital-market-strategic-aspects).
76. One cannot forget the risk that comes from private sources of 'surveillance'. Zuboff's understanding of an 'age of surveillance capitalism' certainly adds to concerns of using the structure of data flows created for the digital environment to be used in a variety of dubious or even unscrupulous ways (Shoshana Zuboff, *The Age of Surveillance Capitalism: The Fight for a Human Future at the New Frontier of Power* (PublicAffairs, 2019)).
77. Monika Zalnieriute, Lyria Bennett Moses and George Williams, 'The Rule of Law and Automation of Government Decision-making', *Modern Law Review*, 2019, v. 82(3).
78. Calo, for instance state that there is a difference between robots and technologies such as the internet, because robots can cause physical harm, their 'habitat' is not the cyberspace, but the same plane as us, the physical world. (Ryan Calo, *Robotics and the Lessons of Cyberlaw* (2015), 103 CALIF. L. REV. 513: 515).

79. The internet of things is a term used to describe the usage of sensors and algorithms to connect everyday objects to the internet. This means they can execute many of their functions online and receive and impart information online.
80. Lee mentions for instance the fast transition in China to a O2O economy (online to offline) and predicts that in no time we will be having a OMO (Online Merges Offline). Kai-Fu Lee, *Artificial Intelligence* (2017): 88.
81. Thas A. Nirmalathas, 'How Is the Networked Society Impacting Us?', *Proceedings of the IEEE* 106, no. 3 (2018), https://ieeexplore.ieee.org/stamp/stamp.jsp?tp=&arnumber=8303874.
82. Some business models are being tested that connect to. They have fridges that can send alerts when you are running out of supplies. Or Amazon's Alexa, for instance, can place a call and order food for you. It is seamless integration with our environments and our homes.
83. From the standpoint of the public-private space available in stores, for example, strategies are being developed for shopping malls to survive in the digital age. Roberto Fantoni, Fernanda Hoefel and Marina Mazzarolo. 'The future of the shopping mall', *McKinsey&Company Report* (November 2014), https://www.mckinsey.com/business-functions/marketing-and-sales/our-insights/the-future-of-the-shopping-mall.
84. There are many possible benefits and some highlight the fact that such technologies coupled with artificial intelligence make them capable of evolving not only serving as specific tools to stop crime, but also to prevent it. About such evolving capabilities see: Markus Christen, Thomas Burri, Joseph Chapa, Raphael Salvi, Filippo Santoni de Sio, and John Sullins, 'An Evaluation Schema for the Ethical Use of Autonomous Robotic Systems in Security Applications', *University of Zurich Digital Society Initiative White Paper Series*, no. 1 (25 November 2018).
85. Zittrain cautions us about too much haste in judgment. He has called our attention that the impacts of technology can only be understood through their use due to the fact that while we use them we change actually change them. The example he gave was how the internet has changed from providing access points to information to a collaborative effort that all can share their views and thoughts, from passive to active. (Jonathan Zittrain, 'The Generative Internet', *Harvard Law Review* 119 (2006): 1975 ff.).
86. Jessica Fjeld, Nele Achte, Hannah Hilligoss, Adam Christopher Nagy, and Madhulika Srikumar, *Principled Artificial Intelligence:Mapping Consensus in Ethical and Rights-based Approaches to Principles for AI* (Berkman Klein Center for Internet and Society at Harvard University: 2020), 20, https://cyber.harvard.edu/publication/2020/principled-ai.
87. AI demands much data in order to train the algorithm, some of the data is personal. Another characteristic of this technology is the need for constant interaction in order to continuously learn. Thus, constant access to data. One of the questions is whether one can eliminate data that is in the basis of the AI, that was used to iterate and train the algorithm. It might render it less effective for everyone.
88. Balkin, talking about robotics hinted that we should not fall into the alarmists of neither side, nor the ones can only see opportunities, nor the ones that only see harm with such new technologies. (Jack M. Balkin, 'The Path of Robotics', *California Law Review Circuit* 6 (June 2015): 54–55).
89. 'Countries Are Using Apps and Data Networks to Keep Tabs on the Pandemic', *The Economist*, March 26, 2020, https://www.economist.com/briefing/2020/03/26/countries-are-using-apps-and-data-networks-to-keep-tabs-on-the-pandemic?fsrc=newsletter&utm_campaign=the-economist-today&utm_medium=newsletter&utm_source=salesforce-marketing-cloud&utm_term=2020-03-27&utm_content=article-link-1.
90. IACHR, 'Resolution no. 01/2020: Pandemic and Human Rights in the Americas' (2020), https://www.oas.org/en/iachr/decisions/pdf/Resolution-1-20-en.pdf.
91. Ibid., 4.
92. Ibid., 12–13, item 35.
93. Privacy International, for example, has called attention to the enthusiasm of the implementation of technologies that use biometric data within the developing world and in particular in Latin America. See: Privacy International, *Biometrics: Friend or Foe of Privacy?* (2017), https://privacyinternational.org/sites/default/files/2017-11/Biometrics_Friend_or_foe.pdf.

94. The comparisons between credit card fraud and id theft comes to mind. One can order a different credit card number, but not a different face or actual identity.
95. Most national general data protection legislations in the Americas recognise that there are categories of personal data that are 'sensitive', following a language used within the European context.
96. Inter-American Juridical Committee of the Organization of American States, *Privacy and Data Protection* (2015), CJI/doc. 474/15 rev.2, p.3, https://www.oas.org/en/sla/dil/docs/CJI-doc_474-15_rev2.pdf.
97. There is a wealth of discussion on the matter, but a general view outcry can be found at: O'Neil Catherine, *Weapons of Math Destruction: How Big Data Increases Inequality and Threatens Democracy* (New York: Crown, 2016).
98. Amazon, for example, had to cancel the use of a AI hiring algorithm for a similar flaw (Jeffrey Dastin, 'Amazon Scraps Secret AI Recruiting Tool that Showed Bias Against Women', *Reuters*, October 10, 2018, https://www.reuters.com/article/us-amazon-com-jobs-automation-insight/amazon-scraps-secret-ai-recruiting-tool-that-showed-bias-against-women-idUSKCN1MK08G). For an analysis of similar cases, see: Sara Wachter-Boettcher, *Technically Wrong: Sexist Apps, Biased Algorithms, and Other Threats of Toxic Tech* (London: W. W. Norton & Company, 2017) and Catherine O'Neil, *Weapons of Math Destruction: How Big Data Increases Inequality and Threatens Democracy* (New York: Crown, 2016).
99. Karen Hao, 'This is How AI Bias Really Happens – and Why It's So Hard to Fix', *MIT Technology Review*, February 04, 2014, https://www.technologyreview.com/s/612876/this-is-how-ai-bias-really-happensand-why-its-so-hard-to-fix/; Sara Wachter-Boettcher, *Technically Wrong: Sexist Apps, Biased Algorithms, and Other Threats of Toxic Tech* (London: W. W. Norton & Company, 2017); Danielle Keats Citron and Frank Pasquale, 'The Scored Society: Due Process for Automated Predictions', *Washington Law Review* 89 (2014): 1; Catherine O'Neil, *Weapons of Math Destruction: How Big Data Increases Inequality and Threatens Democracy* (New York: Crown, 2016).
100. Michael Kosinski, David Stillwell, and Thore Graepel, 'Private Traits and Attributes are Predictable from Digital Records of Human Behavior', *PNAS* 110, no. 15 (April 2013): 5802–05, https://doi.org/10.1073/pnas.1218772110.
101. For a general view of the matter with critical overtunes, see: Sandra Wachter and Brent Mittelstadt, 'A Right to Reasonable Inferences: Re-Thinking Data Protection Law in the Age of Big Data and AI', *Columbia Business Law Review*, no. 2 (2019).
102. One major concern for the Americas and particularly for Latin America is the protection of journalists, artists and political opposition. Such technologies may make it easier to find, track and surveil them.
103. One very clear way people see it is their 'news feeds' in social network. It automatically organises the information we see, and this determines what we see first, allegedly so that we can more easily find the information we are more interested in. For more information on how such automated algorithms work and their consequences see: Eli Pariser, *The Filter Bubble: How the New Personalized Web is Changing What We Think and How We Read* (Penguin, 2011), Introduction and Chapter 1.
104. Frank Pasquale, 'Restoring Transparency to Automated Authority', *J. On Telecomm. & High-tech. L.* 9 (2011): 235; Lilian Edwards and Michael Veale, 'Enslaving the Algorithm: From a "Right to an Explanation" to a "Right to Better Decisions"?', *IEEE Security & Privacy* 16, no. 3 (2018): 46–54, 47; Margot E. Kaminski, 'The Right to Explanation, Explained', *U of Colorado Law Legal Studies*, Research Paper No. 18–24 (15 June 2018), 10; Izak Mendoza and Lee A. Bygrave, 'The Right Not to Be Subject to Automated Decisions Based on Profiling', in *EU Internet Law: Regulation and Enforcement*, ed. Tatiani Synodinou et al. (Springer, 2017), 7.
105. The research was conducted by cross checking three databases, namely: UNCTAD, https://unctad.org/en/Pages/DTL/STI_and_ICTs/ICT4D-Legislation/eCom-Data-Protection-Laws.aspx (accessed January 27 2020); DLA Piper Data Protection Laws of the World, https://www.dlapiperdataprotection.com (accessed January 27, 2020); Baker McKenzie Global Data Privacy & Security Handbook, https://globaltmt.bakermckenzie.com/data-

privacy-security%20 (accessed January 27, 2020); Graham Greenleaf, *Greenleaf's Global Table of Data Privacy Laws and Bills (Greenleaf, Graham, Global Tables of Data Privacy Laws and Bills)* (January 2019), https://ssrn.com/abstract=3380794 (accessed January 27, 2020), and individual research by the authors.

106. Republic of Antigua and Barbuda, 'Data Protection Act' (2013), https://laws.gov.ag/wp-content/uploads/2019/02/a2013-10.pdf (accessed January 27, 2020).
107. Republic of Antigua and Barbuda, Information Commissioner.
108. Republic of Antigua and Barbuda, 'The Antigua and Barbuda Constitutional Order 1981', Article 3(c) of the Constitution states as a fundamental right 'his family life, his personal privacy, the privacy of his home and other property and from deprivation of property without fair compensation', https://pdba.georgetown.edu/Constitutions/Antigua/antigua-barbuda.html (accessed January 27, 2020).
109. Argentina, Ley 25.326/2000, https://www.argentina.gob.ar/normativa/nacional/ley-25326-64790 (accessed January 27, 2020). The main regulation Decree is the Decreto Regulamentario 1558/2001, https://www.argentina.gob.ar/normativa/nacional/decreto-1558-2001-70368. Important to mention that in 2018 the Congress has received a proposal of an updated Data Protection Law. An initial analysis of the project by the Civil Rights Association (*Asociación por los Derechos Civiles*) can be seen at https://adc.org.ar/informes/analisis-inicial-del-proyecto-de-ley-de-proteccion-de-datos-personales-de-argentina/ (accessed January 27, 2020).
110. Ibid., Ley 25.326/2000, Article 12.
111. Argentina, Dirección Nacional de Protección de Datos Personales (DNPDP), part of the Agencia de Aceso a la Información Pública (AAIP), https://www.argentina.gob.ar/aaip (accessed January 27, 2020).
112. Argentina, 'Constitution of the Argentine Nation', Article 43, §3° of the Argentine Constitution foresees: 'Any person shall file this action to obtain information on the data about himself and their purpose, registered in public records or data bases, or in private ones intended to supply information; and in case of false data or discrimination, this action may be filed to request the suppression, rectification, confidentiality or updating of said data', https://www.biblioteca.jus.gov.ar/Argentina-Constitution.pdf (accessed January 27, 2020).
113. The Bahamas, Data Protection (Privacy of Personal Information) Act (2003), https://laws.bahamas.gov.bs/cms/images/LEGISLATION/PRINCIPAL/2003/2003-0003/DataProtectionPrivacyofPersonalInformationAct_1.pdf (accessed January 27, 2020).
114. Ibid., Article 17 of Data Protection Act 2003.
115. The Bahamas, Data Protection Commissioner, https://bit.ly/2GeAB12 (accessed January 27, 2020).
116. The Bahamas, The Constitution of The Commonwealth of The Bahamas, https://bit.ly/2twNpxi (accessed January 27, 2020). The Constitution appears to focus at the protection for the privacy of the home, as per Articles 15(c) and 19(7).
117. Barbados, The Barbados Parliament, Data Protection Bill 2019. First draft in 2005. Follow legislative process here https://www.barbadosparliament.com/bills/details/396 (accessed January 27, 2020). First comments at Bartlett Morgan, *Re: Comments on the Data Protection Bill* (9 July 2019), https://ssrn.com/abstract=3418667.
118. In the draft bill, however, there is a provision for such establishment.
119. Barbados, Barbados Constitution, https://barbados.org/constitution.htm (accessed January 27, 2020), Section 2, Article 11(b) states provides as a fundamental right the 'protection for the privacy of his home and other property and from deprivation of property without compensation'.
120. Belize, Constitution, https://nationalassembly.gov.bz/wp-content/uploads/2017/03/Belize-Constitution-2017updated-March.pdf (accessed January 27, 2020), Chapter 4, 3(c) of the Belizean Constitution provides as a fundamental right the 'protection for his family life, his personal privacy, the privacy of his home and other property and recognition of his human dignity'.

121. Bolivia does not have a specific data protection law. However, the General Law of Telecommunications, Information and Communication Technologies (Ley General de Telecomunicaciones, Tecnologías de Información y Comunicación, Ley n° 164) does provide for data subject rights and other rules concerning personal data. See for instance Articles 54(9), 56 and 59(13), https://www.diputados.bo/leyes/ley-n°-164 (accessed January 27, 2020).
122. Bolivia, Constitución Política del Estado, https://www.diputados.bo/sites/default/files/cpe2014.pdf (accessed January 27, 2020). Article 21(2) of the Bolivian Constitution states that all bolivians have the right to privacy, intimacy, honour, self image and dignity.
123. Brazil, Federal Law n° 13.709/2018 (General Data Protection Law), https://www.planalto.gov.br/ccivil_03/_ato2015-2018/2018/lei/L13709.htm (in portuguese) and https://www.lgpdbrasil.com.br/wp-content/uploads/2019/06/LGPD-english-version.pdf (unoficial translation).
124. Ibid., Articles 33 to 36 of the Law n° 13.709/2018.
125. Brazil, Federal Constitution, https://www.stf.jus.br/arquivo/cms/legislacaoConstituicao/anexo/brazil_federal_constitution.pdf (accessed January 27, 2020) Article 5(X) provides the right to privacy as a fundamental right 'X – the privacy, private life, honour and image of persons are inviolable, and the right to compensation for property or moral damages resulting from their violation is ensured'.
126. Canada, Personal Information Protection and Electronic Documents Act (PIPEDA), https://laws-lois.justice.gc.ca/PDF/P-8.6.pdf (accessed January 27, 2020). Besides, it is worth mentioning the Alberta Personal Information Protection Act (Alberta PIPA) and the Quebec Privacy Act.
127. The general standard is that the organisation responsible for the transfer 'shall use contractual or other means to provide a comparable level of protection while the information is being processed by a third party', as per Article 4.1.3 of the PIPEDA.
128. Privacy Commissioner of Canada, enacted under Section 53 of the Canadian Privacy Act (https://laws-lois.justice.gc.ca/eng/acts/p-21/index.html).
129. According to the Office of the Privacy Commissioner of Canada, 'The Supreme Court of Canada has stated that the *Privacy Act* has "quasi-constitutional status", and that the values and rights set out in the Act are closely linked to those set out in the Constitution as being necessary to a free and democratic society'. Office of the Privacy Commissioner of Canada, 'An Overview of the Office of the Privacy Commissioner of Canada and Federal Privacy Legislation', https://www.priv.gc.ca/en/about-the-opc/publications/guide_ind/ (accessed January 27, 2020).
130. Chile, Law 19.628/1999. Available at https://www.leychile.cl/Navegar?idNorma=141599 (accessed January 27, 2020).
131. Chile, Constitución Política, https://www.senado.cl/capitulo-iii-de-los-derechos-y-deberes-constitucionales/senado/2012-01-16/093413.html (accessed January 27, 2020). Included as a constitutional right in 2018. Article 19, 4° states that '4°.- El respeto y protección a la vida privada y a la honra de la persona y su familia, y asimismo, la protección de sus datos personales. El tratamiento y protección de estos datos se efectuará en la forma y condiciones que determine la ley'.
132. Colombia, Law 1581/2012, https://www.secretariasenado.gov.co/senado/basedoc/ley_1581_2012.html (accessed January 27, 2020). Also worth to mention Law 1266/2008, which regulates gathering, treatment and circulation of personal data in relation to financial and credit, commercial and service information, as well as that obtained from third countries, https://www.secretariajuridica.gov.co/transparencia/marco-legal/normatividad/ley-1266-2008 (accessed January 27, 2020).
133. See Article 26 of Law 1581/2012.
134. Colombia, Superintendencia de Industria y Comercio (Superintendent of Industry and Commerce – SIC). See more at https://www.sic.gov.co/tema/proteccion-de-datos-personales.
135. Colombia, Constitution, https://www.constituteproject.org/constitution/Colombia_2005.pdf (accessed January 27, 2020). Article 15 of the Colombian Constitution states that all individuals have the right to 'know, update, and rectify information collected about them in data banks and in the records of public and private entities. Freedom and the other guarantees

approved in the Constitution will be respected in the collection, processing, and circulation of data'.

136. Costa Rica, Protección de la Persona frente al tratamiento de sus datos personales (Protection of the Person over the processing of their personal data – Law n° 8968), https://www.pgrweb.go.cr/scij/Busqueda/Normativa/Normas/nrm_texto_completo.aspx?param1=NRTC&nValor1=1&nValor2=70975&nValor3=85989&strTipM=TC (accessed January 27, 2020).
137. The general rule is that there must be a valid and express authorisation for the transfer and that it respects the Costa Rica law's principles and rights, as per Article 14 of the Law n° 8968.
138. Costa Rica, Agency for the Protection of Personal Data of Inhabitants (*Agencia de Protección de Datos de los habitantes* – Prodhab), https://www.prodhab.go.cr.
139. Costa Rica, Constitución Política de la Republica de Costa Rica, https://www.pgrweb.go.cr/scij/Busqueda/Normativa/Normas/nrm_texto_completo.aspx?nValor1=1&nValor2=871 (accessed January 27, 2020). Article 24 of the Constitution provides the right to privacy as a fundamental right, namely the right to intimacy, freedom and secrecy of communications.
140. It is worth mentioning, however, that according to local scholars 'There are several sectoral rules that address information in a general sense and indiscriminately protect certain personal information depending on whether it is sensitive data or if it appears in databases of these sectors' (Free translation, Zahira Bello and Yarina Fernández, 'La protección de los datos personales en Cuba desde la legislación vigente', *Justicia juris* (2017), 91, https://www.scielo.org.co/pdf/jusju/v12n2/1692-8571-jusju-12-02-00087.pdf (accessed January 27, 2020)).
141. Cuba, Constitución de la Republica, https://www.cuba.cu/gobierno/cuba.htm (accessed January 27, 2020). Articles 56 and 57 of the Cuban Constitution establishes the right to privacy in what refers to individuals' houses and communications (cable, telegraph and telephone).
142. Dominican Republic, *Ley sobre Protección de Datos Personales* (Law n° 172–13), https://www.tribunalconstitucional.gob.do/transparencia/marco-legal/leyes/ley-172-13-sobre-protección-de-datos-personales/ (accessed January 27, 2020).
143. See Article 80 of Law n° 172–13.
144. Article 29 of Law n° 172–13 establishes as a control organ for data concerning credit the Superintendency of Banks (*Superintendencia de Bancos*), but there is no DPA.
145. Dominican Republic, Constitución Dominicana, https://dominicana.gob.do/index.php/pais/2014-12-16-20-52-13 (accessed January 27, 2020). Article 44 of the Dominican Republic Constitution provides for the right to intimacy and personal honour, expressly recognising citizens' right to access personal data and right to be informed about its use.
146. Ecuador, Bill proposed in September 2019. See draft bill at https://ppless.asambleanacional.gob.ec/alfresco/d/d/workspace/SpacesStore/0735e2b3-6545-4f66-afe4-0d7eee51e6c5/Proyecto%20de%20Ley%20Org%E1nica%20de%20Protecci%F3n%20de%20Datos%20Personales%20Tr.%20379637.pdf.
147. Ecuador, Constitution, https://pdba.georgetown.edu/Constitutions/Ecuador/english08.html (accessed January 27, 2020). Article 66(19) of the Constitution guarantees 'The right to protection of personal information, including access to and decision about information and data of this nature, as well as its corresponding protection. The gathering, filing, processing, distribution or dissemination of these data or information shall require authorization from the holder or a court order'.
148. Luis Andrés Marroquín, 'Ley de Protección de Datos tendrá su propria superintendencia', *elsalvador.com* (04 February 2020), https://www.elsalvador.com/noticias/nacional/ley-proteccion-datos-superintendencia/683392/2020/ (accessed May 03, 2020).
149. El Salvador, Constitution of the Republic of El Salvador, https://constitutionnet.org/vl/item/constitution-republic-el-salvador (accessed January 27, 2020). Article 2 provides as individual rights 'The right to honor, personal and family intimacy, and one's own image is guaranteed'.
150. Grenada, Grenada Constitution of 1973, https://pdba.georgetown.edu/Constitutions/Grenada/gren73eng.html (accessed January 27, 2020). Article 1(c) of the Grenadian Constitution states as a fundamental right the protection of privacy of home and other property.

151. Guatemala, The Initiative 4090 (*Iniciativa 4090*). Under discussion since 2010. See more at https://dca.gob.gt/noticias-guatemala-diario-centro-america/piden-aprobar-ley-de-proteccion-de-datos/.
152. Guatemala, Constitución Política de la Republica de Guatemala, https://www.ine.gob.gt/archivos/informacionpublica/ConstitucionPoliticadelaRepublicadeGuatemala.pdf (accessed January 27, 2020). The Constitution establishes as individuals' rights the non-violation of property (Article 23) and the secrecy of correspondence and telephone, radio, cable and other modern technology communications (Article 24) (free translation by the authors).
153. Guyana, Constitution of the Co-operative Republic of Guyana Act, https://parliament.gov.gy/constitution.pdf (accessed January 27, 2020).
154. Haiti, La Constitution de La République D' Haïti (1987), https://www.oas.org/juridico/PDFs/mesicic4_hti_const.pdf.
155. Honduras. The *Ley de Protección de Datos Personales* (Data Protection Law) is under discussion. See more at https://www.elheraldo.hn/pais/1246129-466/ley-de-vivienda-y-otras-quedaron-pendientes-en-el-congreso-nacional and https://www.accessnow.org/honduras-igf/ for first comments on the Bill.
156. The Institute for the Access to Public Information (*Instituto de Acceso a la Información Pública – IAIP*), already established in the country, would be the Data Protection Authority according to the Bill.
157. Honduras, Constitución Política de 1982, https://www.poderjudicial.gob.hn/CEDIJ/Leyes/Documents/Constitución%20de%20la%20República%20de%20Honduras%20%28Actualizada%202014%29.pdf (accessed January 27, 2020). Article 182 of the Constitution foresees the right to *habeas data*, namely that 'Toda persona tiene el derecho a acceder a la información sobre sí misma o sus bienes en forma expedita y no onerosa, ya esté contenida en bases de datos, registros públicos o privados y, en caso de que fuere necesario, actualizarla, rectificarla y-o suprimirla'.
158. 'Data Protection Bill to Go Before Parliament Soon', *The Cleaner Jamaica* (January 25, 2020), https://jamaica-gleaner.com/article/news/20200125/data-protection-bill-go-parliament-soon (accessed January 27, 2020). Since 2017, the Data Protection Bill is under discussion. Jamaica, Data Protection Bill, https://japarliament.gov.jm/index.php/publications/bills/public-bills (accessed January 27, 2020).
159. Jamaica, The Jamaica Constitution Order in Council 1962, https://moj.gov.jm/sites/default/files/laws/Ja%20%28Constitution%29%20Order%20in%20Council%201962.pdf (accessed January 27, 2020). Section 13(3)(j)(ii) establishes as a right of everyone to 'respect for and protection of private and family life and privacy of the home' and Section 13(3)(j)(iii) to 'protection of privacy of other property and of communication'.
160. Mexico, Federal Law on the Protection of Personal Data held by Private Parties (Ley Federal de Protección de Datos Personales en Posesión de Particulares – LFPDPPP), https://www.diputados.gob.mx/LeyesBiblio/pdf/LFPDPPP.pdf (accessed January 27, 2020). Besides, the General Law on Protection of Personal Data Held by Obligated Parties (*Ley General de Protección de Datos Personales en Posesión de Sujetos Obligados*), 2017, https://inicio.ifai.org.mx/MarcoNormativoDocumentos/LEY%20GENERAL%20DE%20PROTECCIÓN%20DE%20DATOS.pdf (accessed January 27, 2020).
161. Ibid., Articles 36 and 37 of the LFPDPPP.
162. The National Institute of Transparency for Access to Information and Personal Data Protection (*Instituto Nacional de Transparencia, Acceso a la Información y Protección de Datos Personales* – INAI). See more at https://inicio.ifai.org.mx/SitePages/English_Section.aspx
163. Mexico, Constitution, https://www.constituteproject.org/constitution/Mexico_2015.pdf?lang=en (accessed January 27, 2020). Article 6 establishes the right to information and to freedom of expression, foreseeing that, in order to accomplish that provisions, 'Information regarding private life and personal data shall be protected according to law and with the exceptions established therein'. Besides, Article 16, which refers specifically to the right to privacy, states that 'All people have the right to enjoy protection on his personal data, and

to access, correct and cancel such data. All people have the right to oppose the disclosure of his data, according to the law'.

164. Nicaragua, Law n° 787, https://www.pgr.gob.ni/PDF/Constitucional/ley%20787.pdf (accessed January 27, 2020).
165. Ibid., Articles 13, 14 and 15 of Law n° 787.
166. The Directorate for the Protection of Personal Information (Dirección de Protección de Datos Personales) has not been enacted yet, but it is foreseen in the Law n° 787 (Art. 28).
167. Nicaragua, Nicaragua's Constitution of 1987, https://www.constituteproject.org/constitution/Nicaragua_2005.pdf (accessed January 27, 2020). Article 26 states as individuals' rights the right to private life (Art. 26(1)) and to 'know all information that has been recorded about it in private and public entities, as well as the right to know why and for what purpose this information is used' (Art. 26(4)).
168. Panama, Law n° 81 of 2019, Data Protection Law (*Ley 81 de Protección de Datos Personales*), https://www.panacamara.com/ley-81-de-2019/ (accessed January 27, 2020).
169. Ibid., Articles 31, 32 and 33 of Law n° 81.
170. Panama, Constitución Política de la República de Panamá, https://www.oas.org/es/sla/ddi/docs/P1%20Constitución%20de%20Panamá.pdf (accessed January 27, 2020). Article 42 of the Constitution establishes the Right to Informational Self-Determination, namely that 'Toda persona tiene derecho a acceder a la información personal contenida en bases de datos o registros públicos y privados, y a requerir su rectificación y protección, así como su supresión, de conformidad con lo previsto en la Ley'. See also Article 29.
171. Other domestic laws regulate the matter (see e.g. Law n° 4868/2013 and Law n° 1682/2001), but a Data Protection Law is under discussion since 2019. See more at https://www.senado.gov.py/index.php/noticias/noticias-comisiones/2924-debaten-proyecto-de-ley-de-proteccion-de-datos-personales-2019-04-30-19-17-59.
172. Paraguay, Constitución de la República del Paraguay, https://digesto.senado.gov.py/archivos/file/Constitución%20de%20la%20República%20del%20Paraguay%20y%20Reglamento%20Interno%20HCS.pdf (accessed January 27, 2020). Article 33 of the Constitution establishes that 'Personal and family intimacy, as well as respect for privacy, are inviolable' (free translation by the authors).
173. Peru, Law n° 29733, Personal Data Protection Law (*Ley n° 29733, Ley de Protección de Datos Personales – LPDP*). Available at https://www.leyes.congreso.gob.pe/Documentos/Leyes/29733.pdf.
174. Ibid., Article 15 of Law n° 29733.
175. Peru, National Authority for the Protection of Personal Data (*Autoridad Nacional de Protección de Datos Personales*).
176. Peru, Constitución Política del Perú, https://www.minjus.gob.pe/wp-content/uploads/2019/05/Constitucion-Politica-del-Peru-marzo-2019_WEB.pdf (accessed January 27, 2020). Article 2(6) establishes as a fundamental right that 'That computer services, computerized or not, public or private, do not provide information that affects personal and family privacy'. The Personal Data Protection Law is considered to be a normative development from that provision.
177. Saint Kitts and Nevis, Data Protection Bill 2018. The Bill is inspired in the Organization of the Eastern Caribbean States Model (available at https://www.oecs.org/en/oecs-library/e-gov/data-protection-act) See more at https://www.thestkittsnevisobserver.com/st-kitts-and-nevis-legislators-pass-data-protection-bill-2018/.
178. Saint Kitts and Nevis, Information Commissioner.
179. Saint Kitts and Nevis, Constitution, https://www.oas.org/juridico/PDFs/mesicic5_skn_constitution_annex1.pdf (accessed January 27, 2020). Article 3(c) of the Constitution establishes as a fundamental right the 'protection for his or her personal privacy, the privacy of his or her home and other property and from deprivation of property without compensation'.
180. Saint Lucia, Privacy and Data Protection Act, https://www.govt.lc/media.govt.lc/www/resources/legislation/PrivacyAndDataProtectionBill.pdf (accessed January 27, 2020).

181. Ibid., Article 28 of the Privacy and Data Protection Act.
182. Saint Lucia, Data Protection Commissioner.
183. Saint Lucia, Constitution, https://www.oas.org/es/sla/ddi/docs/SL1%20Constitution.pdf (accessed January 27, 2020). Article 1(c) of the Constitution establishes the right to privacy as the right to 'protection for his family life, his personal privacy, the privacy of his home and other property'.
184. In Saint Vincent and the Grenadines, the existing law related to the matter is the Freedom of Information Act (2003).
185. Saint Vincent and the Grenadines, Constitution 1979, https://www.oas.org/es/sla/ddi/docs/SVG%201%20Constitution.pdf (accessed January 27, 2020). Article 1(c) of the Constitution establishes the right to privacy as the right to 'protection for the privacy of his home and other property'.
186. Suriname, The Constitution of The Republic of Suriname, Bulletin of Acts and Decrees 1987 no. 166, https://www.oas.org/juridico/PDFs/mesicic4_sur_const.pdf (accessed January 27, 2020). Article 17 provides that 'Everyone has a right to respect for his privacy(…)' (Art. 17(1)) and that 'The confidentiality of correspondence, telephone and telegraph shall be inviolable' (Art. 17(3)).
187. Trinidad and Tobago, Data Protection Act (DPA), https://www.ttparliament.org/legislations/a2011-13.pdf (accessed January 27, 2020).
188. Ibid., Article 46 of the DPA.
189. Trinidad and Tobago, Office of the Information Commissioner.
190. Trinidad and Tobago, Constitution of the Republic of Trinidad and Tobago Act, 1976, https://laws.gov.tt/pdf/Constitution.pdf (accessed January 27, 2020). Article 4(c) recognises 'the right of the individual to respect for his private and family life'.
191. United States of America, Privacy Act of 1974, available at https://www.justice.gov/opcl/file/631151/download (accessed January 27, 2020). Other laws make part of the data protection framework in the country. In the state level, it is worth mentioning the California Consumer Privacy Act of 2018 (CCPA).
192. Federal Trade Commission and other sector-specific regulators.
193. The United States of America Bill of Rights, in its Fourth Amendment, establishes the right of the people 'to be secure in their persons, houses, papers, and effects, against unreasonable searches and seizures'. For a short opinion article about the matter, see Josephine Wolff, 'Losing Our Fourth Amendment Data Protection', *The New York Times* (April 28, 2019), https://www.nytimes.com/2019/04/28/opinion/fourth-amendment-privacy.html (accessed May 03, 2020).
194. Uruguay, Law n° 18331, https://www.impo.com.uy/bases/leyes/18331-2008. Personal Data Protection Law (Ley n° 18331 – *Ley de Protección de Datos Personales*).
195. See Article 23 of the Law n° 18331.
196. Uruguay, *Unidad Reguladora y de Control de Datos Personales (URCDP)*. See more at https://www.gub.uy/unidad-reguladora-control-datos-personales/
197. Uruguay, Constitucion de la Republica, https://www.impo.com.uy/bases/constitucion/1967-1967 (accessed January 27, 2020). Article 1 of Law n° 18331 establishes the data protection right as a inherent right to the human being, being it comprised at Article 72 of the Constitution, which establishes that 'The enumeration of rights, duties and guarantees made by the Constitution does not exclude others that are inherent to the human being or derive from the republican form of government' (free translation by the authors).
198. Venezuela, Constitucion de la Republica Bolivariana de Venezuela, 1999, https://www.oas.org/dil/esp/constitucion_venezuela.pdf (accessed January 27, 2020). Articles 47 and 48 of the Constitution guarantees the inviolability of home and of communication in all forms.

Disclosure statement

No potential conflict of interest was reported by the author(s).

ORCID

Carlos Affonso Souza http://orcid.org/0000-0001-5421-4782

Index

Note: Page numbers followed by 'n' denote endnotes

For Product Safety Concerns and Information please contact our EU representative GPSR@taylorandfrancis.com
Taylor & Francis Verlag GmbH, Kaufingerstraße 24, 80331 München, Germany

www.ingramcontent.com/pod-product-compliance
Lightning Source LLC
LaVergne TN
LVHW080653011026
849160LV00014B/1416
9781032171906